Good Kids, Bad Behavior

HELPING CHILDREN LEARN SELF-DISCIPLINE

PETER WILLIAMSON, Ph.D.

A FIRESIDE BOOK
PUBLISHED BY SIMON & SCHUSTER
NEW YORK   LONDON   TORONTO   SYDNEY   TOKYO   SINGAPORE

To Charlene, Sasha, and Jamie with love

FIRESIDE

Rockefeller Center
1230 Avenue of the Americas
New York, New York 10020

First Fireside Edition 1991

Designed by Nina D'Amario/Levavi & Levavi
Manufactured in the United States of America

10 9 8 7 6 5 4 3 2 1
10 9 8 7 6 5   Pbk.
Library of Congress Cataloging in Publication Data
Williamson, Peter A.
   Good kids, bad behavior: helping children learn self-discipline/Peter A.
Williamson.
      p.   cm.
   Includes index.
   1. Discipline of children.   2. Parenting.   3. Parent and child.   I. Title.
HQ770.4.W55   1990
649'.64—dc20
                                                        90-32180
                                                        CIP

ISBN: 0-671-70220-3
ISBN: 0-671-74818-1 Pbk.

Contents

a new understanding. "Clear" is not the same as
"harsh." Why punishing does not mean "hurting."

Guidelines for when to ignore misbehavior and when
to step in. Learning how you "pay attention" to a
misbehaving child.

PART III.
The Mechanics of Discipline

How to stop misbehavior before it starts. From "bad
days" to "holidays," the routines of daily living as the
best first line of defense.

A simple discipline routine to manage most of the
minor problems in daily living.

Manipulative or just overstimulated? The causes of
and remedies for this overlooked aspect of your child's
misbehavior.

Unique strategies to solve severe or chronic behavior
problems.

Sometimes even the most competent parents need
extra help. How to know when to get help and how to
get the help you need.

Introduction

When I decided to write this book, I knew it would not become just another self-help "pop psych" book. I don't believe in clever tricks or quick fixes when it comes to bringing up children. In my own practice, though, I needed a book that would help parents develop a positive attitude toward discipline—parents need to be able to feel good about themselves as disciplinarians. They also need to accept the fact that their children are going to misbehave—and to feel *good about that,* too. This book takes a fresh look at the individual differences among children and the purposes of misbehavior. It seeks to help parents develop a constructive attitude toward the process of discipline.

I approach this subject not only as a child and adolescent psychologist who works with a broad range of children, but also as a parent sharing the same everyday problems as anybody else. I'm the father of two small children, neither of whom is an angel. They are bright, spunky, and assertive. They misbehave and they test limits the same as all children in all families. They have misbehaved in restaurants, in supermarkets, and in the car. They have had temper tantrums in the morning and when they went to bed at night. After I had been gone for a few days on a trip, my two-year-old son let me know his displeasure by throwing a temper tantrum in a doctor's office. While I wrestled him into his snowsuit, my five-year-old daughter cried, "Don't hurt him, Daddy!" Heads turned. I smiled weakly. As he flailed and cried, one of the clinic technicians came over and told me she could not carry out a particular task because my son was making too much noise. I doubt she had children of her own. On the outside I was cool, and I explained to her what was going on, but on the inside I was Ralph Cramden: "Bang—

zoom, right to the moon!" Within a few minutes, of course, we worked the problem through, and my son settled down quickly, but the impression of the situation never left me. No, my children do not have severe behavioral problems, only the normal everyday ones. But experiences like this always increase my empathy for parents whose children do this sort of thing day in and day out. This book is written for all parents, but it is especially for them.

Certainly none of us are totally immune to irritation, embarrassment, or frustration in such situations. But how can we best deal with children's behavior problems? How can we cope with our emotions? And how can we develop a consistent point of view that will carry us through the seemingly endless difficulties that occur?

While many parents today are fairly well read and well informed about behavior modification and other techniques, they still feel a kind of desperation when it comes to discipline. Often they have already tried all of the popular techniques. Some have worked and some haven't. Most parents are enormously frustrated by this scattershot approach. They sense there's something wrong in needing to use thirteen different techniques to get Johnny through his day. They begin to feel incompetent as parents and even angry at the source of their frustration—their child.

What most parents need is a constructive way to think about the process of discipline. They often equate it with punishment. The very idea of punishing leaves many parents feeling angry and guilty, so they avoid it as much as possible. They tend to think of discipline as a form of crisis intervention. The problem is that with children who frequently misbehave, the crisis is never-ending.

This book was written to help parents develop a more upbeat attitude toward the process of discipline, *to give them a way to think about their misbehaving children in a positive light.* Helping parents change their attitudes is especially important in my work as a psychotherapist. Because of the nature of my practice, my method is essentially short-term and problem-focused and there isn't much time to work through resistance. My approach demands a lot of cooperation on the part of the parents. I have found through experience that when parents believe in what they are doing, and feel good about themselves and about their children, they are able to quickly deal with most problems.

With this book I hope to inspire parents about the mundane job of disciplining children. It is not a treatise filled with research reports.

The language is simple and direct, and I hope readers will find it not only useful but enjoyable to read.

This is not, however, a typical self-help "recipe" book, because there are never enough recipes to account for every situation. Of course the book contains many practical suggestions and illustrations, but its major thrust is to give you an overall strategy and to help you develop a more positive attitude toward the process of discipline. There is much more to discipline than punishment. Most day-to-day discipline problems can be dealt with through ritual, routine, and anticipatory structuring. Special emphasis is given to teaching children how to pace themselves and to regulate their expression of feelings. But no book can provide a panacea, and if anything, this book debunks the notion that there are any quick fixes or shortcuts in discipline. For serious behavior problems, therapy may be the right option, and a whole chapter is devoted to helping parents decide when to get help from a therapist, and learn how to overcome their reluctance to seek therapy and how to choose a therapist wisely.

Discipline is a two-decade-long teaching process. So much of the time, we seem to take the short view: if we just say this clever thing or try that smart trick, the whole problem will be solved. Too often, self-help books present the notion that if you just perform the right tricks, your family will be happy and problem free, just like those on TV. But this is not true: the war will not be over in a week; the troops will not be home by Christmas. Children do obnoxious things and misbehave because they are supposed to—it is the natural way in which children learn.

Finally, there is a message in this book that may be somewhat less obvious. This is the notion that it is not necessarily the things we actively teach which will have the greatest impact on our children. Sometimes the things which have the greatest impact are more indirect—in many cases, the background mood of the family, that often indescribable though ever-present atmosphere of the home. In some respects, this may be attributable to the clear attitudes of the parents toward the children, but often it is communicated through the regular rituals and routines that are a part of every family's life. This regularity provides a sense of safety because it is so predictable. A family sits down to dinner a certain way; everyone has his or her own chair. Bedtime routines have a certain orderly flow. There is repetition and rhythm to daily life.

   The importance of routine became clear to me before my first child was born. I wanted to make peace with my own parents, and as part of the process, I wanted to let them know what they had done for me that had enriched my life, had made a lasting impact. My parents were not perfect. They made their share of mistakes. But I realized what they had provided me with was a sense of order. Our family had its share of turmoil, but it also had a strong sense of predictability, even of certainty. This communicated a sense of orderliness, a sense of safety in a very unsafe world. I wonder how many children hunger for that sense of safety.

   I have written this book with a deep sense of respect for the difficulties parents and children experience as they grow and learn together. This respect comes not only out of my own experiences as a therapist but also from my experiences as a child and as a father to my own children. Problems are a normal part of family living. They are not aberrations—embarrassments to be swept quickly under the nearest rug. The more we can approach the process of parenting with assertiveness and zeal, the more we can profit from this long and often difficult journey.

PART 1

Getting Oriented:

Building a Positive
Mental Attitude

1

When Children Are Not Good

We live in the Age of Good Managers. If we pick up any magazine or watch any daytime TV talk show, we will be instructed in how to manage all aspects of our lives. Management "experts" provide techniques to help us invest our money, climb the career ladder, dress for success, work on the relationship, and lose those pounds without losing our minds. We are led to believe that if we learn the right techniques, we will achieve the right results! We expect to be competent at whatever we try to do, to be on top of any situation. *We will not be like our own parents,* who seemed overwhelmed and confused by the rapid and enormous changes in the world around them. We have grown up with change and we are not surprised by it. We seem to measure our self-worth by how efficiently we can manage our affairs.

Then, in the midst of our crisp, efficiently run lives, we have children; what should make this experience unlike any other? Today many parents feel compelled to manage all aspects of their child's development. There is, for example, among many a considerable push for more formal academic instruction during the preschool years. Never mind that the worth of this early academic pressure has never been established (even though the stress that children experience when pressured too early *has* been established *and is substantial*). Preschools in competition with one another offer not only basic prereading and premath skills, but also foreign languages, music instruction, and education in computer science.

And the intrusion goes even deeper—into children's play. Knockabout activities that were once left up to the child alone are more frequently now organized by adults. Children take lessons in art; drama; and sports such as soccer, baseball, and karate. Children are structured, guided, and taught at every turn. Apparently there is a fairly widespread belief that if you do not do these things for your children, they will lose ground to others. As a result, it is not uncommon to see parents moving their young children through a day that includes lessons of one sort or another, a preschool experience, a library program, a regularly scheduled playtime, and finally dinner at home and some "quality time" with the folks before bed. Then, right in the middle of the schedule, the child decides to do what children have done for thousands of years: the child starts to misbehave.

In the Age of Good Managers, there is no room for childhood misbehavior. It clogs the smooth workings of the system. It makes the family machine spark and sputter. Parents, being consistent, start searching for techniques to deal with the problem. There is no lack of resources available to combat this nasty rebellion. As with all other aspects of life, there are the magazines, TV talk shows, and, of course, books by psychologists offering advice on appropriate ways to shape and structure a child's behavior.

The efficient family manager often feels pushed into short-term solutions. Many times it is clear to the uninvolved observer that the parents need not only to read the books but also to work with a professional therapist. Unfortunately, this is often the last approach they are willing to take. Perhaps it is due to pride or simply the time constraints that many parents work under these days, but many parents are reluctant to recognize how difficult some of these behavior problems are. The pace of day-to-day living is so rapid and the pressure to be competent so intense that many of them attempt to treat complex and persistent behavior problems by asking for simple techniques. It is as though they were saying, "If I only knew the one right thing to say or do, I could make this problem go away."

WHY MOST HOW-TO ADVICE DOESN'T HELP

When parents finally come for the professional help of a therapist, advice about the right techniques will not be enough. They have failed to efficiently manage their own child; their self-confidence has been undermined. Even though they have come for help, they are skeptical of quick fixes. Many times in my own practice I have seen the crossed arms and narrowed eyes of those irritated mothers and fathers. Most of the families I work with have tried all of the do-it-yourself tricks and found they do not work.

When children are showing severe and chronic behavior problems, the right technique and the right thing to say invariably seem to fail. Parents nowadays are not ignorant, and they have many resources at their fingertips. They know all about "time-outs," rewarding good behavior, the perils of punishment, etc. They have not failed for lack of trying. It is not uncommon for them to say, when asked what sorts of techniques they have used, "We have tried everything." They mean it, too!

When I see this situation in our first meeting, I know I've got a bumpy road ahead. How do you convince these parents, who feel they have exhausted every sweeping strategy or tiny tactic, that they can teach their child to behave appropriately? How do you convince these exhausted people that their child will turn out to be anything but an irresponsible sluggard at best, a criminal at worst?

Are the techniques themselves to blame? No, that would be like the workman blaming his tools. Certain facts about teaching children to behave are fairly clear: positive reinforcement increases the likelihood that certain behaviors will recur; punishment decreases the likelihood of recurrence. Experiments in learning have been carried out in university laboratories for the better part of this century using pigeons, rats, horseshoe crabs, and even human children. In the laboratory, the techniques work like a charm.

So what goes wrong when you try the techniques in the comfort of your own home?

Well, practically everything.

It isn't that the techniques fail, but the parents and children hold attitudes and expectations that don't allow them to work. Consider the following. In the first place, the poor horseshoe crab in the aversive-conditioning experiment is not being experimented upon by his mother or father. As we will see, children have a great deal to gain by challenging their parents' authority. Therefore, before you can deal effectively with persistent and severe behavior problems, you have to understand the purpose of the misbehavior and why children seem to need to act in this self-defeating, irritating way.

In the second place, most parents view the process of discipline with a certain amount of distaste. They equate discipline with punishment, and punishment—so we have been told for the past thirty years—is "bad." Punishment hurts children; if you do the wrong things to your child at an early age, you could damage her for life. We are not discussing abusive or neglectful parents here, but parents who spend a great deal of time attending to their children, satisfying their needs, and fussing over their complaints; parents who love their children and tend to blame themselves when things go wrong.

Perhaps more than ever before, parents are tentative around their children. Today's parents do not learn child care from their own families of origin, they learn it from television, magazines, discussion groups, and parenting classes. There are experts at every turn telling them how to carry out this task, how to deal with that problem. Again—this stress on *managing* the situation, on finding the *right technique*. But all of this contradictory expert advice has made parents gun-shy. They no longer trust their instincts; they hesitate before they act. It becomes impossible for them to do what Dr. Spock advises: "Trust yourself, you know more than you think you do."

Before they can make good use of any technical advice, parents have to *believe* in what they are doing. They have to have some sense of *hope*. To build this new faith in themselves, they must do away with the beliefs and attitudes that have shaped their parenting efforts thus far.

Fortunately, there seems to be one central set of beliefs that colors many families' approach to child rearing. This is the idea that "goodness" has something to do with the way children behave and learn. First, let's be clear about what we mean by goodness. There is an important difference between teaching our children to *do* good things and expecting them to behave because they *should be* good. After we settle this issue, we will examine how faulty beliefs about goodness interfere with our parenting.

"GOODNESS HAS NOTHING TO DO WITH IT"

How often do we use the terms "good" and "bad" to describe our children's behavior? Nearly all the time! "Now, be good, Billy," we caution our three-year-old as he grabs a toy away from another child and pushes his face in the sand. In explaining to me what she had tried in order to avert the recurring supermarket temper tantrum, one mother said she had told her child, "*If you are good,* I'll give you some gum at the checkout." One father, after angrily listing off a number of his child's obnoxious behaviors, reassured me, "Now don't get the wrong idea—*he is really a good kid.*"

Certainly we all want our children to be able to make appropriate moral choices when they are older. We want them to be kind to others, respectful, socially responsible, and honest. We want our children to grow up to be responsible citizens and to raise families of their own. We want them to have clear moral convictions and even, perhaps, certain religious beliefs. These are all very desirable goals of our parenting efforts. When the term "goodness" is used in the following section, you should understand that this has nothing to do with the moral purposes of child care.

Children do not learn to become responsible because of their "inner goodness." They learn to be this way because in the long run it works better to behave than to misbehave. Children don't learn this intuitively, they learn by trial and error. A lot of errors! That is why human childhood lasts almost twenty years.

Now, what has goodness got to do with any of this? Nothing, of course. But often parents act as if children are naturally supposed to be good. They are shocked and angered when their children misbehave. They believe children should be endowed with a quality of inner goodness, and that if they bring out this goodness, then this is a reflection of their own goodness as parents. Let's see what sorts of problems these beliefs cause.

SHOULD CHILDREN BE GOOD?

Every neighborhood has a family that appears to be "perfect," and of course it is not *your* family. You can picture them on windswept Saturday afternoons in March flying kites together in the park. They are always busy together doing creative projects on rainy days. They have cheerful faces and singsong voices, and seem to be happy with one another. They do not evade chores; no, they volunteer. When there are disagreements, the children do not have tantrums or mess themselves. The parents squat down, establish eye contact, and talk to them reasonably in soft voices. The children listen to their parents, hear the reasons, and do what they are told.

This is pure fiction. It is a fantasy we buy into when we envy others we do not know so well but conceive of as having more free-flowing, trouble-free lives than we do. This type of fantasizing may be a source of inspiration to us by providing us with something to strive for. But it is also a source of despair. We are aware of our own shortcomings and do not believe we could ever achieve this fantasized perfection that we attribute to others. Can these families be as perfect as they seem? Certainly not. People are not happy and reasonable all the time. Children are not always well behaved. This is as accurate a portrait of real people as "smiley face" buttons are! Families, in which the individuals become as entangled with each other as strands of spaghetti, are infinitely more complex and interesting.

Is it possible or even desirable for the family we envy to be as perfect as it seems? In reality, what happens is that there are such strong prohibitions against unseemly behavior within a family like this that such behavior never comes to light. Does that mean it is not there? No! The people in other families are probably not much different from the people in your family, and they have the same wants, wishes, needs, drives, and conflicts. What they do, though, is put an inordinate amount of energy into avoiding conflict.

When the Jensen family first appeared for therapy, they had trouble thinking of anything to talk about. Dad wore a nicely tailored suit and Mom wore an attractive skirt and blouse. The twins were pretty, neatly dressed, and well mannered. Everyone was happy. Everyone got along so well. But the tension in the room was so oppressive it could have melted plastic flowers. Thank heavens for little Billy! He was the problem that had brought them in. After five minutes of silence he flew out of his chair and raced around the room. He taunted the twins and made them upset. He climbed on his mother and messed up her hair. His father began to sweat and stammered, "Billy—now sit down, son. We don't act this way in public."

In order to avoid conflict, however, you have to avoid certain thoughts, feelings, and behaviors associated with conflict. You have to live as one-dimensionally as possible. You can do this only by repressing and denying those aspects of yourself that might lead you into conflict with another family member. This means you have to close off a lot of yourself to others. You have to live only a fraction of a life. Think of the price you pay in the loss of intimacy. Think of the stress such denial places upon you. In part you might be able to offset the stress and emptiness by frenetic activity. It becomes essential to find new and exciting things to do, new ways to present your family to the outside world. This may work for a short time, but eventually the stress will win out. Families that do not know how to deal with conflict are also unable to cope when things start to unravel.

GOODNESS HAS ITS PRICE
ON THE PERSONAL LEVEL, TOO

What price do children pay in order to be good? For one thing, they cannot behave as normal children do and learn appropriate behavior through trial and error. Often they may appear polite and "nice," but they may also seem dull and uninspired. They lack initiative and do not engage in exploratory behavior. Some children react to the stress with bodily symptoms such as headaches or chronic stomachaches. Others may act out with shocking, inappropriate behavior during adolescence. Still others who do not succumb in this way report a pervading sense of emptiness. When such an emphasis is placed on "good" behavior, the child is forced into extinguishing any form of "bad" behavior. The child does not do this for altruistic reasons or because such behavior is not functional. She represses the behavior simply because it is "bad."

There is another consequence inherent in this faulty pattern. The child has to act as though she does not have this "bad" side. The child cannot be accepted or loved as a whole human being but only as a "good" one. In order to carry out this lie in day-to-day living, the child has to pretend in front of her parents and in front of others that this side does not exist.

Janice was a single woman in her early twenties who came in for treatment of headaches. As the initial interview progressed it became apparent that the headaches were the least of her worries. She was also very anxious and depressed. She could not sleep at night and her appetite was very poor. In the office she was easily moved to tears. Despite this, she seemed to have no awareness of her emotional turmoil, only her headache pain. She described her internal state only as empty—as though she was missing something but didn't know what it was.

As a child she had always been the "good girl" in the family. Her older brother was a failure in school and a disappointment to his parents. Her father disliked his job and drank heavily, but no one talked about that. Her mother often sat at the kitchen table staring gloomily out the window. But Janice was the good girl at home and at school. She never had problems and never caused trouble. Her parents could at least be proud of her.

She learned to be a good girl as a child by walling off any of her other feelings. But as she grew to adulthood she felt empty and dissatisfied. Even though she experienced enormous feelings of anger and sadness, she could not acknowledge them. She only had headaches.

How does such a child, as a result, come to think about herself? In the words of D. W. Winnecott, the great English psychoanalyst, the child grows to view herself as "not-good-enough." But the child soon finds herself in a double bind—she is not able to acknowledge her anger or despair. She is, after all, supposed to be "perfect" and so cannot admit to the less-than-perfect feelings. Hence, the child does not feel anger or despair, only a pervading emptiness.

There is nothing inherently desirable about a child's learning just to be "good." There is also nothing desirable about having a family that seems to be "perfect." In fact, when children do not learn to cope with conflict, the results can be extremely destructive. Viewed in this way, the behavior of the typical healthy, terrible two-year-old can be almost reassuring.

ARE CHILDREN MOTIVATED BY INNER GOODNESS?

There is a sentimental belief that children are innocent, sweet, kind, loving, and in all ways good—that this is the basic inner nature of the child, and his behavior is merely a manifestation of the degree to which this inner nature has been stimulated and allowed to grow. It brings to mind the turn-of-the-century postcards with dewy-eyed and rosy-cheeked little children playing merrily, rolling hoops and chasing butterflies. Their innocent wondering is disarming and exposes the deviousness of politicians and industrialists. Even mild misbehavior is tolerated since it is seen as innocent, charming, and totally without malice.

To the adult who buys into this belief, the innocence of childhood represents the purity of nature before society exerts its corrupting influence. As a parent, you are charged with the responsibility of guarding against these corrupting influences. To carry out this role, harsh discipline and punishment are not necessary. If you simply give the child a lot of love, his inner goodness will be stimulated and will bubble up into his surface behavior. If the bubbles don't surface, though, and your child continues to act as other ordinary children do, then you have obviously failed to stimulate this inner goodness. You have failed to guard your innocent child against the corrupting influences of the world. You may have failed as a parent.

This belief, like the previous one, is *nonsense,* and because of that, there is an opposing myth, which is perhaps even *more* dangerous: that children are intrinsically evil. This myth is evident not only in much television comedy but also in a number of recent best-selling books that have worked up the "child-as-a-devil" theme. This view probably dates back to a long and ancient series of legends and myths about the demon-child. Yet when battle-weary parents come out of the cold and start looking for help, they often feel their children behave the way they do purely out of spite. These parents are afraid that their children seem to enjoy being nasty, destructive, and hurtful. The children seem to defy the parents' attempts to "give them love," and become angry

with their parents when told they are good for anything other than
nothing. As we explore further, we find that these parents, at bottom,
are fearful that there is something intrinsically evil about their children.

> Chad came strutting into the office with a big smile on his face. His
> mother was right behind but she was neither smiling nor upset. There
> was no visible anger despite the fact that he had just been suspended
> from school for the third time—and he was only in second grade. His
> mother described all of his awful behavior at home. She seemed tired,
> worn out. Chad, though, seemed very proud, as though she were de-
> scribing how he won a trophy.
> "That's right, Doctor," he said, "I'm bad, bad, bad. I'm mean and I
> beat kids up. They're all scared of me and my teacher hates me, too. I
> got her scared, too."

It is both ineffective and illogical for parents to base their teaching
practices on some assumptions about a child's basic nature. It forces
them to see their children not as they are but in some idealized or
imaginary form. This also places a burden on the children, since they
cannot live up to the ideal. It sets everyone up for disappointment. If
a child is seen as "all good," parents may oversentimentalize important
conflicts within the child and miss important teachable moments. It
also makes it very difficult for the child to change his behavior. Children can learn to behave themselves at the table, do their chores, or
get their homework done. But it is very hard for them to "be good."
There's a clear difference. Certainly children can learn appropriate
behavior and can develop the potential for doing good in the world. It
is the parents, though, who must first dispense with this kind of
ineffective and destructive belief.

IS A GOOD CHILD A REFLECTION
OF A GOOD PARENT?

The following belief focuses on the competence of the parents: if
you know and do the right things, you will have perfect children. All
those obnoxious temper tantrums in the supermarkets, refusals to
comply, crying scenes, and other embarrassing displays in public are

avoidable. How many of us, when we were young and childless, upon viewing such behavior said, "No kid of mine would ever get away with that?" A few years later we find ourselves pleading with our own toddler not to tear down the deodorant display—in front of *all these people*. This myth goes deeper: children are totally malleable stuff of limitless potential. All you have to do is stimulate them, teach them the right things, and they will be remarkable and brilliant in everything they do. They'll be polite, respectful, responsible, ordinary children—who just happen to be geniuses! Unfortunately, this belief, like the other two, has its very dark side. After all, who is to blame when *your* child exhibits the same typical obnoxious and embarrassing behavior you said you would not permit? What happens when *your* child shows average ability or, heaven forbid, actually has learning problems? Of course, the blame all rests firmly on the parents' shoulders. When parents, having exhausted all their own resources, seek help from another, their underlying question at the onset is often, "What did we do wrong?" The problem for them is not that the child has had some trouble learning appropriate social conduct, but that they, the parents—through their incompetence—have created a monster capable of great evil. It is assumed the parents, not the child, are responsible for the child's misbehavior.

> Joanne and Basil were coming in for therapy to learn how to cope with their six-year-old daughter, Celeste. She had terrible temper tantrums and was very destructive when she was upset—she would smash the nearest object. The trouble was that almost anything seemed to set her off. When she was upset she was unable to settle herself. An exhaustive evaluation revealed she had always been this way; even as an infant she had been extremely difficult to care for. Although her parents were warm and caring people, they could not escape the feeling that her behavior was somehow their fault. They were sure it was something they did that made Celeste this way. They continued to have doubts even though they could not think of anything they did that was so terrible.

What, actually, have the parents done to create this aberration, this thing of great evil? In most cases, *probably nothing*—and I mean that quite literally! First of all, there is—as we shall see subsequently—nothing aberrant about most forms of oppositional, noncompliant behavior. Behavior problems are not only very *usual* but also quite *nec-*

essary in order for children to grow up into mature, independent adults. In addition, children vary in terms of their developing ability to regulate their feelings and their behavior. In most cases, there is nothing abnormal about children with difficult temperaments, but it is often harder for them to learn to control themselves. This means the teaching needs to be done more carefully and the process may be somewhat more lengthy and difficult.

Finally, the problem is often not that the parents have *done* something but that they have missed opportunities to discipline and thus teach their children. As I noted before, many parents have become gun-shy. They have become cowed into hesitation and uncertainty by the fear that they might do something which is psychologically damaging.

But most children are a lot tougher psychologically than their parents think. They have to be, after all, to endure the bumps and bruises involved in normal growing. Often the first step in helping parents change the behavior of their children is teaching the parents to see their children as tough, resilient, and capable of learning.

That some parents blame themselves for their child's behavior is certainly irrational, but it does not mean there is anything abnormal about these parents. In fact, the people I see in my practice are normal, healthy people, competent in almost all respects. They certainly mustn't be blamed for falling prey to these faulty beliefs, which did not originate in their minds but were shaped by some powerful social forces.

In American life, the never-ending quest for self-improvement is deemed a sacred duty. People are expected to be able to juggle careers and home life and also to be perfectly healthy. The idea of being a new, improved parent is just a logical extension of this type of self-improvement. It is not enough to love our children and enjoy them while getting on with the day-to-day business of living; we must hold down full-time careers and still manage to spend "quality time" with our children. This type of pressure probably explains why so many trim-looking mothers wrapped up in their business suits trot off to their jobs with irritable bowels.

The push to be a new, improved parent has somehow become confused with the idea that this makes us better people.

Stimulating children at an early age is not necessarily bad. What is destructive is the idea that unless parents and children behave in certain ways, they are "not-good-enough" as people. To cement your self-worth to the oppositional, irresponsible behavior of little children is ridiculous! There is always going to be strong pressure for self-improvement, and when we find areas in our lives in which we are having some trouble, trying to do a little better is certainly not bad. But to try to live up to the demands of this faulty belief is ultimately deceiving and destructive.

To Sum Up: Let Us Be Parents, Not Managers

The sign of a good manager, so the story goes, is that the office runs so smoothly he does not need to be there. Unfortunately, this is not the case with most families. Indeed, it is not even a desirable goal. But in the Age of Good Managers, this is often poorly understood. Instead, it is expected that if parent and child are only good enough, if they do their job well enough, conflicts can be quickly resolved—it is only a question of finding the right techniques to solve the problems. Since the attitudes and expectations about parenting do not change, this is often a futile search. Parents encounter failure after failure and end up feeling hopeless and ashamed.

The mechanics of teaching are probably the simplest part of parenting to master. But the major reason parents have difficulty changing their teaching is that *their attitudes and expectations are unrealistic*. Parents often hold a central set of beliefs—for example, that a child's behavior is governed by "inner goodness." This leads them to shy away from conflict and to set up expectations for their children and themselves that are impossible to uphold.

The bottom line on child rearing is that goodness has nothing to do with it. Of course Mae West's original bawdy remark had nothing to do with children, but this line does make us aware that teaching children is not lofty but earthy business. It begins with children regulating their bodies—bowels, mouths, and bladders. They learn to regulate volcanic tempers, pouty bad moods, and uncontrollable giggle fits. They learn to respect their parents, to hold their own with their peers, and eventually to assert themselves with their colleagues. But it is work—inch by inch and row by row.

• • •

How are parents, then, supposed to develop realistic expectations for their child? The first step is to understand the role of misbehavior in normal child development. First, all the irritating oppositionality and noncompliance has a healthy purpose and is *crucial* to a child's development. Second, understanding how children differ in terms of temperament and learning style is essential. This is important since many parents are often discouraged when they compare children across families. All children do not learn the same way, and you must establish appropriate expectations for your own child. Finally, parents need a sense of purpose to give them the energy to discipline. Let's face it: childhood lasts for at least eighteen years. It is a difficult job—and in the end they leave you. If you approach the task in a tired, defeated way, those eighteen years will seem like an eternity. If you can approach the task with some amount of zeal, you may be able to get through it with a smile!

2

Bad Behavior Is Good for Your Child

When your child misbehaves, she is carrying out one of the healthiest activities of childhood. It is the way in which children learn to regulate themselves and understand others. By misbehaving they are able to test the continuity of their boundaries. It is in the nature of children to oppose the limits their parents set, and look at how they do it! Set a rule before a child in clearest black and white, and it usually isn't too long before the child finds that barely visible band of gray and wedges herself firmly into it. How irritating to the parents, how important for the children.

One morning, Ginny presented herself with a big chapped ring around her mouth. She looked like a clown.

"Now, Ginny," said her mother, "don't lick your lips. I'm going to put some cream on them."

"I don't want any cream," insisted Ginny. "I hate it."

"But your lips are chapped," said her mother. "You need cream— and stop that licking!"

"Look, Mommy," said Ginny, "these are my lips, right?"

"Right."

"And I'm a different person from you. I'm not the same, right?"

"So?"

"So your lips may be chapped 'cause you're a different person. These
are my lips and they're not the same as yours. They're not chapped and
they don't need cream!"

What intelligence and creativity! Yet, too often we cannot appreciate
the *ingenuity* in this form of learning. We tend to see this type of
behavior in terms of its "goodness" or "badness."

In other words, we see it on some type of moral scale. It is not
uncommon for parents to view each temper tantrum or power struggle
as a rebellion of the great unwashed against the established world
order. The misbehavior of the preschooler or young school-age child
is seen as a foreshadowing of blacker things to come in adolescence:
drug and alcohol abuse, uninhibited sexual behavior, and spiky purple
hairdos! I have heard many parents ask, "If he is like this now, what
will he be like when he is fifteen?" Never mind that the child is
probably only three and still has daytime accidents—the parents still
worry. But though we worry for our children, we can learn to respond
to their impish behavior in a more rational, evenhanded way. We must
first understand what misbehavior is all about.

THE IMPORTANCE OF PREDICTION AND CONTROL

Consider the function of misbehavior from the child's point of view.
Misbehavior is the primary mode through which children learn self-
control and the ability to predict how other people will respond to
them. As parents, we worry about such things as developing morality
and other qualities of good citizenship. But to young children, these
concepts are hopelessly abstract; indeed, even if they could conceive
of such ideas, they would not be the least bit interested in them. What
they are concerned with is regulating their own behavior and mastering
some basic social independent living skills. In the early part of this
century the psychologist John B. Watson stated that "the prediction
and control of behavior are the two goals of psychology." This is especially true of children. Prediction and control are, in fact, the two
great organizing principles in the psychological development of the
child. Misbehavior, then, is the means by which children can ask
"What if . . . ?" If we look at "bad behavior" this way, we can see that
it is very *healthy* for our children. This is how they learn.

Consider the importance of prediction in your own life. Don't you have a sense that your life flows in a fairly orderly way? Certainly you expect the sun to rise in the morning, and you can plan your day around certain events that happen at fairly consistent times. There are probably routines that you follow. You are able to think ahead through the coming year and plan for holidays and vacations. You can even anticipate certain problems. Pleasant or unpleasant interactions with certain people can be anticipated. Financial planning can provide for a college education for your children ten or fifteen years from now and retirement income for you thirty years from now. Certainly we cannot predict every event that is going to happen, and at times our lives may feel in a state of flux. But as adults, we have usually developed a reservoir of experience so we can get through the routines of day-to-day living, anticipate problems, and in general view the world in a reasonably consistent fashion.

Developing children are just beginning to struggle with aspects of prediction. Though they are not nearly as skillful as adults in anticipating problems or thinking far into the future, they are nonetheless busy with the work of learning how the world works. This probably has a larger purpose than merely to know what bit of behavior to carry out in the next moment. Even at a very early age, children develop a primitive worldview: often toddlers believe that clouds hold fire, that the wind is alive because it moves, or that the sun follows them from place to place. They develop a sense that the world tends to operate in a certain orderly fashion: a three-year-old boy might believe that when he grows up to be "a big man," his parents will grow down and become "little boys." Children also tend to see themselves as certain types and thus start to develop a rudimentary self-concept: it is not uncommon for preschoolers to talk about themselves as shy, bad, strong, nice, big, or good. All of the above depends upon their developing the capacity to understand and to predict events in the world around them.

The concept of control is no less crucial. If we search our own experience, we will realize how important feeling in control of a situation is to us. In order to control a situation, though, we have to understand it and be able to predict the consequences of various courses of action. Our ability to act effectively in a situation is intimately tied to our ability to understand it. Again, most of us, through our understanding of the world, are usually able to regulate our behavior to some

degree. We get up for work and try to get there on time so we do not
get fired. We plan meals and eat so we do not get hungry.

Certainly some aspects of our lives may get out of control at times.
Marriages end in divorce, we can be fired from our jobs, and we may
abuse drugs and alcohol. But as adults, we know there are certain
steps we can take in order to regain control of our lives. We can obtain
counseling, go into treatment for our alcohol problems, seek the advice
of friends and clergy. When we get back on our feet, we speak of it
as "getting in control of our lives." We learn to take responsibility for
ourselves.

The process for children is quite similar. At each stage of development, children go through what the Swiss psychologist Jean Piaget
termed *the process of adaptation.* As children take in new information
about the world around them, they must learn to adjust their concept
of the world in some way. As they are able to make these adjustments,
they begin to adjust their behavior as well. A preschooler who refuses
toilet training goes to a nursery school where he sees other little boys
in colorful underpants—guess what he suddenly insists on learning.
What children find is that as they improve their ability to predict
events, they are better able to act in order to control the situation. A
boy snatches a toy away from a younger child, then realizes that his
father has seen the act and is moving toward him. He quickly looks
at the other child and says, "Please?" His father sits down. As children
become able to efficiently control encounters, their ability to predict
a pattern in subsequent situations improves.

The processes of prediction and control are intimately related. As
a child learns to predict the behavior of others, he learns to set limits
on his own behavior and improves his self-control. The development
of self-control is crucial to the child's subsequent ability to establish
and maintain relationships with other children and adults. As children
are increasingly able to do this, they achieve a certain level of social
mastery. This breeds self-confidence and the willingness to assume
responsibility and independence. This scenario, however, assumes that
all goes well.

But often all *doesn't* go well. Children also learn very quickly that
they are "bad" and that it is wise to avoid responsibility at all costs.
They can learn that people don't like them and can easily prove this
by acting as obnoxious as possible. It is important to understand that
children are always engaged in the business of predicting the world

around them and regulating their behavior accordingly. Though you may think of your child as a little stinker, in actuality he or she is more like a little scientist. Children develop hypotheses, test them out, and evaluate their results. The answers they come up with lead in turn to the development of new hypotheses, or to the scrapping of a whole line of theory. Misbehavior is the medium of the child-scientist. Predictable, consistent discipline is the means by which you can provide predictable, orderly answers.

EARLY DEVELOPMENT AND THE ROLE OF MISBEHAVIOR

Let's explore the ways in which misbehavior and child development seem to go together. Certainly children develop particular abilities according to an orderly schedule. They also misbehave in fairly predictable ways. These coincide with their mental and physical development.

Children move through—or rather slide through—some fairly clear stages in their psychological development. They do not appear to leap from stage to stage as though they were going up a staircase. Instead, they seem to gradually evolve more complex mental skills. But as on a river passage, there are certain features of the channel or landmarks along the way by which you can mark progress.

Jean Piaget described several such stages in cognitive development. Initially, the infant is bound by *sensorimotor* (sensory-motor) behavior. With the development of language, the toddler passes into a transitional phase described as the *preoperational thought* stage. The young school-age child exhibits concrete operational thinking. This is when the child develops most basic academic skills in reading, spelling, and arithmetic. He is still, though, tied to factual information—the great list learner, baseball card collector, or name memorizer. It is not until early adolescence that the child begins to show the capacity for formal operational thought, which involves a greater degree of abstract thinking. Our concern is primarily with the toddler and young school-age child, to show how characteristic patterns of misbehavior are not only normal but *essential* to their psychological development at each stage.

During infancy, children are bound by their senses and their limited motor behavior. Though even newborns show brain responses to human speech, they aren't able to use language to relate to adults or to organize their behavior. Infants show a clear pattern of sensorimotor development during the first year. Usually, though not always, children roll, sit, crawl, stand, cruise, and then walk. Toward the end of infancy, they are often able to use simple words or sounds to identify specific objects or actions. Infants will often use an initial word to represent many meanings. An early word such as "up" can mean "Will you pick me up," "Oh, I hear an airplane," or "Take my plate, I'm finished." Often words are used to describe actions rather than things. As children move and sense in their immediate surroundings, they gradually develop some integrated, organized patterns of sensorimotor behavior. They begin to discover cause-effect relationships. How does a child first get his parents' attention? He cries and, much to his pleasure, finds that Mother comes running to pick him up, change his diaper, feed him, or just cuddle him. With some practice, the child learns to do this intentionally.

At about seven to nine months, children are able to think about objects that are out of their immediate sight. For example, they are able to search for an object that has been placed under a cloth. It is important to note, though, that they are not able to think about whether their behavior is good or bad. In fact, they don't have the language necessary to "think about" their behavior at all. They can conjure Mommy by crying and are delighted to see her when she appears. When they repeat this a dozen or more times, it is not through devilishness but through the pleasure of getting a happy result.

> Jean, the mother of eleven-month-old Marcus, could not get any rest at night. She had to hold the child until he fell asleep. If she put him down and tried to leave the room, he abruptly woke up and bellowed until she picked him up again. Eventually she began to sleep with him, not daring to move or breathe for fear he would wake up.
>
> This did not sit well with her husband, who insisted they talk to their doctor. The doctor suggested they just put the child down and let him cry. When they tried this, they were amazed to find that after two nights he went to sleep without protest. Moreover, he seemed happy and playful in the morning.

Infants do not cry to be annoying or to upset their parents, but only to make them attend to their needs quickly. What children learn during their infancy is that when they behave in certain ways, their environment tends to respond in certain ways. They learn to exert some control over their world and to achieve some measure of predictability.

Infants exert control over their world in ways that can perplex and annoy their parents. The infant food strike is an example of this. Often an infant will go through a period in which he refuses the breast or the bottle and then cries as though dissatisfied, as if he wants something else. This is easily misinterpreted as a signal that the child does not love his mother. Sometimes a mother will even fall for an old superstition: her milk must be bad! In fact, the child may simply be doing exactly what he appears to be doing: exerting some control over his own feeding. Many parents find that if they patiently wait the child out, he will "choose" to regulate his feeding correctly.

During toddlerhood, the child undergoes rapid growth and development in a number of areas. He begins to discover new ways to exert control over his immediate world and, in the process, presents a host of problems for the parents. The most obvious changes are purely physical: he is now able to walk and to run. This provides him with great freedom to move, to explore the world, and to bang his head on every surface and sharp edge in the house. During the latter part of this period, he is able to develop bowel and bladder control and becomes ready for toilet training, which will further increase his capacity for independent behavior.

It can also create a lot of headaches for the parents. Most children realize fairly quickly that controlling their bowels or bladder is not something you can *make* them do. For perhaps the first time, they have found an area in which they have *complete control* and which can also drive their parents *crazy!* Some children learn to use the toilet very quickly and are soon out of diapers and into underwear with their favorite cartoon character leaping off the front. Other children, though, show hesitation and a lot of stop-start behavior. This is very frustrating and annoying to parents, especially if it is important to them to have "trained children." Unfortunately, though the parent feels all the urgency and responsibility, the child has all the control. Some toddlers refuse to use the toilet until they are nearly four years old. Then abruptly one day they start using it. Although many parents worry about damaging their child's psyche through poor toilet training, *there is no evidence to support this fear*. Most children's variations are quite normal and have no lasting effect.

The major developmental issue that toddlers wrestle with is their own confidence in working out independent behaviors. For the first time, they are able to do things for themselves, and this can be an exciting, even exhilarating time. For some children who are more anxious and tentative, it can also be a very scary time. Transition and change are upsetting to children, and in their behavior they show a lot of progression followed by rapid regression. This type of inconsistency is often unsettling and frustrating for parents, who find themselves hesitant and uncertain as to whether to baby the child or demand that he act like a big boy. What the child may actually be doing is trying to develop skills in prediction and control by taking smaller steps. Some children are afraid of sudden leaps and prefer to go through change gradually, with a lot of rehearsal. We will discuss these frustrations further when we look at individual differences in temperament.

While all the above adjustments are important during toddlerhood, the most vital development is in the area of language. It is through language that children are able to communicate with other people and to "think about" their world. Some children seem to have a remarkable ability to string words together. But even though they appear to use language well, their capacity to think about their experience is still very limited and concrete. Their thinking is confined to the here-and-now, physical aspects of the situation. At this age you can still fool them into thinking you can see their shadows under a door. Although they may be able to toss off fairly abstract concepts like "being good" or "cooperation," they usually don't understand what they are talking about. Toddlers will often use words or phrases they have heard others use but that they can't yet adapt to specific situations. As a result, their phrasing is often inappropriate. A little boy talking about his recently disciplined sister might ask, "Anna go her room? He a naughty boy?"

The most significant behavioral trait of children during the toddler period epitomizes what is known as the "terrible twos." This is the negativistic and oppositional behavior which begins when a child is approximately sixteen to eighteen months old and lasts through late adolescence. Their operative word during this period is "no," and the phrase "I can do it myself" is frequently heard. This is especially important to heed since this is exactly what the child is doing: developing a sense of self.

Buddy was a fierce, defiant two-year-old always ready to do battle when his mother tried to get him to eat his vegetables. After an hour at the table, the conflict would become open war:

"Eat your vegetables."

"No!"

"Eat them, or else."

"No! Can't make me!"

"How about if I spank that little fat bottom of yours."

"It won't hurt me. I still not eating it . . . yucky."

"I'll take away your bunny for a week."

"I don't care, I not eating it."

"If you eat it I'll give you pie."

"I all done. Gimme pie."

"Eat your vegetables first."

"No, I all done. I not hungry. Gimme pie."

"If you're not hungry for vegetables, you're not hungry for pie."

"I hungry for pie, just not for this . . . yuck!"

It is very easy for parents to become extremely frustrated with the sheer defiance of children during this age. As in the example above, a frustrated parent might threaten all sorts of horrible reprisals only to be stunned by the child's rubberheadedness. Doesn't this kid realize how big and powerful I am? Apparently not! Most parents don't intend to carry out half of the awful things they say, but the hostility they feel shocks and shames them. What has happened to Little Baby Boo-Coo? What have you become?

This defiance can also create a lot of problems for parents who expect their young children to cooperate and to share with others. This is a time when parents often get their two-year-olds together to play. After all, they are beginning to talk and are showing some developing symbolic play. Parents expect their child to get along with others and be a "good" playmate. They want their child to share and are embarrassed when she snatches a toy away from another child and then pushes his face in the sand. Parents work overtime modeling "please" and "thank you," yet their toddlers seem to take no notice and are abrupt, surly, and rude.

Unfortunately, this is exactly what children are supposed to be doing during this period. They develop a sense of themselves through their possessions. It takes a while for children to learn social interaction skills. Initially they may consider another child nothing more than an object with whom they have to compete. From a cognitive standpoint, their thinking is extremely egocentric. They are unable to take another's perspective or to understand another's feelings.

Children learn to control their own behavior as they grow more able to understand and predict the specific consequences of their acts. But notice how concrete and mechanical their behavior is. After a child burns his hand on the stove, he consistently points to the stove and says, "Owie, hot, no touch it." It all happens on a level of "If I do this, then this is what happens." They are able to use language in concrete ways; they don't understand abstract ideas or metaphors. Time concepts such as "later," "in a while," or "tomorrow" are lost on a toddler. If you say you are "juggling too many things right now," the toddler waits for the balls and duckpins to appear. While some children may attempt to regulate their behavior after parents appeal to their special relationship, this is still very inconsistent at best. "Now, son, you be nice to your little sister—for Daddy." Big smiles and assurances. Two minutes later he's whacking her with his laser saber.

During the preschool and early school-age years, children show increasing development of complexity in their language. They are able to extend their questioning from a self-limiting *what, when,* and *where* to the ever-expanding forms of *why* and *how.* There is tremendous growth in classifying and organizing all manners of experience and behavior. This is the stage at which parents often become concerned that their children seem to be excessively competitive.

When Veronica came home from first grade she was very excited. She had learned all about school and was eager to tell her parents. Now, she was going to a school in which competition was de-emphasized. Teachers graded "qualitatively" and even the reading groups' levels were disguised with animal names. None of this fooled Veronica, who chattered away at the dinner table spilling all of the secrets the school tried to hide: "You know I'm the third-best speller in my class. Mary and Elizabeth are ahead of me but Mary cheats. I'm gonna tell, too. And Becky keeps saying she's a better speller than me, but she's lying. None of the boys are good spellers except Matthew. Billy says he is but he's in the slow reading group. They call it 'the Eagles' but it's really the slow group. But I'm only the sixth best in math. Matthew's the best, then Michael, then Angela, Mary, and I think next comes Marcie or maybe Nathan. I asked Mary but she wasn't sure either. Then it's me.

Becky says she's gooder at math than me but she isn't, I'm better, and
Mary says so too . . ."

This type of behavior is *essential* to a child's intellectual growth. As
children are describing themselves as bigger, better, faster, or smarter,
they are moving from nominal categorizing (for example, naming fruits,
vegetables, and colors) to categories based on some order of elements.
They are able to arrange them in sequences and begin to be able to
predict what comes next. They learn to use rules to organize their
behavior and their thinking. If, for example, they learn to order elements on the basis of size, they are able to identify which should come
next in a series by comparing the size of the remaining elements.
"Size" becomes the organizing principle. They are no longer solely
dependent upon concrete, immediate cause-effect relationships. In
their day-to-day behavior, they are more able to operate on the basis
of rules and are not so dependent on how their parents react in each
and every specific circumstance.

Of course, as they improve their capacity to organize their thinking,
they learn to ask more complex questions. As they learn to ask more
complex questions, they increase their capacity to test out their parents
in complex ways. They are now more apt to look for the subtleties
when they ask themselves, "What happens if . . . ?" Like little scien-
tists, they begin to test hypotheses and develop theories about how the
world works.

The general pattern of behavior, though, even at ages four and five,
is still controlled by the immediate consequences of their actions: the
rewards and punishments. Up to seven years of age, even though they
become increasingly able to articulate abstract rules, their immediate
behavior is still governed by immediate consequences. But as they
develop, they are also increasingly responsive to individual relationships: a boy takes care of his sister because his mother asked him to.

In other words, they may choose to do something or to refrain from
doing something because of the anticipated impact it might have on
some specific person; a girl doesn't join in a group that is picking on
another child, because they are "hurting" her and hurting is wrong.
But please note how difficult it is for children to do this. As parents,
often we expect our young children to do as we ask out of love, and
yet they are simply not ready from a developmental standpoint to do
this.

To Sum Up: The Development of Self-Regulation and Social Mastery

Children, from infancy through their early school years, are limited in their intentional behavior by their level of cognitive development. Most young children are not able to regulate their behavior on the basis of abstract rules or even appeals to relationship. They react best to concrete, immediate responses to their actions.

We have all fallen under the sway of moralizing to our preschooler. Towering over a four-year-old and turning purple in the face, we have lectured on social responsibility, the Golden Rule, and the importance of individual moral behavior in the larger context of blah, blah, blah. But what does the child listen to? Our abstract message? No, this is a four-year-old, remember, and her thinking is extremely concrete, bound to the specific situation. It is the tone of voice, the words, the sustained attention she is given that catch and hold her attention.

Certainly children are interested in and listen to our messages about what is good and bad. They may even be able to repeat these word for word. But small children, even normal and "easy" ones, are often not able to adjust their behavior on such abstracts as "goodness" and "badness." They are much more responsive to the direct consequences of their behavior. How did it feel after it was over? Was it worth what Mom and Dad did when they found out? Did the consequences have such an impact that they would be less likely to do the same thing again? So often we want our children to understand the meaning of an act and what they respond to is just our behavior at the time.

The consistency and predictability of the parents' response to the child then becomes the critical issue. This is the feedback that children use to regulate their own behavior. The more children are able to anticipate these predictable patterns of behavior, the more they are able to control their behavior in advance. They can increasingly recognize the cues that certain things are going to happen and can adjust their behavior accordingly. During infancy, toddlerhood, and the early school-age years, the two motivating principles seem to be learning to control events and learning to predict how others are likely to respond. This is evident at every stage, from the infant's crying and watching for Mother, to the toddler's limit testing, to the preschooler's incessant questioning and arguing. See how the child proceeds in a scientific fashion. He starts with specific behaviors, forms them into patterns, tests variations, and as his language develops, distills these patterns into fairly concrete rules. But it is not until the child approaches middle childhood that he is able to more fully respond to the rules themselves or to appeals on the basis of relationship. Initially and throughout most of early childhood, it is the predictability of the response to his behavior that enables him to develop consistency and self-control.

Now that we have seen how children use misbehavior to explore and control their parents, let's look at some important ways in which children differ. Each young child starts out with a unique temperament and gradually develops an individual personality. In addition, children continually differ in the way they react. Some children tend to be more introverted, while others are more extroverted. Finally, children differ in the ways in which they think. These factors influence how they organize their experiences, behave or misbehave, and respond to your discipline.

3

What Makes Your Child Different

All children are unique. Ask any parent, and they can list the differences between their children. While it is not a good practice to *expect* one child to perform at the level of another sibling, all parents compare their children. It is only natural. They know which child is more active, more emotional, more creative, more of a daredevil. These differences do exist and to understand them is very important, because just as children vary in temperament, they also differ in the way they interpret their experience. They each learn differently. If you understand how they learn, then you will know how to teach them.

A child misbehaves in a restaurant. All children do this at some time because restaurants are noisy, stimulating places that disrupt a child's normal mealtime routine. The way children misbehave is pretty much the same. Simply put, they do not *contain* their behavior. They get down from their chairs and want to run around; they yell or make other noises that attract attention; they have noisy tantrums when they don't get exactly what they want. But the reasons they misbehave vary greatly. One child may be upset because the ritual of mealtime is disturbed and he doesn't know what to expect from this unfamiliar person in the black and white outfit. Another child, insensitive to uncertainty, may be stimulated to explore someone else's table, the potted plants, or the waitress station. Still another child may be so overstimulated by the noise and confusion in the restaurant that her self-control dissolves like a Fizzy. Though the form of misbehavior looks similar, the underlying reasons for the problems are very different.

As parents, we all get a lot of well-meaning advice on how to raise our children. Usually it centers on the techniques in child control that have been used by others with success. But someone else's child is not your child. One parent may tell you to ignore the misbehavior and it will stop. Perhaps, but then your child may start throwing his plates against the wall, just in case you didn't notice. Another parent may offer the time-honored advice to give the child a few "good cracks" across the rear end. That will make him listen! Maybe. Then again, you may have the type of child who does not respond to physical punishment. There are such children. If that is the case, you may as well go out and spank your car tire.

Understanding what makes your child different from other children not only enriches your relationship, but also helps you understand his developmental needs. These needs concern not only what are likely to be problems for your child but also how your child experiences, organizes, and learns. The differences between children arise from several sources. Much of the child's evolving personality is learned. He assimilates a particular set of experiences and learns to accommodate the demands of his environment in certain characteristic ways. In Piaget's terms, he learns to adapt. But there also appears to be a *genetic component* to the child's developing personality. Children are each wired in a slightly different way, and this may determine how they experience the world from birth, how they respond to their experience, and the types of experiences they seek out in the future. For example, some children are more introverted, others more extraverted; some more emotionally reactive, others more flexible and adaptable.

Even though temperaments are evident shortly after birth, a child's personality is not genetically *fixed*. Children have a tremendous capacity for growth and change, but certain temperamental characteristics do influence how a child learns and may be especially prominent during the preschool and early school-age years. Understanding these characteristics may provide important clues if you are trying to untangle the knot of complex, chronic behavior problems.

BABIES AND THEIR TEMPERAMENTS

From the moment a baby sees daylight upon emerging from her amniotic bath, she is a unique individual. Initially, this can be seen in the way the baby reacts to the sights, sounds, smells, feel, and taste of the environment. During the first few months of life a clear behavioral style emerges, and this has been termed the child's *temperament*.

T. Berry Brazelton, a pediatrician by training and the author of numerous books on infant and child care, developed a method for assessing how infants respond to their world. In a nutshell, the technique involves shaking up the infants and otherwise startling them with bright lights, loud noises, and strong smells. The initial startled response of the infant is rated. The infant is then picked up and cuddled, and her ability to become soothed and settled is evaluated. Though this seems like a fairly unfriendly way to welcome a newborn into the world, it does give an idea of how an infant is wired to respond to the buzzing and booming confusion around her. Some infants are hypersensitive and show an exaggerated startled response, often also exhibiting difficulty getting soothed or settled. At the other end of the spectrum are those infants who show extreme withdrawal behavior. Most babies fall somewhere in the middle. As infants grow, their activity and their response to the world around them develop a characteristic style. In the book *Infants and Mothers,* Brazelton describes three types of infants, which he terms the quiet baby, the active baby, and the average baby. The quiet baby is characterized by a sluggish response to the world around her and more withdrawal-type behavior. The active baby, on the other hand, shows much more exploratory behavior and a brisk emotional response to her environment. The average baby's responses fall somewhere in the middle. The book describes vast differences in the way each of the three types progresses through the first year of life.

Perhaps the most significant work on infant temperament arose from the studies of Stella Chess and Alexander Thomas, two prominent New York psychiatrists. Beginning in 1956, they began a longitudinal study of infants in the New York area. The study was undertaken to understand how children with different temperaments grew up: how they got along with their families, established friendships, performed at school, etc. The study also looked at what types of problems these children typically encountered and how they learned to cope with them. Chess and Thomas were impressed by the clearly different behavior infants displayed shortly after birth. They categorized these differences and then watched to see how they influenced the children as they grew. Later, an infant temperament scale was developed by psychologists W. B. Carey and S. C. McDevitt. The characteristics dealt with the following:

1. *Activity level:* Infants show great variation in their simple physical activity shortly after birth. Some wiggle and squirm constantly, never seeming to rest. Parents are often startled and amazed because their baby acts as though she had forty volts running through her. Other parents, though, become concerned because their child is so quiet they mistake her for a pillow in the corner of the crib.

2. *Rhythmicity:* Children vary greatly in their biological rhythms. Some children come home from the hospital and, after one or two bluffs at midnight feedings, start sleeping through the night with great regularity. Others are completely unpredictable, waking up six times one night and then sleeping for forty-eight hours straight. Still other infants show a predictable pattern of nighttime awakening with the frequencies diminishing over the first five or six months. Variations are also seen in feeding time and in the frequency of bowel movements.

3. *Mood:* Some babies are happy little souls, bubbling away and sucking on their toes. Others, however, are not so happy and spend a good deal of the first year of life crying and complaining, whining and moaning, and otherwise fussing constantly.

4. *Intensity:* Some children tend to be placid little creatures who float through their first year on a glasslike pond of tranquillity. At the other extreme are those infants who come into the world on an emotional roller coaster that has immense peaks and valleys. They have a cry that could shatter glass, and a laugh that is no less intense. As they grow older the intensity of these extremes seems to increase.

5. *Threshold:* This refers to the point at which a child will respond to a given stimulus. To all children the world is new, and they need some capacity to tolerate the line drives of life ricocheting off their newborn bodies. Some infants seem exceptionally tolerant, while other infants react to even minor changes as though a bomb had gone off in

their diaper. As older children the latter become much more upset than others over seemingly minor problems. "Oh, that doesn't hurt," we may say when such a child falls. Well, to her, it *does* hurt.

6. *Approach/withdrawal:* This is a very critical element in a child's temperament. Some children greet novel stimuli in their environment with delight. They have what is called an *approach style.* They move toward and explore with eagerness. Other children display a *withdrawal style:* they retreat from and are very upset by novelty.

7. *Adaptability:* Adaptable children are those who seem to take change in routine in stride. They are the ones who are not especially upset by changes in feeding or sleeping schedules or other disruptions in their routine. These are the ones the parents can take to cocktail parties and leave sleeping on a pile of coats. Other children, though, show marked inability to adjust to change. If you say the wrong word during the bedtime routine, they demand you start the whole process again from the beginning. And this time, please get it right!

8. *Attention span:* By the time a child is six or seven months old and sitting up, she is usually able to stay engaged with an object for some measurable period of time. She explores it, shakes it, sticks it in her mouth, and generally monkeys around with it. Some children show a heightened ability to stay with an object and can often occupy themselves for long periods of time. Other children show very limited capacity to sustain their attention, and bounce from object to object like a Ping-Pong ball thrown into a room full of mousetraps.

9. *Distractibility:* A better term for this would be *soothability.* Some children, when they are upset, are quickly soothed. When their parents pick them up, their bodies conform to the parents' and they quiet themselves. Other infants, though, take an extremely long time to become settled and soothed. They may arch and pull away from their parents or they may simply persist in crying for long periods of time.

An infant's temperament can be defined by how she behaves in terms of these nine characteristics. As Chess and Thomas assessed children over several decades, they found that three patterns of interest emerged. First of all, they found that most children fell into a sort of middle group, showing some areas in which they were difficult and others in which they were easier. A small group at the positive end seemed to show very consistent "easy" characteristics. These were infants who were normally active; established regular biological rhythms quickly; were generally happy, stable, and tolerant; reasonable approach behavior; adapted well; and had an approp attention span.

At the other end of the spectrum were children with difficult temperaments, who were characterized by a high activity level; difficulty regulating their biological rhythms; negative moods; high-intensity emotional reactions; and a low threshold of responsiveness. Often they showed a short attention span and had a low tolerance for frustration. They showed significant problems adjusting to change and coping with novelty in their environment. In the original study, about ten percent of the children showed severely difficult temperaments—these are the children who give you gray hair *before* they reach the terrible twos.

Still other children showed a "slow-to-warm-up" temperament. These were children who were generally not as difficult but did have problems adjusting to change or tolerating novelty in their environment. They showed much less exploratory behavior and were more likely to withdraw. This is the type of child who, when you are trying to make a great impression on your favorite wealthy maiden aunt, takes one look at her face and screams in abject terror. The lesson here is important, especially if you are trying to butter up a wealthy relative: always give a slow-to-warm-up baby time to adjust to new people or situations. Given time, these children usually adapt adequately, perform admirably, and may earn some of their college tuition in the bargain.

TEMPERAMENT AND THE DIMENSION OF EMOTIONAL REACTIVITY

What is most important about the Chess and Thomas work is that it showed that many of these temperamental characteristics persisted throughout childhood. Children who had difficult temperaments during infancy tended to exhibit similar characteristics during their early childhood. They were often the ones who were more likely to have trouble regulating their feelings and adjusting to changes in their world, and who showed significant problems regulating the quality of their mood, the intensity of their reactions, and their threshold of responsiveness.

...an thunderstorm ready to burst. As a baby he had
...ecause of his constant crying and his many night
...tor had given the family some medicine because
...colicky. He was now three years old and still did
...night. But most of all, the parents were concerned
...violence. He was always killing his stuffed animals
...tables for weapons. His parents would not allow
...artoons or to play with guns. Still he would chew
his peanut butter sandwich into the shape of a gun and "shoot" his little sister.

The dimension we are looking at when we examine children with difficult temperaments is one that we could title "emotional reactivity." At one end of this dimension children are much less reactive and appear to be more emotionally stable. At the other extreme are children who from infancy onward are extremely reactive and tend to be more changeable in their feelings. Sometimes these children are labeled *hyperactive* since they often have difficulty settling down, exhibit problems getting along with others, and seem to become disorganized in stimulating, confusing situations. These children are more likely to have prolonged and intense emotional reactions when they don't get their way. While other children can accept being told no, or can adjust to changes in plans, these children have an exceptionally difficult time of it. Most important is that they appear to have had this difficulty since birth. Their trouble regulating their feelings and their behavior also affects their ability to get along with other children, especially in groups. Often parents report their child can get along well on a one-to-one basis, but as soon as there is more than one child, trouble is sure to follow. These children are more likely to have adjustment difficulties during their childhood, and the problems crop up not only in the family but also in the school and community.

But there is also a bright side to the children with difficult temperaments. As was found by Chess and Thomas, and later echoed by Stanley Greenspan, these difficult children could adjust as long as their environment accommodated their special needs. When the environment could not accommodate their temperaments, then these children were certainly more likely to have major adjustment problems during childhood. But when the fit between the family and the difficult child was reasonably good, they often learned to adapt and grew up to be healthy, normal adults. Of course, they were somewhat more emotional than other people, but they were not at all abnormal.

The more a child has difficulty regulating his emotions, the more he requires effective teaching from his parents. This is not as difficult as it sounds. When children are extremely reactive, they have difficulty soothing and settling themselves when they become upset. They also have difficulty tolerating stimulating settings and pacing themselves during stimulating tasks. Parents need to concentrate on structuring the level of stimulation these children experience and eventually to teach the children to do that for themselves. An important area of discipline is in structuring activities so they are more predictable; children who are extremely reactive tend to do better in situations that have more routine. Parents also need to attend to the pace of activities so these children do not get overstimulated and out of control. It is imperative to plan enough breaks for them so they can soothe and settle themselves. Finally, these children tend to escalate their behavior when the level of stimulation increases. This means it is important to lower the level of stimulation when you are attempting to help the children get themselves under control. It is usually unwise to yell at these children since this will probably only get them more disorganized than before. Using a soft voice and clear, concise commands will be far more helpful. In general, the more emotionally reactive the child is, the more the parent has to attend to controlling the level of stimulation.

INTROVERTS AND EXTRAVERTS

What is seen during infancy as an approach or a withdrawal style is often seen during childhood as an early form of introversion or extraversion. Like emotional reactivity, this style probably has a strong biological component. That is, introverted parents tend to have introverted children, and extraverted parents tend to have extraverted children. As with emotional reactivity, however, there are a lot of misconceptions about introversion and extraversion. This is an important topic to consider because it is probably one of the few aspects of personality that has been related to how people learn.

How do we normally think of extraverted people? If we watch commercials on television, we can gain some important clues. Most commercials will portray happy, active young people with white teeth and apricot-colored tans bashing volleyballs on the beach, diving into the surf, racing fast cars, or dancing the night away. The introvert is the skinny guy with corrective lenses who cowers behind the books in some musty library corner. Clearly, to be extraverted is to be sociable and desirable; to be introverted is neither.

But initially introversion and extraversion have very little to do with beaches or barrooms. Even during infancy you can see a range in the way children respond to stimulation. Some infants tend to be more quiet, exhibit a long attention span, and withdraw more from anything novel, especially if it is complex and noisy. Other infants show unrestrained approach behavior and heightened exploratory activity. The critical feature in the development of introversion or extraversion seems to be the developing child's capacity to tolerate novel stimulation and to sustain his attention.

Introverted children seem to show a great natural ability for holding their attention on an object. While they are attending to something, they become annoyed if something else comes into their sensory field and disrupts their attention. Later, as these children develop greater language skills, they seem to devote more attention to their own internal thoughts and feelings and are much less likely to orient their attention to the outside world. They seem to be stimulated enough from the inside, so that added outside stimulation has a disrupting influence. If introverted children are less social it is not because they don't like people. They do like people and they are very interested in other children. But they can tolerate only so much stimulation, and noisy groups of children push the needles right off their meters.

> Carlos was a very quiet little boy who had trouble getting his work done in school. He seemed to daydream a lot and was easily distracted if there was any sort of noise in the classroom. His teacher didn't know what to do with him. He liked to play with another quiet child but did not take part in the group games on the playground. He preferred to stay inside at lunchtime. Sometimes he wouldn't get his work done so he would have an excuse to stay inside. The teacher tried sticker charts and tokens to get him to work faster. He was always agreeable but then would act like he didn't care. She began to wonder if he didn't have an attention problem.

In contrast, extraverted children will probably show an approach style from fairly early on. They enjoy complex, noisy environments and seem to crave this kind of stimulation. They are more likely to show exploratory behavior and less likely to sustain their attention for very long. As they learn to use language more effectively, they show more social behavior—probably because it is a very good way to keep the flow of novel stimulation going. These approach-oriented, extraverted children do not tolerate isolation well and also do not tolerate boredom. They seek stimulation from the world around them, not from their own thoughts.

>   Micki was a bright, active little girl who was at her best in groups of children. She loved to talk to the other children and was very friendly to everyone. She found schoolwork uninteresting, though she always did well on her weekly spelling tests. She learned her math facts very quickly and did well on her "mad minute" tests on Friday. But she had trouble staying with a task and preferred talking to the girls on either side of her desk. She could also be impatient and would blurt out answers without waiting her turn. Her teacher thought she might have an attention problem. She tried using sticker charts for following rules and listening. This worked like a charm for one week. Then Micki said she was bored with it and asked if they could try something else.

During the toddler years, another important difference between introverts and extraverts becomes evident. When I talk to parents about their children, I find that as a rule extraverted children are much less responsive to physical pain. When they do hurt, they are more likely to bounce back and continue their exploratory activities than introverted children. In contrast, the introverted children often need a lot of coaxing and seem to be very sensitive to physical pain. They often will not try a new activity unless they are guaranteed of success. In addition to physical pain, they seem to be more acutely sensitive to emotional pain. Introverted children show more anxious, fearful behavior in novel or threatening situations. The extraverted children show much less fearfulness and are more likely when hurt to simply get angry.

In terms of learning, the degree of introversion and extraversion seems to be strongly related to how children respond to rewards and punishments. As a rule, extraverted children seem to be much more responsive to external, positive reinforcement. These are the children who are likely to try something in order to get something they want. These are the kids who are more likely to gamble and less likely to consider possible negative consequences of their behavior. In contrast, the introverted children are much more acutely sensitive to the possible negative consequences and much more wary of punishment. Not surprisingly, they also don't work very hard for the usual "positive reinforcement."

This creates a lot of problems for parents and teachers. Most adults have been taught that behavior modification has something to do with charts and stickers and giving loud, noisy praise whenever a child does something appropriate. This is the type of reinforcement that works very well for extraverted children but not always so well with introverted children. These children seem to be motivated much more to avoid pain and punishment than to achieve some tangible reward. These are children who learn much better when the personal meaning of the task is enhanced, and this seems to be the key to motivating them. If you have an introverted child, you must work to ease his fears and show him how completing the task will help increase his competence. If you do this, you will find he is more likely to give something new a try.

Children's orientation toward positive or negative reinforcement has other effects as well. For example, extraverted children are more likely to improvise and are better at short-term learning. These are the kids who never study until the last minute yet always seem to get A's. Introverted children tend to need more rehearsal time and a slower pace to their learning. They seem to plod along, but when they learn something, it becomes set in stone.

While introverts have a longer attention span, they also retain information differently. Extraverts lean more toward a "load and dump" strategy that is compatible with short-term learning. They learn, take the test, and then forget. In contrast, introverts seem to learn best when they can relate some new bit of information to a lot of other information they have learned before. The first time you test these children they may or may not do well, but if you give them a surprise test two weeks later, you will find they do as well as, if not better than, before. They simply don't forget.

Introverted children, as a result, seem to obsess more over their learning. They also obsess over emotional pain. Not surprisingly, given their short-term learning style and high tolerance for pain, extraverts are more likely to forget punishing experiences, which roll off them more easily. In fact, extraverts will tend to evaluate situations much more positively than introverts do. Introverts tend to be more self-critical, especially when it comes to their work. They also remember their pain in exquisite detail. "Hey, Dad, remember when I was two and you slapped my hand for touching your cigarettes?" The child remembers this and you've forgotten you ever smoked. Introverts and elephants never forget an injury.

Perhaps the most crucial difference between introverts and extraverts is that as a result of their initial disposition to tolerate certain amounts and types of stimulation, they develop very different orientation biases: an introverted child who becomes upset by complexity and confusion is likely to seek out different types of experiences from a more extraverted, stimulation-seeking child. This orientation bias probably has a strong influence over most aspects of social behavior and may also affect how a child competes in school. But this does not mean that many aspects of introverted or extraverted behavior cannot be altered through learning.

In our society, there is a strong social preference for extraverted behavior. This is clearly evident in most television commercials. To be outgoing, warm, and lively is highly desirable. Introverts are often misperceived as cold fish. As a result, many introverted children actively work on changing their social behavior during their early adolescent years. Through typical introverted ways, they study, rehearse, and act out specific social routines until they can master them with apparent ease. Eventually they look as though they are completely spontaneous. But though they often show very outgoing social behavior, they still maintain many of the learning characteristics of the introvert. They tend to dislike noisy, confusing environments; are much less likely to gamble; perceive unclear situations pessimistically; and prefer to learn new activities in quiet.

In some cases, extraverts can learn to modify their study behavior so they can sustain their concentration, tolerate isolation, and inhibit their behavior. Extraverted children can learn numerous skills to plan, monitor, and evaluate their more impulsive behavior. Even though the basic tendency toward introversion and extraversion is probably biological, many of the outward behaviors, especially social behaviors, can be modified, though with some degree of difficulty.

The dimension of introversion-extraversion is very important since it tells us how to motivate our children. The more introverted the child is, the more the parent will probably have to focus on helping

her take initial steps to try a new task. This means helping her overcome anticipation of possible negative outcomes. It also means teaching
her the difference between taking a reasonable chance and a hopeless
gamble. Introverted children do not respond very well to external
rewards, and these do not necessarily need to be used. These children
are more likely to learn if the task is meaningful to them. When
teaching these children, emphasize the value of the task to their developing sense of competence. These children will also put more effort
into a task if they value their relationship with the teacher.

The more extraverted the child is, the more she will respond to
external positive reinforcement and the less she will probably respond
to punishment. If children are extremely extraverted, most forms of
punishment should be discontinued. This is not because of any moral
injunction against punishment but simply because it won't work. This
does not mean these children should not be given time-outs. It is
important to understand, though, that a time-out is merely an inter-
ruption in the child's behavior, not a punishment; it is a way to interrupt the flow of negative behavior so the child can be redirected to
more positive behavior. Extraverted children learn best when their
attention is occupied by appropriate behavior for which they can be
positively reinforced.

COGNITIVE STYLES

While children differ in their emotional reactivity and their ability
to tolerate external stimulation (introversion versus extraversion), they
also differ in their intellectual ability and in what has been termed
their *cognitive style*. There are a number of factors which influence
how children understand their experience and organize and respond
to their world.

First of all, children differ in the rate of their *cognitive development*.
Consider the tremendous variation among two- and three-year-olds.
Some children are toilet trained by the time they are eighteen months
old, while other children may leave parents holding dirty diapers until
they are nearly four. Some children say clear, intelligible words by the
time they are nine months old, while others do not begin speaking
until they are nearly two. By kindergarten, there are those who know
the alphabet, can count to a zillion, can write their name, and can do

the cartwheels they learned in gymnastics class. In contrast, there are others who do not yet know their primary colors. Does this mean that the preschool superstars will all be geniuses? Fortunately, it does not.

Keep in mind that most preschool measures of ability are very poor predictors of academic performance at the third-grade level. This is because what is seen during the preschool years is an unfolding process. Some children mature at a fairly rapid rate, while others develop more slowly. Certainly a parent whose child is not walking by eighteen months or has no speech by age two has a right to be concerned. Children who show these kinds of lags may be exhibiting some type of developmental disorder or may be at a higher risk for learning disabilities. But, within limits, there is considerable variation in the rates at which children develop their cognitive abilities. They mature at different rates.

The second factor concerns the child's *cognitive style*. All individuals have a characteristic way in which they go about the business of learning. Some tend to think in pictures, and ideas are easily translated into a stream of mental visual images. When others try to see with their mind's eye, they find theirs needs glasses: no images appear, like a TV caught between channels. Often these people think in words. They talk to themselves constantly. Both types of mental imaging are called *mediation,* and many people have definite preferences. Differences in the way children mediate their experiences are important since they provide clues as to how they learn.

Some children, especially those who rely on verbal mediation (who also, incidentally, tend to be more anxious), tend to show a more focused, analytical cognitive style. In the extreme, these children tend to obsess on minute details and may have trouble seeing "the big picture." Often these are children who are very conservative in their problem solving. They may be more likely to plod through slowly in a step-by-step fashion. As long as the work load is meted out in a slow, predictable stream, they are able to maintain a high level of organization. When the work load increases, though, they are very susceptible to disorganization. This is because they are focusing on each detail as it comes in and have a limited capacity to integrate and organize information. This may mean they will be brilliant in their academic work when they have adequate preparation time. But they may be completely at sea when trying to cope with concrete immediate problems in day-to-day living. These children can have a lot of trouble in fast-moving group sports like basketball or soccer. They may have very good splinter skills but get lost in the game itself.

In contrast, there are those who tend to neglect detail and focus on the larger picture. They seem to respond intuitively to the flow of a situation and do not approach problems in an organized manner. This is a cognitive style that works extremely well in social situations. These children are very attentive to all nonverbal aspects of communication, such as tone of voice, posture, facial expression, and social grouping. They may develop strong skills flowing with complex situations. They are the ones who are called "instinctive" by others. You can see this in the way they play soccer or basketball. These children tend to adopt a riskier problem-solving style: they rely less on organization of details and prefer to use intuitive leaps. This can result in their being very disorganized and careless in their schoolwork. They are simply not careful.

As with extraversion and emotional reactivity, these cognitive styles represent extreme ends of a dimension. Most children fall somewhere in the middle and exhibit some analytical skills and some intuitive sense. It is inviting to equate analytical problem solving with introversion and intuition with extraversion. More often than not this equation may be accurate, especially in the extreme, but what we are exploring here are simply the differences in thinking and problem solving and not the larger personality structure; so for the time being, let us consider cognitive style as somewhat separate from personality. This brings us to one final aspect of cognitive difference: competence.

As much as we would like our children to all be above average, they simply aren't. Competence in various intellectual tasks usually shows the same pattern as other dimensions. The majority of children cluster somewhere in the middle, with some trailing off below average and others showing higher ability. Moreover, it is completely normal for children to show variations in their abilities. Some children are more proficient at mathematics, while others excel in language-arts areas. Certainly a child's developing competence is going to affect his motivation. A child who is very successful in mathematics is probably going to show a preference for this activity, especially if he gets a lot of attention for the work. Such children tend to show more striking patterns of strengths and weaknesses.

There are also children who show specific learning disorders which have nothing to do with motivation or general intelligence. They may have specific skill deficiencies in reading, spelling, or mathematics. Instead of showing only average ability in these areas as compared with their other strengths, these children can't achieve at their grade level.

In terms of behavior there appear to be two types of learning disorders that have a major impact. Some children have significant problems with both forms of mental mediation, language and visual imaging. The importance of mediation cannot be overstated. It is the way in which children understand, organize their behavior, act, and evaluate the results.

Children who have these learning problems often appear hyperactive, spacey, and out of touch. They tend to act and then see what happens. They do not think things out in advance. They simply cannot organize their thinking and don't pay attention to what is important around them. They often miss cues to regulate their behavior. Because they have problems thinking things out in advance, they have trouble predicting what will happen if they behave in certain ways. Because they cannot predict the consequences of their behavior, they often fail to develop adequate controls over it. These children often arouse the wrath of adults because they are disorganized, don't complete their work, don't plan ahead, etc. Many such children, who have visual-perceptual motor problems, don't understand social situations and so are easily victimized by children their own age. In addition to being hopelessly irresponsible, they are often social outcasts.

Overall, it is important to consider not only children's feelings and their personalities but also these three aspects of intellectual functioning. One must assess a child's level of cognitive development since it is useless to try to get him to understand concepts for which he is not developmentally ready. One must try to understand a child's particular cognitive style: how he mediates his experience and goes about the business of solving problems. Finally, one must consider a child's level of cognitive competence. This means understanding not only his intellectual strengths and weaknesses but also his capacity to organize his behavior and to predict and control his immediate world.

Jared was a nine-year-old and a tremendous thorn in the side of his fourth-grade teacher. He would not listen to directions and did not get his work done. He was always involved in other people's business. When she would discipline him he seemed oddly happy and would answer with a smug "I don't care." He was falling farther and farther behind because he was not getting his work completed. His teacher had conferences with his parents and found they were unable to get him to work either. Eventually she referred this disruptive child to the school psychologist. A careful evaluation revealed he had a significant disability in both auditory language processing and reading. He was given extra help through the school's learning-disability program. His behavior improved dramatically.

Children with specific learning disorders are also more likely to present certain types of "behavior problems." It is essential to recognize learning disorders when they occur because these children will often develop some inappropriate acting-out behavior to defend themselves against the humiliation of being incompetent. Here the term *incompetent* is a subjective evaluation since this is the way most learning-disordered children see themselves. They see others able to do things they are not. If they are behavior problems, at least they appear to be in control of the situation. Any child would rather feel naughty than defective!

If there is a general rule that can be applied to this, it is that cognitive factors determine how information needs to be organized for the child. Some children can respond to fairly general concepts of behavior. All you have to do is explain once why you can't pick up kitty by the ears and they understand. Others, however, require more frequent, concrete cues. With some learning-disabled children, it is crucial to be very explicit with these cues in order to help them organize appropriately. Once again, the use of well-established routines can help them predict a sequence of events and regulate their behavior accordingly. The impact of cognitive factors on behavior cannot be overstated since they determine a child's capacity for and style of mental organization.

To Sum Up: Individual Differences and Discipline

All parents know that each child is a unique individual very different in many ways from other children. Often, though, these individual differences are not taken seriously, and they are especially neglected in matters of discipline. Instead, parents are told to concentrate on techniques of discipline that, for some odd reason, just don't seem to work. They don't work because these individual characteristics that make your child unique in her personality also make your child unique as a *learner*. In this chapter we have covered three different dimensions of a child's uniqueness that strongly influence how she experiences the world around her and learns. Simply put, children show differences in their emotional sensitivity and responsiveness. They also show differences in their tolerance for external stimulation and their responses to reward and punishment. Finally, children vary in their ability to think about and organize their experiences, and in the style in which they do it.

Now you can see why it is necessary to understand your child as a whole person. These factors are extremely important to take into account if the child is to profit from discipline. Please remember what discipline is all about: helping your children to predict and control their own experience in the world. In order to do this effectively, you have to take into account how they experience the world on many different levels. The goal is not to simply control your child but to teach your child *self*-control.

Above all, enjoy the individuality of your child. As you well know, this is not a laboratory animal or a trained pet. This is your child, the one who carries your brightest hopes. The fact that your child is having behavior problems does not mean these hopes are dashed. Children can learn. They can control their feelings, develop strong social skills, and learn to organize their behavior. In order to help them, you must try to understand the unique way in which they interpret the world around them. How they do this will provide you with the information you need on how to teach them. But before we plunge into the mechanics of discipline, let us take stock of the other important person in the relationship—you. You are, after all, the one who will lead your child down that difficult road. You are the most important person in your child's life.

4

Psyching Yourself Up

Your attitude toward your child, yourself, and the whole disagreeable business of discipline is what will make the entire process work. The child isn't going to discipline himself. The answer lies with you and your belief in yourself. So for the moment, forget about how you are going to punish *this* behavior or reward *that* one. Let's concentrate on you.

How were you raised as a child? Did your parents dote on your every want or need? Did they bend over backward to occupy your time? Probably not. If you were like most children then, your parents were far too busy with the day-to-day business of working and homemaking. The traditional attitude toward discipline is, "If it ain't broke, don't fix it." In other words, when children are behaving themselves, it is time to concentrate on laundry, cleaning, and cooking. It is time to get something done. Granted, if the child has been hurt or comes in for comfort, he needs attention. It is also appropriate to pay attention to some clever piece of artwork or new stunt, but this is usually done at the child's specific request. The parent in the traditional model does not actively seek out the child to find out what he is doing.

Discipline, then, is equated with punishment. Parents pay attention to children when they are acting up or behaving inappropriately. The message is clear and simple: "You stop that right now or else." Some sort of nasty consequence is tagged on, designed to deter the child from further inappropriate behavior. The child stops in his tracks, considers what the parent has to say, changes his behavior, and life gets back to its normal hum. In the traditional model, the threat or application of punishment is designed simply to deter deviant behavior.

Now, what about the positive approach? Most everyone has heard that positive reinforcement is supposed to promote good behavior. Parents know it is important to praise their children and that techniques such as sticker charts can help them achieve certain goals. At a more practical level, many of us received allowances while growing up and remember having to take out the trash or walk the dog in order to receive our pittance. As teenagers, some may have earned money toward that first car by successfully completing a work-related agreement ("I promise I won't get below a C—okay, a B, I won't get below a B, Dad, not in any subject, my whole junior year. How about it? Okay, a B+, Dad . . ."). We have also heard that positive reinforcement, in addition to promoting good behavior, can be used to persuade a child to correct some improper behavior.

Let us say there is a child who does not clean his room, but instead leaves his clothes balled up under the bed, sheets and blankets a rumpled mess, toys spread out across the floor. Nagging and threatening to dock his allowance don't seem to work. Then comes the suggestion, "Why not try positive reinforcement?" The parents know the boy would like a new bicycle and so they offer him the new bike if he will only keep his room picked up.

Initially he is quite enthusiastic about this, but seems to lose interest as time goes on. The parents find they seem to be nagging him more and more to clean up his room. They remind him repeatedly that he might not get the bike if he does not keep his room clean. After all, he does want the bike. Doesn't he?

How well do you suppose this is going to work? There is something seriously wrong with this approach because the outcome isn't clear. The problem with traditional discipline is that it is not geared to deal with persistent, extraordinary problems. Now, there is nothing wrong with the basic principles of reward and punishment. These are the universal means through which we reinforce or discourage different types of behavior. What is awry here is the attitude toward the disciplining process: that some reward or punishment is supposed to "make" a child feel a certain way and that this is supposed to have a lasting impact.

It is very difficult to make any child feel a specific way. In the end, it is the parents who end up feeling all of the urgency over their own attempts at reward and punishment. Who has the problem? Who is responsible? These are the bottom-line questions that must be dealt with before parents will be able to cope with persistent behavior problems.

Many of the traditional attitudes may be very successful with your neighbor's children and, as you were probably told by your own parents, supposedly worked on you when you were little. (Of course, you are probably the best the judge of that.) Once again, this is a discipline method that is geared to respond only to infrequent misbehavior. It is based on the belief that children are naturally able to learn how to behave themselves and get along with others. You do not need to step in unless someone steps out of line. As a result, it is more crisis oriented.

But when the behavior problems don't seem to go away, you may find you are spending an inordinate amount of time disciplining your child. It is not unusual for the child to misbehave: it is the norm. So if you approach discipline in the traditional way, you are in a state of crisis most of the time. This is so exhausting that no one can carry it out successfully for very long. To develop a more constructive attitude toward the process of discipline, you need to take stock of both yourself and your child.

Perhaps your child, for various reasons, is having more difficulty learning how to control his own behavior and to predict the behavior of others. This child may need extra help from you to learn how to behave appropriately. It is not sufficient to simply try to get the child to stop doing what you don't want him to do. You need to teach him how to regulate his own behavior. In thinking this through, you need to deal with certain questions:

1. Who is the most important person in your child's life?
2. How can you help your child?
3. Who has the problem?
4. Who feels the urgency?
5. Who is responsible?

In subsequent chapters we will deal with some of the mechanics needed in a comprehensive discipline program. For now, it is important to focus on the attitude that will make such a program work. What follows is a list of questions and statements that can help you monitor and regulate your own attitude as you teach your child how to behave appropriately. Actively consider, rehearse, and play them out whenever possible.

1. WHO IS THE MOST IMPORTANT PERSON IN YOUR CHILD'S LIFE?

All children are engaged in the business of learning how to regulate their behavior and relate effectively with others. They learn these skills from you. You are both parent and teacher. How does your child relate to you? Often children with behavior problems plague their parents with oppositionality, tantrums, negative attitudes, and socially embarrassing behavior. Favorite aunts, grandparents, or neighbors with the reputation of "being good with kids" don't experience any of this. To your dismay, other adults not only may claim not to know what you are upset about, but in a condescending way may offer you helpful hints. At worst, they may patronize you with sympathetic looks as if to say, "Aren't kids tough?" But they don't seem to be having any trouble at all. Stop a moment and think this over.

Why does your child act this way for you and not for them? Remember that misbehavior serves a necessary purpose and is an essential way in which your child learns. If your child acts out for you, it is because you, as parent, are also the most able to teach. It is from you that the child is most able to learn. No grandparent, neighbor, relative, or therapist can claim that. What is your child to gain from acting out for these people? Nothing! So most children will put on their "good" behavior, and this gets them treats, compliments, and other goodies.

This is nice for the time being, a short stay, but not good for the duration because they learn nothing. They should not have to be on their guard. They should be able to experiment: to try, fail, and try again. They should always be accepted. This does not mean, of course, that you accept *all of their behavior.* They need you to help them understand the difference between acceptable and unacceptable behavior. This is not likely to happen with anyone but you, and that is why you are so important. Please try to remember this the next time you get some well-meaning advice.

2. HOW CAN YOU HELP YOUR CHILD?

So often we think of discipline as negative. This comes about naturally since most people think of what we *don't* want our children to do. We don't want them to have temper tantrums, chew with their mouth open, hit their little brothers or sisters, or bother us when we are trying to talk on the telephone. We want to stop them from doing something, and the effort required can be exhausting. In a very real sense, discipline is negative because it is punishing to parents.

But it does not have to be this way. Remember that the word *discipline* comes from the Latin word meaning "instruction." This is precisely what discipline is all about. It is a way to teach your child the necessary skills for independent living. Some children need much more assistance learning skills that seem to come naturally to others. How will your child learn to get along with other children, get organized for school, pay attention to the teacher, recognize danger, be responsible at home? These things need to be taught, and for your child, they are as important and as difficult as any academic subject. As a parent, your great gift is that you are the one who is able to help your child learn these necessary skills.

So often we think of our child as sly and cunning, and we become weary of his great scheming—Machiavelli in Oshkosh overalls. Look at it in a different way. The tantrums, irresponsibility, rudeness, and sneakiness are really signs that your child needs to learn some important adaptive living skills. You would never tolerate tantrum behavior from another adult. Imagine if one of *your friends* suddenly threw a noisy temper tantrum on the floor of your living room! It would probably send you backpedaling toward the door making excuses about a sick mother-in-law. If an adult is incompetent on the job, she is soon out of work. If your child behaves as rudely toward older, unfamiliar children as he does toward you, someone is going to settle his hash! It is important to see this obnoxious behavior not as craftiness but as the nonproductive flailing of a struggling, ignorant child.

How fortunate this child is to have someone who can help him! Consider this the next time your child has to be taken out of a restaurant or has a temper tantrum in the supermarket to the point where you would like to leave him in the frozen food case with the pizzas. Look at this pathetic creature you are wasting so much anger on. Keep in mind that this is the same child you love deeply and would do anything to protect. When your child behaves in this manner, you can certainly see how much he needs your protection. Thank heaven he is lucky enough to have someone like you who can help him through this. When he does get out of control, it may even be helpful to use the phrase "You are out of control, and I am going to help you" as a way of putting the proper perspective on the problem. This child is not an embarrassment that needs to be covered up with a tarpaulin. He is a child unable to regulate his behavior appropriately and he needs your help in order to know what to do. This is your opportunity to teach.

3. WHO HAS THE PROBLEM?

If your child is comfortable and you are distressed, your child is not ready to learn and will not change. This is often the case when a family first goes into therapy. The parents sit bolt upright in their chairs, flushed and gesturing frantically. They bitterly recount their difficulties getting their child to dress in the morning, sit still at the dinner table, sit still in the grocery cart, take her bath, or go to bed on time. They have tried everything and nothing works. They have tried spanking, bribing, and taking away her toys. They make real threats, idle threats, more threats, and on and on. Who can help this girl with these problems? What will she be like as a teenager? Perhaps the therapist can talk some sense into her?

As the therapist's eyes sweep the room, what does he see? A passive, quiet child slumped in a chair idly kicking her legs to and fro with a benign smile on her face. Who has the problem? The child clearly feels no distress, so why should she change?

The only reason children feel the slightest compulsion to change is that they feel uncomfortable. Children expect the world to operate in certain ways and they learn quickly how to manipulate their environment to conform to their expectations. Some children expect to be yelled at, so they do things to make you yell at them. As odd as this may sound, there are many children who feel more comfortable when they are being yelled at and spanked—at least they know where they stand.

The first critical issue is that the child must feel the need to change. But the impetus to change is not likely to come from the child. It must come from the parent.

No matter what problem you are approaching, you must be able to frame it from the child's point of view. Of course, this demands some introspection and reasonable judgment on the part of the parent. You have to be able to separate a "child's problem" from a "parent's problem." Suppose a child is being a sloppy eater at the dinner table, and spoonfuls of chicken à la king are falling on your Oriental rug. It is not the child's problem that there is food on an expensive rug. It may be the child's problem, though, that if she doesn't find some way to clean it up in two minutes, she will not be permitted to finish dinner, and only little girls who finish their dinner get to watch their favorite program on TV. Similarly, if a child is having a noisy temper tantrum in a supermarket, it is not her problem that the other customers in the store are probably thinking the child's father is a helpless clod. It might be the child's problem, though, that if she is out of control, she will need to sit in her car seat by herself (with Dad right by the car though out of the child's sight) until she can settle down. If the child has some specific chores she must complete in order to get her allowance, it is not her problem if the parents feel the urgency to remind her at every turn what needs to be done next. It might be the child's problem to complete the chores she neglected (after all, what is your time worth these days?).

It is extremely important before approaching any type of problem behavior that the parent relax and ask the question, "Who has the problem here?"

Many times children will try to turn things around so their problem is suddenly *your* problem. A good example of this is when a child, frustrated at not being able to get her way, threatens to commit some heinous crime such as going to her room and breaking all of her toys. Often we as parents feel a powerful urge to jump right in and threaten the child with consequences. In effect, we say, "Don't you dare think of using that out-of-control behavior, because—if you—I'll . . ." We then have to scramble all over for some type of logical consequence that fits the crime. The child, meanwhile, sits back and watches us struggle with our conscience and our failing intelligence.

Why be so ready to assume ownership of the problem? The child doesn't learn anything from this and neither do we. It is the child, after all, who must learn to think several steps down the line to where her behavior will lead. We can already do this. Do we really need any more practice? Why not have the child do the thinking for herself? Invite her to think about carrying out the misbehavior. "Go ahead, I certainly can't stop you if you decide to do that, but you better think about what is going to happen if you do it."

This step helps children understand the reality of the problem. They certainly have the freedom to behave appropriately or to misbehave. You cannot be their brain and control their behavior for them. What you *can* do—and this is very powerful—is to make the consequences of their behavior either highly desirable or highly undesirable. In the end, it is they who have to learn to make the choice.

4. WHO FEELS THE URGENCY?

So often we develop elaborate behavior-modification schemes complete with goals, expensive rewards, and charts with colorful stickers, only to have our children say, "So what?!" We feel tremendous anger and frustration, and the child seems to be unaffected. We can correct the situation once we engineer matters so the child feels the ownership of the problem. We gain some more emotional distance from the frustrating aspect of discipline when we approach it from a positive, teaching standpoint. But it is still important to have some way of monitoring the situation from the gut level. This is what the sense of "urgency" is all about.

Behavior management works only when children feel a sense of urgency to accomplish some goal. But they will often lose that sense of urgency someplace along the way. Sometimes they simply act as though they feel no urgency just to see how their parents will respond. In effect, they ask, "Are you really going to follow through?" The meaning inherent in any limit testing is, "Can I trust you?"

All parents want their children to succeed. If your child feels the urgency and is ready to work, then all is going well. If you start feeling the urgency to "help" your child succeed, however, stop and immediately examine what you are doing. When you feel the child's urgency slipping away, you can fall into a trap by trying to replace it with our own. You plead, cajole, threaten, or simply reason with your child in order to get him back on track. But the more you express your own urgent feelings, the more you can feel his urgency fade into bland indifference.

Sometimes it is difficult to tell who is carrying the sense of urgency. The best internal guide parents can have is their emotional state. If you find you are using your own emotions to persuade the child to behave more appropriately, you very well may be feeling too much of the urgency to solve the problem. You will probably discover that giving vent to your negative feelings does not improve the situation. Many times children actively seek out their parents' frustration and anger because this is their way of staying in the spotlight. Other children who are more anxious and introverted may become immobilized or withdraw when their parents become angry. When a parent invests a lot of frustration and anger in the behavior-modification plan, it is usually counterproductive, a sign that things are going wrong.

Therefore, pay attention to your own feelings, especially anger and frustration. We will discuss this further when we deal with obstacles. For the time being, suffice it to say that the one who feels the urgency in any learning situation is the one who is ready to change. When the child feels that sense of urgency, it is a sign the mechanics of the behavior-modification scheme are running smoothly. When the parent feels the urgency, it is a good signal the mechanics need some adjusting.

5. WHO IS RESPONSIBLE?

Let's face it, there isn't anything especially fun or fulfilling about disciplining a misbehaving child. There is also a lot of bad advice going around. Parents are sometimes asked to excuse a lot of irresponsible, nonproductive behavior because, after all, the child can't help it. They are asked to reduce work loads at school, to not expect compliance with chores at home, and to in all ways reduce demands on the child. Though this advice is well-meaning, it may not help our children learn. All children need to learn how to cope with situations that are noisy and confusing and need to make appropriate judgments about what is a reasonable challenge or a hopeless gamble. While we do not expect children to perform beyond their biological capabilities, we can expect them to develop the skills necessary for living.

An area in which this is especially important is in learning how to regulate social behavior. One of the overall lessons we need to teach our children is that they are responsible for their behavior even though they may have difficulty with self-control. The process of teaching our children how to control themselves is also a process of teaching them that they make choices and are responsible for the choices they make. Children make these choices by their behavior. They need to understand that even *doing nothing* is a choice.

> PARENT: Do you want to wear your green pants or your red ones?
> LITTLE JUSTIN: NO!
> PARENT: Do you want to wear your dinosaur shirt or your Avengers of the Galaxy shirt?
> LITTLE JUSTIN: NO!
> PARENT (*frustrated*): Dammit, put your green pants on now.
> LITTLE JUSTIN: I not dammit. I a little girl.

Children also make choices by acting out their behavior rather than talking out their feelings. This is what happens when a child has a noisy temper tantrum because he cannot have a candy bar at the supermarket checkout. The child probably cannot say, "Mother, it fills me with great disappointment that I am not allowed to have that piece of candy." Instead, he throws himself to the ground and acts as though he is having a grand mal seizure. Certainly one of the goals of any discipline program is teaching children to talk out feelings and thoughts rather than act them out through their behavior.

From a mechanical standpoint, a parent may decide that the consequence for temper tantrums is removal to some controlled place for a time-out. But it is equally important that the parent use language to define not only who has the problem but also who has made the decision for the consequence. Children must understand that such consequences do not fall out of the sky unpredictably. Most of these situations are under their control. They choose consequences by choosing to act in certain ways.

I encourage many parents to say to their children, just before they impose a consequence, "I see by your behavior that you have decided to be out of control and that you want me to help you." This sentence not only sets the emotional tone but also defines roles and responsibilities. It does not have to be shouted. In fact, it is best stated in a soft, somewhat disinterested tone of voice.

Settling the question of who is responsible brings a serious reality home to the misbehaving child. It is how you convey to him that he needs to develop certain necessary skills for living. In effect, you say to the child, "Yes, you may have trouble controlling yourself and that may mean you will have to work a little harder or make more adjustments right now, but you still need to learn how to take care of yourself. You are responsible."

OBSTACLES TO A POSITIVE MENTAL ATTITUDE

A number of factors may substantially interfere with your ability to maintain a positive teaching attitude toward your child. For example, you may find that despite your best intentions, you feel an uncontrollable amount of anger about even minor irritations. There may be other times when you simply do not feel like being around your child, when you want to let somebody else take over. These emotions may leave you feeling upset and guilty. You must be sensitive to your own emotional needs as a parent and especially to how your feelings erect obstacles to your ability to take care of your child. The feelings you have as a parent are not bad or wrong, they are simply there, and they are yours. By understanding your emotions and by working through them appropriately, you may not only be able to more effectively manage your child, but may also understand your relationship with your child with a new sense of richness.

The most common feelings that I encounter in therapy are those of frustration and anger. Typically, by the time parents seek therapeutic help, they have exhausted every other means available to them. They have been frustrated in their attempts to manage their child. They feel they have failed. By the time the parents come to therapy, they are so sensitized to and irritated with their child's behavior that the slightest motion of noncompliance sets off conflagrations in the family. Though we often like to think the parent teaches the child, the process is a two-way street. The child teaches the parents a lot, and in these cases, some of it is very painful. What many parents express is that their anger seems automatic, that they have no real control over it. The child does some silly, irritating thing and the parents feel a reaction of enormous rage. From a technical standpoint, this would be called a *conditioned emotional response,* but knowing this does not help the parents. What it means is that because the parents are so accustomed to certain patterns of negative behavior, they now feel all the anger and frustration at the first signal, even before the behavior occurs.

Clearly, this kind of anger is going to be self-defeating in several ways. First, this conditioned response makes it very hard for the parents to remain emotionally detached from the situation in order to be able to teach positive behavior. Instead, they become engulfed in it and lose their objectivity. Second, an automatic sequence may be set up. The child's irritating behavior ignites a particular response in the parents, which in turn sets off the child, and this in turn upsets the parents further. Both the child and the parents respond automatically without a great deal of rational thought. Soon a self-perpetuating pattern develops. The child and the parents behave like falling dominoes. Finally, this type of automatic anger greatly arouses the parents, and this breeds a strong sense of urgency to change the situation. As I noted in the previous section, when the parents feel the urgency, it is generally counterproductive.

It is crucial that you learn to replace your own automatic, emotionally laden behavior with more rational, intentional behavior. The assistance of a therapist or highly skilled teacher is often necessary. Before you can teach your child, you must be able to handle your own feelings of anger and frustration.

Other important issues may interfere with your ability to teach your child in a rational way. A major one is the loss of your expectations. Granted, when a child is born, her parents always selflessly insist they wish only that their child should be happy in whatever she chooses to do. The parents, lying through their teeth, say it does not matter to them what the child does as long as she is happy, kind to people, and a good, productive citizen.

This, of course, is pure baloney. As new parents of young infants, we all have dreams of what it will be like to be with our children when they are older. Some may have fantasies about teaching them how to swing a bat or throw a knuckle curve. Others may fantasize about after-dinner discussions of politics and world affairs, with the child earnestly asking questions about a country's situation, the parent considering the issue thoughtfully and rendering an opinion.

Perhaps we dream they will have opportunities we wished for but never had, or that they will have virtues we have admired in other people.

When children exhibit self-control problems or serious oppositional behavior, it often appears as though they will be unable to live out the dreams we have for them. Many parents experience feelings of grief and a sense of loss. It is important to realize that these feelings of sadness and grief must be worked through before we can replace them with new hopes. Again, this often may require the help of a skilled therapist, teacher, or clergyman. You may need to work with someone you feel comfortable with and trust.

Other issues that interfere with your ability to parent your child may have nothing at all to do with your anger or your dashed expectations. Let's face it, your child is not the only star in your personal universe. You may have other children, a job, a marriage, other family relations, civic or social commitments. These all have an impact on your life and need attention. Most parents find themselves caught between the demands of difficult jobs and all the other varied responsibilities in their lives. These competing demands create tremendous pressure on parents and substantially interfere with their ability to devote all their attention to the child. Suppose all is going well. For most parents this still means a certain amount of juggling and decision making is necessary, requiring a lot of time and energy. But suppose all is not going well. Suppose, for example, that there are significant problems in your marriage, stresses on the job, or troubles elsewhere in the family. Certainly these types of stresses are going to interfere with a single-minded parenting program.

To Sum Up: Seize Every Opportunity to Teach Your Child

One of the first questions in this chapter was, "Who is the most important person in your child's life?" By now, I hope you realize not only that the answer to the question is *you, the parent,* but also *why* it is the parent. As a parent, you are the only one who can provide the kind of teaching and support your child needs in order to develop self-control and social mastery. Other parents may have an easier time of it than you do. Many parents are able to get along with a laissez-faire approach to parenting, interfering only when the child's behavior gets a little too far out of line. Because of the kinds of problems your child is having, you cannot do this. Indeed, if your child presents many more behavior problems and you continue with a defensive, reactionary approach, you will soon find yourself overwhelmed and exhausted at every turn.

Consider a more active, teaching approach. You are not trying to destroy your child's inappropriate behavior. You are trying to help him develop the skills necessary for independent living. In order to do this, you must develop a positive mental attitude toward the process of disciplining. Discipline must be viewed as instruction, as helping your child to become more confident in self-control and social mastery skills. Many of you need to change the way you think about your role. This will be easier if you actively use the questions and phrases given in this chapter. By viewing the process as positive, by placing the responsibility in the hands of the child and allowing him to feel the urgency to change, you will help the mechanics of behavior management to flow more easily.

One more point begs to be made. The process of teaching your child will go more smoothly the more you are able to bring a certain amount of passion or zeal to your teaching. Use your disciplining assertively: seize every opportunity to teach your child some appropriate way to behave. The more you can value those difficult moments in the grocery store when you teach your child shopping skills and avoid a temper tantrum, the more satisfying the whole job of parenting will be. You'll discover that the process need not be irritating or embarrassing to you. In fact, it is through this type of teaching that you will see your children become more competent. This process of instruction will help your children understand the world around them, control their behavior, and interact more effectively with others. So give yourself a pep talk and believe in yourself. It is fortunate that your children have someone like you who can teach them.

PART 11

Back to Basics

5

Positive Reinforcement: To Bribe or Not to Bribe

Many parents confuse rewards with bribes. They are not the same and the difference is important. Bribery is doomed; positive reinforcement can't fail. But positive reinforcement is not merely praise, stickers, money, or pizzas on Saturday. Whether or not these work depends on the child. You need to consider what a child is willing to work for, how often she needs incentives to keep working, and how you are going to keep her interested in the program. You will see that the best reinforcers are not expensive—your attention and the privileges she already enjoys are usually sufficient. Many of the technical aspects of putting together a positive-reinforcement program are covered later in the book. In order for them to work, though, both you and your child must approach the problem with the right attitude.

Consider this example:

Let us call her little Jasmine and say she is a normal four-year-old. At the grandparents' house, she is delightful, vivacious, and sweet. But when she goes to the local supermarket with her mother, little horns seem to pop out of her head and a pointy tail pokes its way through her Oshkosh overalls. She will not sit in the cart, and she will not stay by her mother. She runs up and down the aisles demanding this cereal, that juice, or those cookies. She runs away and hides. She bites through the cellophane wrapping of the cheese. At the checkout counter, she brings fistfuls of candy bars for her mother to buy. If her mother refuses, she acts as though she is being electrocuted. Sometimes her mother will give in, buying her one or four, depending upon how many people are staring at her. She has tried the usual approaches to the problem: nagging, pleading, begging, threatening, and holding a gun to Jasmine's favorite dolly—all to no avail. When someone suggested to her that she try to give little Jasmine some candy for "being good" in the store, she found—much to her surprise—that it worked like a charm. One time. The next time the bait was offered, Jasmine screwed up her face as if she had just eaten a lemon. "I dunno . . . what else will you give me?" After that, Mom went back to nagging, threats, and the gun to the favorite dolly. As our discouraged mom said to her best friend the next day, she had tried that "positive-reinforcement stuff" and it didn't work. Besides, she didn't believe in using bribery.

Does this sound familiar? It is not uncommon for parents during the initial stages of behavioral training to express a negative attitude toward what they have heard about positive reinforcement. Many times parents will say they have tried "all of that" in the past. On further questioning, it becomes clear that they have tried many different types of techniques, including sticker charts and offering money, bicycles, toys, or trips to Disney World, to encourage their child to clean up her room or do her homework.

Whether or not these techniques work depends on how the system is set up initially, how it is *sold* to the child, and how it is maintained over time so that the novelty does not wear off. In the story above, which describes a fairly common problem for parents of preschoolers, the particular approach worked once, and then the novelty wore off. After that, of course, the mother returned to familiar territory. Many parents will try one strategy of positive reinforcement, and the moment it doesn't work, they will abruptly change to some radical new strategy. Some parents try a whole spectrum of elaborate charts, foods, money, and expensive gifts in a very short period of time. Given what we know about the child's need for predictability and control, these rapid changes are doomed to failure. Other parents simply say they don't believe in bribing their children to do what is naturally expected of them. They look upon a child's misbehavior or lack of compliance as some type of blackmail: "Gimme a buck or I'll scream."

Because many parents confuse *bribes* with *positive reinforcers*, I will start by distinguishing the two terms. They are similar in that both involve giving something in the hope that the child will return to a particular behavior more often. But they are different in some very critical ways. The most important difference, of course, is that bribes don't work, and positive reinforcers do.

WHY BRIBES DON'T WORK

Everyone knows what a bribe is. If you want someone to do you a favor and you feel they are unlikely to do it just because you asked, you offer them "a little something to make it worth their while." You clearly want them to take the bribe, and you hope they will do what you want. They have to consider whether what you have offered really makes it worthwhile. Should they do you the favor or simply walk away?

The dynamics of bribery are the same when we use it with our children. The parents want the child to do something that the child is uninterested in doing. The parents offer some reward, and the child decides whether or not to comply: "If you're quiet while Mommy's on the phone, Mommy will give you some pennies." The key issue here is urgency. The parents have a problem, and they want the child to do something to help *them*. The parents take the responsibility of attracting a child's attention with some incentive. The parents in effect say to the child, "If you do *this* for me, I'll give you *that*." In situations like this, the child is in control. The child may say either yes or no. The child has the freedom to either comply or resist.

The children are not behaving inappropriately here. In fact, they are behaving like any good businessperson. Their services are being solicited, and they naturally test the market to see what it will bear. It is the law of supply and demand. In emergency situations, a bribe can go a long way. A cash incentive at a Las Vegas hotel can transform "no available tables" into "a table right in front." But if you want the child to continue doing something over a long period of time, don't be surprised if you are soon asked to raise the stakes. "I'm bored with that," says the child. "What else do you have to offer?" You feel the urgency, the child is still in control, and you have to dig a little deeper. From the child's standpoint, it is simply good business.

This is the nature of bribes.

WHAT IS POSITIVE REINFORCEMENT?

While everyone knows intuitively what a bribe is, the nature of positive reinforcement is more difficult to grasp. This is because positive reinforcement doesn't have as much to do with the behavior of the parents as with the effect it has on the child's behavior. If a child is willing to behave in a certain way in order to get something, then that "something" is positively reinforcing. If the child won't behave even though the lure is offered, however, then that "something" is *not* a positive reinforcer. Something is positively reinforcing if—and only if—the child behaves in a certain way in order to get it.

The best way to understand positive reinforcement is by your own internal sense of urgency. Let us go back and rethink the problem of bribery. Who feels the urgency? Who is in control of the situation? When you attempt to bribe someone, you feel all of the urgency to obtain a certain end product. A parent chases a child all over the house reminding her she has to clean her room before she gets ice cream. The parent is frantic, the child is indifferent. The child, in a fairly calculating way, can control how much the parent offers as a bribe by resisting him. In effect, her resistive behavior *positively reinforces* bribing behavior. A child completes her chores for a quarter the first week but won't lift a finger the second week. She says she wants a raise.

As you can see, bribery has exactly the opposite effect from positive reinforcement. From a mechanical standpoint, reinforcement is defined by the effect it has on a child's behavior. If the child behaves *better*, then what the parent did was positively reinforcing. It is defined after the fact. If the child doesn't exhibit the desired behavior anymore, then what the parent did was not positively reinforcing. Positive reinforcement has nothing to do with how much parents praise, how much they think the child wants a toy, or how much money they are willing to spend. Reinforcers are measured not in dollars and cents but by what the child does. If you follow this line of reasoning, you will see it is logically impossible for "positive reinforcement" not to work. Bribes may work once or twice and may fail often. Positive reinforcement always "works," because that is part of its definition. The issue, then, is not whether or not positive reinforcement works, but how to set up the mechanics of the program.

WHAT DETERMINES WHETHER REWARDS WORK?

Many parents have difficulty deciding what will be positively reinforcing to their child. They often solicit ideas from other adults or use their own intuition to generate some possibilities. Parents often gravitate toward using sticker charts, money, toys, or some very special (expensive!) prize in order to entice the child to behave appropriately. It is easy to confuse *material* value with *reinforcing* value. Parents often feel more expensive toys should be more attractive and should motivate the child to change. How parents are crushed when their plans go askew! In order to better understand what does work, let's look at seven types of typical reinforcers. Whether they work or not depends on the child, the situation, and how they are presented.

1. *Verbal praise:* Everyone has heard that children hate to be criticized and love to be praised. Parents are often exhorted to praise the child loudly when the target behavior is carried out. Parents jump up and down, clap their hands, and praise the child from one end of the house to the other. Many children love praise and will actively work to get it. But children can also get tired of praise. Moreover, if children are not used to getting praised, the loud and noisy variety will feel phony to them. Children will not work for such praise. Finally, it is important to consider the temperament of the child. Some children are unable to tolerate a lot of stimulation and when praised noisily can easily erupt into a temper tantrum. Some more-introverted learners are genuinely not interested in receiving external praise. Instead, their behavior is controlled more by their internal sense of meaning and their own feelings of competence.

2. *Sticker charts:* Most children seem to love stickers, and there seems to be no shortage of interesting varieties to attract their attention. When my daughter was being toilet trained, my wife and I used stickers to help keep track of her dry days. She enjoyed the process of putting the stickers on her calendar each morning. But I am not sure the stickers had any real motivating influence beyond that. Some children

may initially be interested in sticker charts but become quickly bored with them. After all, how much pleasure can you get from looking at a sticker on a chart? What happens when the child is having some difficulty and there are spaces without stickers? If the idea of a sticker chart is not *sold* to the child in a positive way, the child may perceive it as keeping track of his failures. Many parents report it is not long before such charts are found torn up in pieces on the floor.

3. *Food:* Food works well as a reinforcer as long as the child is hungry and as long as he wants what you are serving. There are many children who like the idea of candy but may not be willing to work that hard in order to get some. There are other children who have fairly free access to food, so whether or not they get this or that piece of candy is of little concern.

4. *Money:* As adults, we understand the reinforcing value of money and figure it works the same magic with children. Not so. In many respects, the reinforcing value of money is similar to that of food. Many young children simply have no concept of the value of money and are not able to sustain work effort in order to get it. Other children have free access to money and so they feel no special urgency to behave in order to get some.

5. *Toys:* Many children are willing to work in order to obtain a special toy. When parents attempt to bribe children with toys, this almost never has a lasting effect. The child will behave well enough to get the toy he wants and then will immediately revert to his old inappropriate behavior. And why not? If it got him the toy before, who knows what it will get him next time? But children's interest in specific toys waxes and wanes. What may be special one day may have absolutely no value next week.

6. *Special outings:* These are usually part of a longer-term behavioral contract: "If you don't bring home any notes from your teacher this week, I will take you to the Pizza Hut on Saturday." Now, the offer of going out for a pizza is very attractive to most children and should have a high reinforcing value, but here, too, there may be a number of factors which might affect how well the plan works. Many children do not understand time. To them, a week might as well be a decade. The bait is simply being dangled too far away to have any real alluring effect. While the child knows that by being good he will get this pizza sometime in the future, the thought of it is simply not strong enough to keep him from pounding on Jerry Schmergel in the chair ahead of

him, who, after all, made the worst face at him *just now*. Many children—not only those who are very young or have some learning disorder—have difficulty organizing their behavior around some remote event. The pizza-at-the-end-of-the-week schemes usually fail, and everyone feels deprived and frustrated.

7. *The jackpot:* These are the long-term, super-payoff contracts: "If you make the honor roll, I'll buy you a car." They usually involve sustaining some high level of behavior over a long period of time in order to obtain some very expensive object. This type of reinforcer runs into the same problems as the special-outings strategy. While the child may sincerely want the object, he may be unable to control his behavior over *such a long period* of time without some form of more frequent reinforcement. Certainly there are some children who do very well with this type of reinforcement approach. Unfortunately, it is probably the children with the greatest behavior problems who have the least ability to keep their work effort organized and sustained over a long period of time. And the younger the child is, the less effective the strategy is.

All seven of these categories may not be reinforcing for your child. That is, he may not be willing to sustain an active work effort in order to obtain rewards. In choosing reinforcers for your child, you need to consider reinforcement from his point of view. What sorts of things is he willing to actively work for? How long can you expect him to work before he is reinforced? How will you sustain his interest in the program?

One problem which parents run into is that they tend to think of reinforcers as involving something unique or expensive. In order to make their child behave, they feel they have to go out and buy something special. But there are two classes of reinforcers which do not involve any extra expense and are probably among the most effective in changing a child's behavior. The first is the value of the parents' attention; the second, the privileges and freedoms of day-to-day living that the child already enjoys.

NEVER UNDERESTIMATE THE VALUE
OF YOUR ATTENTION

Your child works very hard to get your attention. Perhaps, like many children, she has found that the best way to grab and hold her parents' attention is by misbehaving. A parent usually becomes very alert when the glass breaks or the little sister screams. This attention-getting is usually on the child's terms. It doesn't have to be this way. You can teach your child to use *positive behavior* to work for your attention. It's the most effective reinforcer of all—and it is on your terms!

When I was an intern at Children's Memorial Hospital in Chicago, I had the pleasure of taking part in some sessions at the Early Intervention Project. This was a program designed to teach parents to effectively manage the behavior problems of their children. Under the active leadership of Dr. Victoria Lavigne, the project later became independent from the hospital and was renamed "Tuesday's Child."

Parents who became involved with the project were usually normal, psychologically intact adults who were having a lot of difficulty managing their children. These children displayed a lot of oppositional, controlling behavior. They did not comply with requests or directions, threw temper tantrums, and in short carried normal disruptive behavior to an extreme. The plan of the program was to teach parents that they could exert enormous influence over their child's behavior simply by virtue of *what* they paid attention to and *how* they attended.

Every week the parents would come to the project and play a game with the child while being observed by a parent trainer. The game involved having the child play with specific toys in a set sequence; the parent would attempt to have the child play with one toy and then, after two minutes, would attempt to have the child switch and play with the next toy on the list.

During the first session, before the actual training began, parents would spend most of their time actively directing the child to play with specific toys. The child usually refused, and would often go off and play with other toys, or sometimes simply run out of the room. All of this was very discouraging to the parents, who spent most of their time paying attention to the child's noncompliant, resistive behavior.

The actual training took quite a while. Parents were instructed to actively attend to the child when she was playing with the appropriate toy. They did not need to use active directing or verbal praise but could pay attention to the child by simply describing what the child was doing. This is very similar to what the psychologist Russell Barkley has termed *sportscasting*. When the child played inappropriately, the parents would simply be quiet and ignore the behavior. If the child ran out of the room, the parents would bring her back and use very brief time-outs of ten to thirty seconds before redirecting her back to the appropriate toy. Over the weeks, a remarkable change would occur in the child's behavior. Invariably, she played more and more with the toys to which the parents paid attention. Similar programs were also carried out at home.

Once the child had achieved a consistent, high level of compliance, the parents were instructed to pay attention only to inappropriate behavior for one week. This is called a *reversal phase*. The results were disastrous and dramatic. Very quickly the child resumed the pattern of oppositional, obnoxious behavior that had led the family to turn to the project in the first place. The reversal phase was quite short but had a stunning impact—it made the link between attention and behavior very obvious. The obnoxious behavior was easily eliminated once the parents resumed the positive-attention approach.

The most potent form of reinforcement we all possess is our own selective attention. It is only natural for children to start out by soliciting our attention through negative means. After all, their first language was crying when they were uncomfortable or irritable. But children are just as willing to actively work for positive attention as they are for negative attention. This type of approach is especially important for parents who have hyperactive children. These children are often underresponsive to pain and punishment but very willing to work for positive attention.

To change from a traditional approach to a positive-attention approach is extremely difficult for most of us. In a sense, it involves turning discipline on its ear. You have to actively pay attention to children when they are playing appropriately. Negative behavior is greeted in a cool, mechanical way by passive ignoring or very brief time-outs. The emotional charge a child receives is earned by engaging in positive behavior.

The reason children adapt to the positive-attention approach has nothing to do with the "goodness" of behaving appropriately. When

you learn to use attention positively, children experience their appropriate behavior as much more stimulating and enjoyable than their
negative behavior. They learn to discriminate between the stimulation
value of positive and negative behavior. Paying positive attention does
require a lot of effort and a lot of change. But it is extremely potent,
and it doesn't cost a dime.

THE PRIVILEGES AND FREEDOMS
OF DAY-TO-DAY LIVING

All children enjoy certain privileges and freedoms in their day-to-
day living. Most children are also willing to work very hard in order
to maintain them.

Think about your own child for a moment. What kinds of simple
pleasures does he enjoy? A special cereal, perhaps, or TV show? How
much time does your child spend playing with friends in the neighborhood? Most children have special toys they like to be occupied with.
At a more basic level, how much do you allow your child to be out of
your line of sight? What time does he go to bed in the evening? Does
he have any choice in what foods you prepare for dinner? Does he
enjoy the luxury of a computer, video game, or VCR? When you think
about it, your child probably enjoys a lot of highly reinforcing activities
already. Why do you need to go off to the store to buy some shiny new
bauble to offer?

When I see parents for individual work on behavior problems, I
often suggest they make a list of all the privileges and freedoms that
the child enjoys in the family already. When they do, they are amazed
at how long the list is. Make a list for your own child and see how
long it is. See what sorts of things your child already enjoys just by
being a part of your family. Now it is quite likely that any one particular
item is not going to have much value as a reinforcer. Any child is
willing to give up one toy if he has others to play with. But the total
value is usually tremendous! When children find they must go to bed
after dinner, have to be in your line of sight, can't have friends over,
and lose some toys, they take notice!

By using many of these naturally occurring privileges as reinforcers,
you are also teaching a very important message about living—that
privilege and freedom are the products of responsible behavior. They

require some amount of work to maintain. If your child decides to behave irresponsibly, then he is asking you to be responsible *for him*. Things are no different in the adult world. We can choose to disobey laws or hurt others, but we will also pay a price for this. By behaving irresponsibly and by requiring others to assume control of your behavior, you give up some of the privileges and freedoms you might naturally enjoy. As adults we could go to jail; children go to their rooms.

THE NUTS AND BOLTS OF POSITIVE REINFORCEMENT

1. *Choose a reinforcer that the child is willing to work for.* Probably the most crucial part of a positive teaching strategy is the bait. It sets up the feeling of urgency in the child to change her behavior. But you need to operate from the child's point of view, not your own. It makes no difference how expensive the reinforcer is, how much other children want it, etc. It is reinforcing only if the child is willing to work in order to get it. A child stays in her room all day long refusing to clean it. Then her best friend comes to the door. Her room is spotless in three minutes. This is why a child's normal privileges and freedoms are so powerful.

2. *Be prepared to walk away.* In order for positive reinforcement to work, the child must feel the urgency and the responsibility for change. In effect, you must be able to say, "Oh, this is something you want? Well, if it is so important to you, this is what you have to do to get it. It is not important to me whether you get this or not. If it is important to you, though, this is what you need to do." A child asks for an ice cream cone on a summer afternoon. Her mother says that it's all right with her but first the toys have to go back on the shelf. The child grumbles and hesitates. Mother says, "Fine," and starts to go. The child yells, "Wait!" and immediately picks up the toys.

3. *Make the payoff fit the achievement.* Using a reward suitable to the accomplishment is important not only with material rewards (i.e., money, toys, etc.) but also with verbal praise. Try to match your emotional tone to the child's expectations: "Great! You did a terrific job! This tells me what a big boy you are." Some children need confetti and noisemakers when they show some progress. Other children who

are more stubbornly oppositional may perform better with very quiet—
or even grudging—acceptance: "Well, I didn't think you could do it
but you proved me wrong. This time, I'm proud of you."

4. *Make the goals achievable.* When children are learning a new
skill, they are going to make mistakes. In the beginning, be prepared
to accept a less than perfect performance. If your child has never made
his bed, accept a rough approximation the first few times. But decide
in advance what level of performance you are willing to reinforce.
Children at all ages need to know exactly what they are expected to
do in order to get the things they want. Remember, you are teaching
prediction and control.

5. *Make the initial payoff certain.* An initial reward is absolutely
critical when you are teaching a new skill or behavior. This is the
hook that engages the child with the program. If he does not succeed
initially, he will lose interest. If he loses interest, he will not change.
The value of stickers and little rewards at the end of the day is clear.

6. *Make the child work for the reward.* As the child proves to you that
she has the capacity to perform at a certain level, make her work a
little harder in order to get reinforced. At first you may expect a poor
but promising performance. As the child's competency increases,
though, you can certainly demand more of her before she gets rewarded. After you've accepted sloppy bed-making for a while, start
demanding cleaner folds and hospital corners. But as you change your
expectations, let the child know in advance.

7. *Keep the child interested.* The major problem in most reinforcement schemes is keeping the child actively interested over time. Once
the child has mastered the basics, you can begin to vary the rate or
the type of reinforcement. Of course, spell out changes in advance so
the child knows they are coming. If your child achieves a certain goal,
you can use games of chance as an added incentive. These act like a
"bonus round" on quiz shows. For example, if your daughter has kept
her room clean all week, let her "play" for her reward. She may have
three possible choices (pizza and a movie, choosing a video, or staying
up forty-five minutes later than usual). You can use a spinner, dice,
or cards. Make sure the most expensive (or most desired) reward is
the most difficult to get. For really superlative work, you can give extra
chances at the wheel (i.e., two or three tries to get the best reward).
You just need to be fair and clear about the rules in advance.

8. *Keep the child (and yourself) honest.* If you say you are going to

accept performance at a certain level, do not accept anything less. Some parents will do this because they feel the urgency to have their child succeed, but in the long run, what happens is that the tables become turned. The child teaches the parent to accept less and less while still paying off. Children need to be able to trust their parents to live up to agreements. If you say you expect a child to pick up *all* the clothes in his room, do not accept his leaving one sock balled up in the corner. And make sure that the payoff happens on time! The above responses are essential because they help your child predict what you are going to do and, in doing this, help him to help himself.

Toward the end of the chapter we will discuss a number of technical issues regarding positive reinforcement. As you will see, the technical aspects of putting together a positive reinforcement program are not very difficult. In order for it to work, however, both the child and the parents must approach the problem with the right mind-set.

The child must want the reinforcer and be willing to work for it. He cannot approach the positive-reinforcement program as he would a bribery situation, with a take-it-or-leave-it attitude. If he does, the program is guaranteed to fail. He must feel all of the urgency and be willing to take on the responsibility for appropriate behavior in order to ensure he is reinforced for it.

As parents, you must also approach the problem with the right attitude. You cannot have a great deal of investment in whether or not the child receives the reinforcer. All you can do is set up the conditions under which the child may be able to receive the reinforcement. You must also play the role of the quality-control supervisor to make sure the child is not cutting corners. Your job is to see that the child works and to keep him honest. If you start assuming responsibility for his getting the reinforcement, you will soon find yourself doing all the work. You will gradually feel more and more of the urgency, while the child will exhibit less and less. Any parent attempting to use a positive-reinforcement approach must guard against this. You must be ready to walk away from the program if the child is not willing to follow through.

Returning for a moment to little Jasmine, the grocery store guerrilla, bribery was clearly ineffective. She took the bait once but then demanded a higher payoff. In order to change to a situation of positive reinforcement, the first step would be to identify something that is

near and dear to little Jasmine, something she would be willing to
work for. Once this is identified, Mother can simply say, "Oh, you
would like gum? Well, you certainly can have a piece, but first I expect
you to behave in the supermarket." Of course, Mother would have to
explain exactly what she meant by "behaving" since this is far too
abstract a term for a four-year-old. Mother could certainly help out
this situation by giving little Jasmine very specific activities to do while
in the supermarket. For a preschooler, supermarkets are more stimulating than a classroom. There are objects to identify and classify;
things to be hunted for; sizes, shapes, colors all waiting to be explored.
A four-year-old child can also find groceries and put them in the cart.
Jasmine can be a responsible part of the shopping team! In addition
to receiving some tangible reward at the end of a successful shopping
trip, it would probably be helpful for little Jasmine to have little verbal
boosts all along the way. This would help her keep track of how she
is doing, keeping her on-task and her interest level high. Considering
that little Jasmine seems to enjoy terrorizing her mother in the supermarket, however, she may be reluctant to change even though the
positive reinforcements are all in place. This will mean that in addition
to positively reinforcing appropriate behavior, Jasmine's mother will
need to decide on some bottom-line consequences should Jasmine
choose to misbehave. This leads us to the darker side of motivational
mechanics, punishment. This is an ugly word that conjures up all
sorts of terrible images, leaving parents shuddering with guilty con-
sciences. Fear not—punishment is a normal part of the learning process and can be carried out in the most humane manner.

To Sum Up: Positive Reinforcement—Let the Child Do the Work!

Most parents I have met have a natural dislike for *bribery*. This is
commendable. Nobody likes to be blackmailed by their five-year-old at
the checkout in Walgreen's. Besides, there is no guarantee that any
bribe will be effective more than once. Usually parents end up promising themselves into hock even though the child has changed little
and cares less. The parents are the ones who fret and feel the urgency
and responsibility for change. Clearly they are working too hard.

But *positive reinforcement* encourages the child to bear the burden of work, while the parent can simply walk away. The important difference between bribery and positive reinforcement hinges on who feels the urgency. If the parent feels it, then the bauble becomes a *bribe*. If the child wants the bauble enough to work for it, then the bauble is a *reinforcer*.

It is very easy to confuse reinforcing value with material value. It doesn't matter how much a toy costs, how many other kids in the neighborhood have one, or how much your child yells, "Iwantit-IwantitIwantit." If the child won't work to get or maintain it, it does not have reinforcing value. The best reinforcers are usually right under our noses: the privileges and freedoms the child already enjoys and the warm glow of your attention.

Once you are clear about the nature of positive reinforcement, the mechanics are simple and straightforward. First you select a reinforcer the child is willing to work for. Then you need to be able to walk away. Now the sense of urgency is flowing in the right direction. Be sure that the payoff fits the accomplishment, that the goal is achievable, and that initial success is certain. This will hook the child into trying the new behavior. After that, it is simply a matter of making the child work a little harder for the reward. You will also need to keep the child interested in the program. Unlike bribes, these programs can be challenging and fun for both you and your child.

But positive reinforcement also involves a lot of work and it may take some time before you see real change in a child's behavior. This is often discouraging for parents and makes them secretly long for the sweet immediacy of punishment: "You did *what?* Well, I've got a little surprise for you, too!" Punishment, when it works, stops misbehavior in its tracks. You can see the results—that is, when it works. We will consider the emotional tug-of-war over punishment in the next chapter. For now, appreciate the value of positive reinforcement. You are teaching your child new skills, building new behavior that will last a lifetime. Teach slowly and patiently: your child is worth it.

6

Punishment: The Dark Side of the Force

There is no topic in all of child care which arouses such strong mixed emotions as punishment. Many people feel children should receive only loving attention from their parents. Misbehavior can simply be ignored. Others, though, think of punishment as the only reliable method of discipline. There has been a lot written about the dangers of using punishment as the sole method of discipline. Many parents are reluctant to punish but haven't found any workable alternatives. When parents reward children and ignore their misbehavior, they feel as though the children are getting away with something. Most parents I talk to do not have pure and simple opinions about punishment. Rather, they embody all these thoughts and feelings at once. What confusion! Parents must have some clear way to think about punishment so they can discipline their children without guilt and conflict.

As we discuss attitudes toward punishment, it is first important to understand why the social view of punishment is that it is "bad." Next, we will explore the many reasons why punishments often fail. We will see that in most cases, parents use punishment for the immediate impact it has on the child. This may hurt the child, but it is usually ineffective as a teaching tool. We will then see how to develop a more effective attitude toward punishment.

Punishment has a natural place in the learning process. It is present in some form throughout the animal kingdom. It serves as the counterpoint to positive reinforcement. Children tend to resist changing their behavior, especially when the old ways are well practiced and comfortable. The purpose of positive reinforcement is to motivate children to behave in some unaccustomed way. Punishment is merely the dark side of the learning process. It is a way to discourage children from behaving inappropriately—by taking the fun out of it. This encourages them to adapt their behavior. Soon they recognize the benefits they receive if they behave in the new way. This makes positive reinforcement all the more effective.

Our primary focus here is on the mental attitude of the parents. Once you have a clear, constructive way of thinking about punishment, you will be ready to use the techniques in the next chapter.

WHY PUNISHMENT IS "BAD"

There is no way punishment can be pleasurable; it does not make children smile. It is physically, mentally, or emotionally painful. In American society, the use of punishment is not taken lightly. At the broader social level there are severe restrictions on the use of any type of aversive consequences by public institutions. In most states there are strict rules governing the use of physical or mental punishments by the public schools. Similarly, institutions for the developmentally disabled are prohibited from the free use of punishment.

Prior to the last decade, the boundary between society and the home was considered sacred. While social institutions were restricted in the use of punishment, how a man disciplined his son was considered his own business. Increasingly, however, there have been concerns over abuses within the family. This has led social forces to intrude into the once sanctified realm of the home.

In the late 1950s, a number of studies indicated that punishment not only was ineffective in reducing negative behavior but stimulated counteraggressive behavior and resentment. Their results showed punishment simply made children hostile and increased the likelihood that they would act out against their parents in devious ways. Children who were punished, it was suggested, copy their parents' brutish behavior and act out aggressively against younger, more vulnerable children. The recommendation of these studies was that parents should use more positive approaches in their discipline and not rely exclusively on punishment. This was misinterpreted, however, and was taken to mean that all forms of punishment are bad. This was bad news for many parents. It threatened to take away the big stick, leaving them with only the soft talk.

What was a parent to do? These woolly-headed psychologists seemed to be telling parents that the one method they knew to control their children not only was ineffective but was actually doing irreparable harm. Parents were caught in a double bind. If they continued to punish their children, they would be guilty of the crime of damaging them for life. If they didn't punish, their children were certainly headed for ruin: opium dens, cathouses, and bad grades. The major problem with the popular view of punishment is that it is associated with anger and retaliation. In effect, punishment is viewed as a way the parents "get back" at a child for some bit of misbehavior. The phrase "teach him a lesson" is synonymous with physical pain. In this popular view, punishment is expected to work because the child is too afraid ever to try to misbehave again. When punishment is used in this manner it *can be* damaging and it *is* ineffective. Fortunately, physical pain and abject fear have very little to do with effective discipline. Punishment does not have to be abusive, and when it is not, it is very effective. When parents rely on pain and fear, they are guaranteeing themselves failure and frustration. Depending on the child, this approach to punishment can also have damaging effects.

WHEN PUNISHMENT DOESN'T WORK

Most of us have a lot of difficulty understanding the real meaning of punishment. We expect it is the intensity of punishment that is supposed to make it work. Some parents come in for therapy and admit that they have tried some terrible punishments and that the whole process simply doesn't work. They are amazed when the child continues the irritating behavior or simply says, "Go ahead, I don't care." They increase the intensity and again their expectations are exploded because their "punishment does not have any impact." The traditional attitude toward punishment tends to focus on *emotional dynamics* ("I'm very angry at you"), *aversiveness* ("If you do that again, I'll get out the belt"), and *intensity* ("You won't sit down for a week"). It is these factors that are often thought to have the impact on the child's behavior. In actual learning, though, none of these are essential to the definition of punishment.

There are a number of reasons why caution must be used in the application of this sort of punishment.

Jenny went with her stepfather to swimming lessons after some prodding from her mother. Since her mother had remarried, Jenny had been very standoffish. She was a naturally shy girl, but her mother was looking for a way to bring stepfather and daughter together. At the lessons, her stepfather told her to jump into the pool, but she was afraid. He began to yell at her and told her to go sit at the side of the pool. She ran into the locker room instead and only came out with the gentle coaxing of her swimming teacher. Though her parents talked to her about "the incident," Jenny refused to go to swimming lessons again.

Sometimes a punishment will have some immediate effect on behavior but can have long-term detrimental results. In clinical experience, this seems to be more true in the case of anxious, introverted children. These children seem to be more self-critical, more pain-sensitive, and more pessimistic about uncertain situations. They are also very susceptible to the effects of punishment. These children quickly learn to avoid situations in which they experience any type of negative consequence. Such children can easily develop inappropriate avoidance responses. For example, if such a child is punished for making mistakes in some group game or sport, it may be extremely difficult, if not impossible, to get the child to play in groups again.

Another problem that might arise is called behavioral rigidity. A child punished for a certain behavior may close off forever to that behavior, even in situations in which it might be acceptable. Some children who experience inconsistent, extremely harsh punishment for normal sexual self-exploration can develop an aversion to all forms of sexual behavior, even when such behavior is appropriate. These children may grow up having a difficult time establishing normal interpersonal relationships with persons of the opposite sex. This can lead to difficulties in intimacy.

Some children simply do not experience physical pain in such a way that they are able to learn from aversive experiences. In extreme cases, this is typical of the classic hyperactive child. Even with normal, healthy, extraverted children, the harsh punishment may result in only a transitory suppression of behavior. This means that the child may be willing to stop a particular behavior for a couple of hours or even a few days, but soon resumes the behavior at the original intensity.

> "I suppose you're gonna tell me that I shouldn't spank my kid," said the gruff, irritable father.
> The psychologist only looked at him with patience and compassion. "You've tried spanking, huh? Any luck?"
> "Well, I'm not just gonna let him get away with acting that way."
> "But does it work? Does he stop acting up?"
> "For a few minutes, then he goes right back and does the same thing again."
> "You want to try something different?"
> The father looked up, softer now. "You got any ideas?"

Other children who are emotionally reactive may be aroused further by punishment. The purpose of punishment is to make the child stop some type of behavior. However, punishment for some children may have a stimulating effect. This can lead to increased amounts of inappropriate behavior—just the opposite of the intended result.

> The angry father grabbed his son by the wrists, hoisted the boy off the ground, and gave him three solid cracks on his still-wiggling bottom. But when he put the child down he was greeted by an angry, defiant glare. "So what, it didn't hurt me," the boy taunted. He then grabbed his startled father's hand and sunk his teeth into it. "There," he said, "I bited you. How you like that?"

Similarly, it is essential that the child be able to integrate and organize his behavior in anticipation of certain consequences. Children should be able to understand that if they do something, their parents are going to *do something* in response. If the child cannot anticipate, integrate, and then organize his behavior accordingly, as is the case with some learning-disabled children, he will have significant problems with this type of punishment.

This way of punishing also tends to foster negative attitudes that can become an enduring part of the child's self-concept. These attitudes are:

1. "Bigger and meaner is better."
2. "Negative attention is better than no attention."
3. "I'm bad."

All three attitudes are used by children to sustain an unhealthy self-image. Punishments that focus on emotionality, aversiveness, and intensity provide the child with a very negative model for relating to others. They teach the child that if you are big you can intimidate smaller people and that this is somehow okay. The child learns to exercise aggressive behavior in order to get his way. Sometimes the child will behave counteraggressively against the parents. All of this is unhealthy.

The second issue has to do with *negative attention*. All children like attention from their parents. Some children, though, don't know how to go about getting their parents' attention in positive ways. They do know they can get attention by misbehaving. Many children, especially young children, cannot distinguish between positive and negative forms of stimulation. Attention is simply stimulating and they go after it, no matter what form it takes. The child's first experience in using behavior modification with his parents is through the use of negative reinforcement. The child cries, the parents come running, the child stops crying. The traditional approach to discipline is also reactive: if a child misbehaves and his mother is angry at him, it is usually a lot more exciting than when he is behaving well.

The final reason has to do with the role the child adopts within the family. Some children will take on the identity of a "bad child." This is especially true if there is another child in the family who has adopted the role of the "good child." Once the child establishes an identity, he will fight to maintain it. Even if the identity is "bad," it is better than no identity at all. Children maintain their identities by acting out in very specific ways that provoke the parents to respond in predictable patterns: prediction and control. This holds true with "bad children" as well as with "good children." When parents try to be nice to a "bad child," they find, to their dismay, that the acting out skyrockets. This evokes anger and punishment from the parents, which in turn reaffirm the child's self-concept. In such cases, children continue to act in ways which evoke punishment because it builds on their identity—even though that identity is unhealthy.

THE MEANING OF PUNISHMENT

Now that we have explored the popular notions of punishment and the ways in which these backfire, we can ask, how does punishment really work? In the driest of clinical terms, some behavior is followed immediately by an unpleasant consequence and this is repeated until the two are associated. The association becomes strong enough so that when the child thinks about the behavior, the thought of the punishment is also evoked. When the child thinks about the punishment, she stops her behavior.

It is important to remember that punishment is defined only by the effect it has on the child's behavior. If the consequence decreases the future occurrence of the behavior, then it is punishing. If the consequence does not decrease the future occurrence of the behavior, then it is *not* punishing. This is critical. Punishment has nothing to do with how hard you spank, how many toys you take away, or how long the child stays in her room. If the child has not changed her behavior as a result, then what you have tried has not been punishing. That is not to say you haven't had an impact on the child. What you have done may have hurt the child or made her angry or resentful. But it is not punishment unless the behavior stops.

Punishment must always be defined from the child's point of view. Children differ in the way they respond to or learn from negative outcomes. Some children are extremely sensitive to physical and emotional pain. Many of these children learn to avoid not only dangerous situations but also reasonable challenges. These are the preschoolers who refuse to imitate a song in front of others, but can be overheard singing it perfectly in their rooms. Other children do not respond to physical or emotional pain and are willing to take incredible risks to get something they want. They do not seem to respond to threats to take away their toys, although when it happens, they get angry. Other children are very reactive to the pain of punishment even though they cannot stop their behavior in advance. Once the punishment is over, they immediately return to the prohibited activity, as if they have learned nothing from the experience. Specific punishment techniques may work all too well, once in a while, or not at all. It depends on how the individual child organizes and interprets this type of experience.

STOP LOOKING FOR IMPACT, LOOK FOR CHANGE IN BEHAVIOR

If you rely on the emotional impact of punishment, you are going to be frustrated. Instead, focus on what the child *needs to learn* from the situation. Punishment, like positive reinforcement, will be effective only if the child feels the urgency and the responsibility to solve the problem. This will not happen as long as you expect your punishment to have *impact*.

When parents rely on emotional dynamics, intensity, or aversiveness, they are betting that their punishments will have impact. They want to see the child cry, feel fearful and sad, or show remorse. They think these immediate signs indicate the child has *learned something*. But this is not necessarily true. Immediate impact may not be a good predictor of what your child has learned. It indicates only how your child feels *here and now*. The way children respond to the same punishment will vary depending on the circumstances, their stamina, and their attitudes. Besides, when your child realizes that you expect your punishment to have impact, she has power in the situation. Once children see your cards in the mirror, they know how to play their hand.

When you have an emotional investment in the impact of the punishment, you are setting yourself up for disappointment. Suppose your child doesn't come home on time at night and, as a consequence, you take away his bike for one week. He squawks and sputters, goes to his room, and slams his door nine times. Does this mean he has learned something? The next day you see him out on his friend's bike. He has borrowed it for the week, trading his GI Joes in return. He is happy as a clam. How do you feel? Suppose your preschooler won't stay in bed at night, so you threaten to take away her favorite dolly. She looks at you earnestly and deadpans, "I want you to take her away . . . Oh, and take away Bear-bear, too." What do you do then? Obviously these punishments have not had any impact, and what is the result? Once parents look for impact, they are taking on the urgency of the situation. Once they take on the urgency, guess who has the problem?

The whole purpose of punishment is to let the consequence, not the parents' emotions, affect the child's behavior. When the parents' emotions become more prominent, some serious problems can result. Once the child senses the parents are looking for the punishment to have impact, the child gains power and leverage in the situation. The issue becomes whether or not they show remorse, admit they did something, or simply cry. By denying the parents the response they want, the child can control the situation. Some children are willing to endure pain just to see the parents get frustrated and take on the urgency and the burden of the problem. The parents escalate, the child becomes more stubborn, the twice-frustrated parents escalate some more. Dangerous territory!

It is vital that parents focus on their attitude toward discipline before settling issues of technique. They need to see misbehavior as normal, the medium through which children learn self-control and social mastery, and they must develop a positive, assertive attitude toward the process of disciplining. Punishment can still be employed with the same positive attitude, but for this to happen, it is the child who must feel the urgency and wrestle with the problem of self-control. When the parent has an appropriate mind-set, the consequences follow the behavior in a mechanical fashion. When the child chooses to behave in certain ways, he also chooses certain consequences. In a sense, the child punishes himself; the parent simply walks away. When you can approach problems this way, the fun goes out of misbehavior.

TEACH YOUR CHILDREN TO BEHAVE THEMSELVES

When you punish a child, what are you really trying to accomplish? Most parents will say they are trying to discourage the child from behaving irresponsibly. If you ask the child, though, he will say, "They are trying to make me behave." If this is the case in your household, you have trouble. If there is one truism in all of child rearing, it is this: you cannot *make* your child do anything. Your child always has the choice of whether to behave or to misbehave. You cannot make the choice, control her thoughts, move her limbs or her tongue. But you do control what happens after she misbehaves. You *do* control whether or not you pay attention to her, and you control her privileges and freedoms. Even though you cannot make a child behave, you can hold her responsible for *how* she behaves.

The most valuable lesson you can teach your child is that privileges and freedoms are tied to responsible behavior. By behaving irresponsibly, the child is simply showing you that she is not capable of making appropriate choices concerning her behavior; she obviously needs you to make these choices for her and also to watch over her more closely. You, of course, are willing to help her because you are her parent and you love her. This means, however, that a number of privileges and freedoms get restricted in the bargain.

What you stress here is not that she is "bad" and in need of punishment. Why give her the satisfaction of seeing herself as some heroic outlaw? Instead, you grant her the power to behave as irresponsibly as she chooses. You are not there to "make her behave." However, if she chooses to behave irresponsibly, she is also choosing to give up her privileges and freedoms. Who is responsible? Who has the problem? When she can behave responsibly, she will be demonstrating to you that she is capable of self-control and ready to resume these privileges.

The attitude of the parents determines whether punishment will work or not. It is the child who must bear the burden of the problem and struggle through the process of learning self-control. Keep the overall purpose of discipline in sharp focus. Punishment is for teaching, not hurting. If you use punishment to retaliate, looking for the emotional impact, you will be assuming all of the urgency. The child needs to feel that urgency in order to want to change her behavior. It is the child who must learn to behave more responsibly—let her wrestle with the problem. Granted, most parents will have a number of questions about the technical aspects of defining rules, setting limits, making contracts, and imposing consequences. There are a million "what ifs" that arise simply because children are very creative in testing limits. The next chapters will deal with the technical problems. But first, concentrate on your attitudes and expectations. When these are clear, the technical process of discipline will flow more smoothly.

To Sum Up: Using Punishment Effectively
Without Guilt

As with positive reinforcement, parents need to develop a constructive view of punishment before they can use it effectively. This is hard
because of all the bad press punishment has gotten over the years.
Like some shadowy stranger at our door who has been preceded by
rumors and gossip, it is not necessarily welcome in our home. We have
all grown up with some experience on the receiving end of punishment
and the memories are often painful. So the task of transforming our
dislike of punishment into something akin to a positive attitude is
formidable indeed.

But punishment has a natural place in the learning process. It serves
as a counterpoint to positive reinforcement. It adds value to incentives
by contrast. Children often will not change what they do unless they
can feel the contrast between the positive and negative responses to
their behavior. How did that feel? Ouch! How does this feel? Hey,
that's not so bad! Punishment is simply the dark side of the learning
process. It is necessary because it helps children appreciate the light.

Pain and fear do not have to play any part in the learning process.
Though we often equate punishment with these qualities, they are
superfluous by-products of misguided efforts. Inflicting emotional pain,
physical pain, and fear is abusive but usually ineffective in helping
children learn more mature ways of behaving. Whether or not a child
cries after a punishment is irrelevant; look for changes in behavior,
not at the immediate emotional impact.

In this chapter there has been almost no mention of technique. Too
often, the controversy over punishment degenerates into a shouting
match over whether it is right or wrong to spank. Instead we should
be asking what we want our child to learn and how we can help teach
her. If punishment has a role in the teaching process, then we need
to consider only a few technical issues. What is generally effective?
Administering something—extra chores, a scolding, a spanking? Or
removing something the child wants—time with friends, TV, money?
Whatever the consequences of misbehaving, they need to be predictable, consistent, and immediate.

Like any other form of learning, punishment needs to be considered from the child's perspective. It doesn't matter how loudly you yell, how hard you spank, or how many toys you take away. If the child doesn't change his behavior, then he hasn't been punished. For punishment to work, it must have deterrent value. The child needs to see that if he does "it" one more time, something unpleasant is going to happen. This gives him time to change.

This is what is so confusing about time-outs. Parents often try to use a time-out as a punishment and are dismayed to find "it doesn't work!" Of course not! Time-outs and other techniques aimed at limiting your attention to your child's naughty behavior have no deterrent value at all. They are still extremely important tools in the learning process, as we will see in the next chapter.

7

Can You Ignore the Blue Horse in Your Living Room?

The most powerful disciplinary tool you possess is not your belt or the sole of your shoe, it is your attention. How you pay attention is crucial to the way your children learn to relate to you and to others around them. What your child sees you responding to is what your child will repeat—again and again. Many children do not care about whether the behavior that hooks your attention is positive or negative. If you respond to noncompliant, obnoxious misbehavior with crackling, electric anger, that is sufficient. Respond to this behavior in this way often enough and you will develop a relationship with your child that will be based on negative attention-seeking. But you can teach your child to seek your *positive* attention instead of just your negative attention.

Teaching your child to seek your positive attention usually means you will have to change how you pay attention to your child. But don't expect him to go along with these changes without some stiff resistance. Before any misbehaving child worth his salt is going to give up the game, he needs to feel that the rules have *really* changed. Your child will need to know you are firm in your resolve. Engaging your attention by behaving appropriately may mean he has to make a full 180-degree turn in his behavior. It is going to take some time and energy to adjust to such a drastic change. After all, you have just demolished his ability to predict and control your behavior. Can he really trust you this time? You must teach him that of course he can.

In this chapter, we will discuss how to distinguish which types of problems can be eliminated by simply being ignored. Certain kinds of behavior problems will go away if you ignore them altogether. Other problems simply won't go away. They linger on to haunt and irritate you. When your child keeps up that awful bugging, can you really ignore it? When I tell you, "Don't think about a blue horse," what image pops into your mind? It is very hard *not* to think about such a graphic image. As with the image of the blue horse, when your child behaves in a hurtful or destructive way, you can't afford to pretend to look the other way, although there are ways to respond to misbehavior without paying satisfying attention to the child.

The primary technique discussed in this chapter is the use of *time-outs*. Probably the most effective yet least understood method for teaching a child, the time-out is not painful and it is not especially punishing. No child will quake in fear at being sent to his room for two minutes. But pain and punishment are not the purpose of time-outs. Properly carried out, time-outs are surprisingly effective in denying a misbehaving child the attention he seeks. As with most aspects of teaching, a child learns as much from your attitude as from the simple mechanics of the procedure. What a child learns is that a parent is warm and responsive when he behaves in some appropriate way, but bland and mechanical when the child chooses to become a blue horse. Children always move instinctively toward warmth.

THE MERITS OF SIMPLE IGNORING

Many parents, on the verge of exploding over their child's latest terrorist act, have been told by well-meaning neighbors, "If you just ignore it, she will stop doing it." The just-ignore-it approach is often espoused in many psychology textbooks as well. The usual example involves the toddler who cries bloody murder at night when being put to bed. The parents, usually frantic to soothe their screaming child, will visit her repeatedly, pick her up, give her glasses of water, sing lullabies, offer live puppies and horses, and eventually end up letting the child sleep with them.

Parents are counseled to let the child know that once she is put to bed, there will be no more visits from the parents. The child, who is used to this very frequent but somewhat unpredictable attention, immediately takes the case before the Supreme Court: she screams bloody murder and waits to see what will happen. When the parents, ears plugged with Kleenex and biting their nails, do not respond, the child redoubles her efforts. After all, perhaps they didn't hear her. The child keeps this up for two solid hours before falling asleep. The parents, shaky and gray, are certain they have done irreparable damage to her frail psyche.

In the morning, though, she is bouncy and happy and ready to play. All seems to be going well until that night, when she keeps it up for three hours. With a little support from their counselor and a lot of bourbon, the parents are able to withstand this emotional torture. They discover, much to their surprise, that the crying time decreases steadily over the next week, until by the fifth or sixth night there is no fussing at all.

In the terms of the psychology of learning, this is called *extinction*. In actual practice, this means that when children don't get rewarded, they stop doing something. In this particular case, the child is working very hard for her parents' attention. When the parents make it very clear that they will not attend to her cries of distress, she quickly gives up the behavior.

The just-ignore-it approach is very effective for other problems as well. It is especially useful when the child is trying out some new routine and wants to see how it will play to the parents. Simple ignoring can eliminate the preschooler's first tentative use of curse words. Simple ignoring can also effectively eliminate some types of "bugging" behavior like whining and name-calling. This holds true especially if the behavior is not well practiced or the child is not very determined. Another situation that can be extinguished by ignoring is sibling squabbles. Often the fighting is designed to draw parents into the middle; once there, they find they are holding a tar baby with no briar patch in sight. If you can recognize these situations when they occur and deliberately ignore them, the squabbling usually diminishes.

THE LIMITS OF SIMPLE IGNORING

Like all simple techniques, ignoring has a place in the process of learning but is not sufficient to cope with all the many and varied ways that children misbehave. Fortunately, ignoring is not the only way to deal with most behavior problems. Consider the following problem situation:

Cindy had always considered herself a "New Age" parent. She had imagined her son chasing bubbles, blowing dandelion seeds, and concocting wild creatures in the clouds on summer afternoons. Jean Claude, age four, had different ideas. He liked to get goofy in the late afternoon, running from room to room and making as much noise as possible. Sometimes he would jump from foot to foot in a spasmodic dance, singing tonelessly. His mother did her best to ignore his behavior. Sometimes she would talk about how nice it would be to have a little boy around the house who was under control. But all the while she was ignoring him, her anger increased, purpling her face and making her voice sound like glass caught under a basement door. Jean Claude missed none of this.

One day, picking just the right moment, he grabbed the vegetables she was washing for dinner and threw them on the floor. This was too much! Cindy's temper burst openly into flames. "You little rat!" she exploded and raced off after him. Jean Claude gave a squawk of half surprise and half fear at the New Age mom transformed into a screamin' demon. He ran away and the chase was on. But Cindy had been training for a ten-kilometer race and was full of fire. She caught him as he made the turn for the living room and, grabbing Jean Claude by the elastic waistband of his pull-up pants, turned him over her knee and gave him four good cracks on his bottom. The cracks made a great deal of noise but afforded very little pain. Jean Claude had not yet *decided* to be toilet trained and wore thick, ultra-absorbent diapers.

Jean Claude stamped up and down and screeched something unintelligible. Cindy felt a rush of guilt and horror. How easily the beast within her could be stimulated to react! To her surprise, though, within a few moments Jean Claude was as happy as could be, singing merrily and playing by himself. Cindy thought to herself that perhaps Jean Claude had learned something. Indeed he had. He had learned that in order to make Mommy turn purple and talk in that funny voice, he had to throw the vegetables on the floor.

The story of Jean Claude and the New Age mother illustrates several problems with the just-ignore-it approach. First, in order to ignore misbehavior, you have to have considerable stamina since children will usually escalate their irritating behavior before giving it up. Second, the child's goal in initiating the behavior must be taken into account. Extinction works only if the child is trying to get your attention. If the behavior is designed to communicate some other thought or feeling, extinction will not work. Third, children learn to get your attention by doing whatever will hook your attention. This means that if you respond only when the child does something serious, then serious misbehaving is what the child will learn to do.

GIRD YOUR LOINS!

You have to have a lot of stamina to ignore misbehavior. Anytime a child is used to receiving attention for some particular behavior, he will actively resist any attempt to change that. You are, after all, supposed to behave according to the simple clockwork of their expectations. This is the way they have learned to control events. When you stop behaving according to their expectations, they will work very hard to bring you back into line.

If you try to ignore a child, he will simply redouble his efforts to get your attention. Children will always escalate the behavior you are trying to extinguish, and depending on how strongly they expect you to respond, they are usually willing to take you to the limits of your endurance. This explains why when you try to ignore some behavior it always gets worse before it gets better. Many parents simply do not have the emotional stamina to tolerate this dramatic increase in awful behavior. To most parents who are unaccustomed to dealing with this kind of escalation, the initial results are truly terrifying. After a brief burst of bad behavior is ignored, the child transforms himself into a monster with an inexhaustible capacity to scream. Therefore, take stock of your own emotional armor. If you don't have the tolerance for this type of situation, there are plenty of alternatives.

SOMETIMES IT'S NOT FOR YOUR BENEFIT

In other situations, the just-ignore-it approach won't work because the child is not directly seeking attention. It is not always obvious at first glance whether or not the behavior is for your benefit. This is especially true when children engage in some self-abusive behavior. When they are frustrated or upset, some children will bite themselves or bang their heads. Unfortunately, this type of behavior is seen both in developmentally disabled children and in neurologically intact toddlers who are prone to temper tantrums. Many healthy children discover that when they bang their heads on the floor, their parents will fall to their knees and beg for mercy.

Often the first line of advice in cases of self-abusive behavior is simply to ignore the behavior. Parents are advised to examine whether the child actually does hurt herself when she engages in the head banging. Usually they find there are no bruises or cuts, unless, of course, the child gets careless. In most cases this attention-seeking head banging results in no physical harm to the child. In these cases a little bit of ignoring goes a long way. Upon finding their parents are giving them the cold shoulder, the children quickly give up the bouncing head.

However, parents have to exercise considerable caution around these types of behaviors. There are many children who are underresponsive to pain and may not be engaging in the behavior simply for attention. It may be a genuine expressive act of frustration. These children often will hurt themselves because the behavior does not give enough painful feedback to stop them. Ignoring the behavior will work only if the goal of the behavior is to get your attention. When it is clear that this is not the case and that the child may hurt herself, some other approach should be immediately employed.

THE BLUE HORSE STAMPEDE!

Finally, there are some behaviors you simply cannot ignore. Some children are willing to escalate their behavior to the point where, in order to save your property or protect lives, you have to respond. If you ignore low-to-moderate levels of obnoxious behavior but react to very high levels of obnoxious behavior, guess what the child is going to do in order to get your attention! When this happens, the best-intended behavior-modification plans can have disastrous results. Consider the following story:

Thaddeus was a charming eight-year-old who also happened to be the reigning nuisance of his third-grade classroom. It seemed he was fond of poking the girl who sat in front of him. Every time he poked her she would squawk, "Thaddeus, you cut that out! I'm telling." The teacher would scold him and Thaddeus, beaming away, would do it again. Finally the teacher discussed the problem with the school psychologist. After considering the situation, the psychologist suggested a very elaborate extinction procedure. The boy was sent out of the room one day and the school psychologist and the teacher talked to the entire class. They identified the problem and involved all the children in a program of "just ignoring" Thaddeus's bugging behavior. If the whole class would comply with ignoring Thaddeus when he bothered other children, they would all earn a treat at the end of the week. When Thaddeus came back into the room, he naturally resumed his poking of the girl in front of him. He got no response from her. No one looked at him. The teacher acted as though he weren't there. He poked the boy in the seat next to him. No response. He wadded a spitball and fired it into the ear of the girl sitting on the other side of him. Again, no response. This was unbelievable! It was clearly time to pull out all the stops. He stood up in his chair and, picking up his social studies book, whacked the girl in front of him on the top of her head. She screamed and cried, the teacher began shouting, the school psychologist came in from next door to see what had happened. Children were on their feet and desks and chairs were falling over. Now things were cooking. That was more like it!

When ignored, Thaddeus stopped his simple poking of children and began hitting them, kicking them, and whacking them with books. Thaddeus did not learn to stop bothering other children. Instead, he learned he had to work a little harder, do something more drastic, in order to get the attention he wanted. He was clearly willing to escalate the behavior and got the results he wanted.

In conclusion, while simple ignoring is often the best initial approach to many low-key, irritating behaviors, it is certainly not the only or the last approach that needs to be tried. Ignoring works best when the child has not yet established the behavior strongly and would probably be willing to give it up quickly. Cases of simple bugging, first curse words, interrupting, and sibling squabbles might qualify. Ignoring also works best in situations in which the child has a limited capacity to escalate. This is why it is effective in eliminating some mild, socially inappropriate behaviors and in teaching children to sleep through the night.

Finally, children will always escalate the irritating behavior before giving it up. If you planned on simply ignoring the behavior, then you must be committed to ignoring it no matter how extreme it becomes. The problem with ignoring Thaddeus and Jean Claude was that they were willing to escalate to the point where they could damage property or hurt others. The adult simply *had to respond* at some point. Unfortunately, what this taught these children was that they had to carry their acting-out past the danger point in order to get a response. This, of course, was not what the adults had intended them to learn. Certainly, simple ignoring may be appropriate for some low-key problems. For many problem behaviors, though, a more active intervention is the wisest approach.

TIME-OUTS: ACTIVELY REMOVING THE CHILD FROM YOUR ATTENTION

By this point, almost everyone knows what a "time-out" is, or at least they think they do. Magazines such as *Parents* and *Family Circle* frequently contain articles that discuss discipline. Often there is a mention of time-outs and it usually involves having the child go to his room or sit on her chair in the corner for around ten minutes or so. The use of time-outs can be a very effective discipline technique if the process is understood and carried out correctly. Unfortunately, there are a lot of misconceptions about time-outs and parents are often frustrated, stating they "just don't work." Let's set the record straight by defining time-outs, and then examine situations in which they will be more useful than simple ignoring. Finally, let's troubleshoot the time-out process, exploring what goes wrong and how to make that process work.

The term *time-out* means that the child doesn't have the chance to receive positive reinforcement for a short period of time. The idea behind having the child sit on a chair or go to her room is that she is removed from the company of others who might reinforce her. This means others don't talk to her or about her, feed her, give her toys, or pay any sort of attention to her. From the dark side, it often means that parents don't yell at her, spank her, or scold her. It is supposed to be a very bland process and that is what makes it unpleasant for the child. It doesn't provide the negative attention she loves or expects. It is a time-out from all forms of reinforcement.

A time-out derives much of its power simply by interrupting the pattern of misbehavior, breaking the rhythm and allowing the parents to redirect the activity. Most parents become frustrated because time-outs do not seem to be an effective punishment. Children do not tremble in fear at the thought of sitting in their rooms. But a disciplinary time-out can serve the same purpose as a time-out in a basketball game. It provides a break in the pattern of action and a chance to change the strategy or at least the pace of the activity. This may be the most important feature of the time-out process, one that is frequently overlooked or underrated.

In a strict sense, simple ignoring is really an informal time-out process. After all, when you ignore your child for saying something inappropriate, you are withholding your most positive reinforcer—your attention. Making a child sit on a chair or go to the bedroom for a few minutes is simply a more formal way of removing her from the aura of your attention.

The formality of a time-out process has some distinct advantages over the more spontaneous simple-ignoring approach. While simple ignoring can be effective in eliminating poorly rehearsed, tentative behaviors, a more structured time-out process is more effective when the child is accustomed to misbehaving; when she is not simply doing it for your attention (i.e., perhaps she is overstimulated); when she is willing to escalate past the limits of your endurance; or when she is potentially destructive and hurtful.

There are three reasons why a formal time-out procedure is more effective in cases like those above. First, structured time-outs help the child learn to predict your behavior and to control her own behavior. When you simply ignore your child, you create a very *uncertain* situation. The child is *uncertain* as to whether or not you heard or saw what she did. The child is also *uncertain* as to whether or not you are going to respond. Faced with this degree of uncertainty, many children are likely to increase their misbehavior until they are sure you notice it and know you will respond. The time-out procedure eliminates the uncertainty. It provides the child with clear feedback that you have noticed the behavior and allows the child to predict the consequences of further misbehavior. Because the situation is predictable, the child can control his behavior before the consequence is imposed. In essence, you set a boundary and the child can choose whether or not to keep his behavior within that boundary.

A second advantage to a formal time-out procedure is that it gives the parent something specific to do. As was noted in the previous chapter, it is very difficult to organize your behavior around "not doing" something. It is as hard for parents *not to do* as it is for children. What are you really doing while you are trying to ignore some misbehavior—holding your breath and counting to a million? Like our poor New Age mother, many parents can ignore only a limited amount of testiness from their children. When parents do respond, it is with a bang as the cork shoots out of the bottled feelings. This leaves children feeling shocked and uncertain and parents feeling guilty. A formal time-out procedure gives you a specific process to follow, something concrete to do. It gives you a way to respond to your child's misbehavior without explosive anger.

Finally, a formal time-out procedure is essentially a more honest approach to your child's misbehavior. As your child is escalating and you are trying not to pay attention but turning purple, what is being accomplished? Does the child really believe you are not aware of what she is doing? Who is fooling whom? More than likely your child is simply waiting to see how much bugging you can take before you blow up. But even though the child may notice you are getting angry, she pretends to see nothing. Both parent and child attempt to deceive each other until finally one gives in, usually in a rage. A structured time-out gives the parent a very straightforward way to deal with the problem. There is no game; you do not have to pretend not to notice something. You can respond immediately to misbehavior in a rational manner. You tell the child what you see, what will happen, and then you follow through.

USING TIME-OUTS EFFECTIVELY

If time-outs are so effective, then why are so many parents frustrated when they try to use them? I believe the answer lies in the parents' attitudes and expectations. Many parents have misconceptions about what a time-out is and how it works. Many parents use it as a punishment, instead of spanking, for example. If they expect that the threat of sitting on a chair for a few minutes *should* deter children from misbehaving, they are sadly disappointed. Consider the following example:

It is 4:30 in the afternoon, the time at which, in most families, all semblance of order and sanity breaks down. You are irritable, late from work, trying to prepare dinner. Your seven-year-old is tired of watching "The Brady Bunch" rerun and has begun chasing his younger sister in a looping figure eight from the living room to the dining room and back into the living room again. The dog is barking. You ask the boy to stop the chase game. You tell him firmly to stop. You tell him that if he doesn't stop, he will have to take a time-out. He doesn't stop. You tell him that this time you *really* mean it and that he has to sit on "the chair" and settle down. He doesn't. Now you are purple and you spit when you talk. You grab him by the arm and march him straight up to his room, where you tell him he will have to stay until he learns how to behave. He yells, "CanIcomeoutcanIcomeoutcanIcomeout?" for four minutes. He is quiet for ten minutes and you discover he has been playing contentedly in his room. This makes you angry, but you let him out anyway. He goes downstairs and immediately starts chasing his sister, the dog starts barking . . .

This example illustrates many of the common problems that parents experience when trying to use time-outs. The parents threaten the child with a time-out, but the child does not seem to care. They leave the child in his room for a long period and are dismayed to find he is able to play by himself or simply goes to sleep. When they let him out of the time-out, he goes right back to the same misbehavior. At this point, parents throw up their hands in frustration.

Does this mean that the time-out does not work? In these situations, it is completely ineffective because it is being used for the wrong purpose—as a punishment. The time-out is not a punishment in the proper sense; it has no deterrent value. It is merely a break in the action, a way to interrupt a pattern of inappropriate behavior. It allows the parent to change the circumstances, to remove the child from the situation, and to pay attention to anybody else who is behaving appropriately. When a time-out is used correctly it can be a very effective tool.

Time-outs don't need to last long. For toddlers, a time-out can mean sitting them in the middle of the living room floor with their heads down for ten seconds. For older children, a time-out of two to five minutes is usually sufficient—roughly equivalent to the penalty times in ice hockey. Because time-outs are meant to be used as interruptions, it is not necessary for them to be of great duration. Parents do not need to keep their children in their rooms for fifteen minutes or half an hour, waiting fruitlessly for them to show some sign of remorse. A time-out is merely a way to interrupt a deteriorating situation, restructure it, and allow a more positive situation to develop.

There may be some circumstances in which a parent will use room time as a punishment. If your child has decided to unravel all of the tape cassettes in your VCR library, an extended room time would be a healthy alternative to murder. There is nothing wrong with placing a child in his room for a lengthy period if that is what you need to do to contain the situation or to get your own feelings under control. But here you are not using room time as a brief time away from reinforcing attention. There is a difference between extended room time as a punishment and brief time-outs.

When parents use a brief time-out as a disciplinary technique, their attitude will determine its success. If they are angry and looking to give the child a piece of their mind, they are quickly frustrated. I have found through clinical experience that when parents adopt a low-key, bland attitude, time-outs are more satisfying to them. Using rote phrases to signal the child into the time-out helps. These can be rattled off rapidly in a tone of bored disdain, much the way a police officer reads off Miranda rights: "Take thirty seconds on the stairs. I am going to count to three. If by the time I count to three you are not sitting on the stairs, then . . ."

What if the child won't sit on the stairs? What if when you put the child in his room he immediately opens the door and comes out? These are very common problems with children of all age levels. Often the first impulse of the parent is to grab the child and try to forcibly hold him in the chair or engage in a tug-of-war over the doorknob of the bedroom door. You cannot *make* the child sit! You cannot control the child, the child must learn to control himself. If you try to control the child from the outside, who feels the urgency? Who has the problem? The child makes a decision to do what you tell him or to disobey. This is the child's decision and his responsibility. But there are consequences for every decision and this is what the child learns from any disciplinary encounter.

Suppose you place the child on the chair and he simply gets up and runs away. If you do not follow, the child will learn that your words are empty. If you attempt to hold him in the chair but then give up after a few minutes, what does the child learn? That if he is persistent, he will prevail. And where does this thinking lead? To the idea that the control over his behavior which you exert from the outside is very weak. Once he bursts through, there are no limits on his behavior. This is why you cannot control a headstrong child from the outside. If you fail, as you are certainly bound to do, the consequences for him are indeed frightening.

Instead, what you emphasize by using time-outs is that this is a chance for him to get *himself* under control, to settle *himself* down. The time-out procedure cannot be done in a haphazard manner. If the child will not sit on the stairs for thirty seconds, what will happen next? Suppose this next step fails; what will happen after that? Think of three or four steps to the time-out process that give the child the sense that if he chooses to disobey, the consequences will be more severe. For example, with very young children an initial step might be thirty seconds sitting on a chair. If they refuse to do this, however, then the next step might be one minute in their room with the door open. If this is challenged, then the next step could be two minutes in the room with the door closed.

But do not expect children will be intimidated by the thought of two minutes in their room with the door closed. Do not emphasize your power to control them. Who has the problem? Who feels the urgency? The child has simply decided he needs more time to settle down, and you are there to help.

Of course, the time-out procedure works more smoothly when children are trained into it at a very young age. It is going to be much more difficult to use a simple time-out procedure to change well-established oppositional behavior. For these types of problems, please refer to the subsequent chapters. It is also very important to define family rules in a simple and clear manner. It should be clear to the child what will lead to time-outs and what will not. Limits need to be very clearly established. Parents must respond immediately to the misbehavior, not allowing the child to keep pushing and testing.

For the present, however, let's focus on the attitudes of the parents. While it is very important to keep a bland attitude during the mechanical process of placing a child into a time-out, the most critical issue is how to get the child *out* of it. Many parents experience the most frustration at this point. It is very common for children to be able to settle themselves down quickly, but as soon as they come out of the time-out they go right back to the activity that led to it in the first place. This is where you need to place your greatest efforts. When a child comes out of a time-out, it is important that you not dwell on your own feelings. Remember, many children actively seek out negative attention. Instead, pay attention to the fact that the child was able to use the time to settle down ("You did a good job of settling yourself down—looks like you're ready to come out of your room"). Do not be disappointed if the child plays quietly in his room or goes to sleep. When you use a short time-out period, these responses will be less likely. But should you find a child playing quietly in his room, notice how he has managed to settle down and behave appropriately. You do not need to go overboard in your compliments, but restrained respect for the self-soothing and settling is important ("You were really upset and I'm surprised that you settled yourself down this well"). You may also wish to clarify the behavior which led to the time-out. Be careful, though, not to get drawn into arguments over whether you should or should not have responded this way. Keep the explanation simple and mechanical. Focus on what the child did. If the child needs to make some amends or reparations, like saying he's sorry or cleaning up a mess, bring that up now. But again, watch the tone. Keep it matter-of-fact.

When the child comes out of a time-out, you need to put a lot of energy and enthusiasm into redirecting him into some more-positive behavior. If you let the child float when he comes out of his time-out, he will be likely to get back into trouble. Don't allow dead space. Get the child interested and involved in some toy or play activity. Most children can be redirected after a time-out without much difficulty. Some children may deliberately test you by balking at your attempts to redirect them. This may mean they need some more time to settle themselves down. They may also be testing some more to feel the difference between your positive-comment, enthusiastic side and your bland, disinterested, mechanical side. Remember, most children do not enjoy mechanics. They move instinctively toward warmth and emotion. If your emotion is predominantly angry and negative, they will move toward that. In order to make time-outs work more effectively, you need to concentrate on the opposite. Make the process *into* a time-out bland and mechanical; make the process *out* of it warm, lively, and enthusiastic.

To Sum Up: Using Your Attention to Help Children Learn Self-Control

If someone were to say to us, "Don't think about a blue horse," what image would immediately pop into our minds? When children misbehave, can we really ignore them? We can hear them, feel them tugging at our clothes, maybe even see them out of the corner of our eye. Children do not care whether attention is positive or negative, whether they are being good or bad. Attention is warmth and light, and children move toward it. The power of our active attention is so great that if we pretend not to notice their behavior, they will often immediately stop it. Watchful and eager for our response, children will repeat behavior that we countenance with our attention. They stop behavior that nets a barren yield.

But when children become blue horses, we cannot ignore them. Then we must respond, but in a way that does not give them active, warm attention. The time-out process is one way of doing this. It is a method that immediately interrupts a misbehaving child and helps her to change her pattern of behavior to one you will shower with your attention. It has the advantage of working in situations in which you must respond. It provides the child with clear, predictable limits and gives you, the parent, something specific to do. It is also much more honest and realistic than ignoring. But it is the expectations and attitudes of the parent that allow time-outs to work. You teach the child to make an appropriate choice between your cool, mechanical response and your warm, lively attention. In the long run, you will teach the child she is responsible for regulating her own behavior and for the consequences she chooses.

PART III

The Mechanics of Discipline

8

An Ounce of Prevention

How are rituals, routines, and daily schedules going to solve any problems in day-to-day living? There are many reasons for using them and many ways in which they help. Think about how your own day goes. Your major activity is not punishing your children; you do not stand around waiting for someone to misbehave so you can take away a bicycle or imprison your child in his bedroom. Your major energies are probably devoted to running the family. This includes not only getting through the routines of dressing, washing, and eating breakfast, but also getting to work on time, working, planning meals, shopping, cooking, cleaning the house, cutting the grass, doing the laundry—the list is endless. Families are involved in the multitudinous activities of daily living. Punishing your children is only a very small part of life—even though on bad days it may not feel that way.

But *discipline* can be a part of everything the family does. Remember that the word means "teaching," and that what you are teaching your children is that they are competent to regulate themselves and to master social skills, control, and prediction. What better medium do you have for teaching them than the naturally occurring events of everyday living?

Besides, look at the types of problems you face every day. Children do not routinely set off fire alarms or level supermarket displays. The majority of problems most parents have to deal with are those grating, nagging, chronic problems that occur predictably each day. Children wake up in bad moods and have tantrums during the morning rush. They dawdle when you are trying to get out the door. They whine and cry in the store and want a special snack, then won't eat their dinner. They won't go to bed. These are not great embarrassments. They are the sort of constant, low-grade conflict that gives parents battle fatigue. When the big disaster does strike, you find you are simply too worn-out to cope. If you can deal with these minor skirmishes, eliminate them as problems, you may find you have a lot more energy for the big battles ahead.

If you felt some sympathy, some agreement, with the paragraph above, then you realize none of that behavior is surprising. You *know* how your children resist the flow of normal daily life. How does your child dawdle, whine, refuse to eat or go to bed? My guess is that you could describe your child's behavior in minute detail. This means *your child is predictable.* This is not unusual. Most children behave in characteristic ways. Most parents know *what* will set their children off and *how* they will behave when they are set off. But this predictability means you can anticipate problem situations. If you can anticipate them, you can set them up so the behavior will be less likely to occur. By using structured activities, daily rituals, and routines, you can eliminate some of life's recurring problems and reduce the intensity of many others.

SOME CHILDREN NEED MORE STRUCTURE THAN OTHERS

Not every child needs to have her day structured down to the last minute or second. In fact, many children are capable of structuring their own activities and finding their own routines. You must take stock of your own child's need for structure and routine.

Most parents find younger children need greater amounts of structured supervision throughout the day. This is not surprising. Infants and very young toddlers need help during mealtimes with the simple act of eating. Close supervision is also required when these very young children are in the bathtub. And, of course, there are diapers.

"Daddy, I goed poop."

"That's nice, honey. Go tell your mother."

"I heard that, Jim!"

"All right, all right. Come with me, Rosebud."

But even at early ages, individual differences among children emerge. Some children are more adaptable and appear to occupy themselves without difficulty. Other children need rigid schedules and to have each activity planned out in advance. Still others seem unable to occupy themselves for very long and require constant attention from their parents. Striking differences in temperaments are evident even in siblings.

Molly and Jack were siblings, yet they couldn't have been more different. Molly, age nine, could occupy herself for long stretches at a time. On a rainy Saturday morning, her mother could send her off to play and feel confident she would keep herself amused until lunch. This meant Mother would have time to get some things done around the house. And she would have done them, too . . . except there was Jack. He was Molly's chronically bored seven-year-old brother. When it was sunny out, he could be sent outside. There he could run, climb, throw things, yell, and annoy the neighborhood. But trapped indoors on a rainy day, he seemed lost. As his mother went from the basement laundry room to the upstairs linen closet, he followed close at her heels, whining, "I don't know what to do." His mother tried suggesting activities. "Why don't you go play with your Legos?" For a moment he was enthusiastic and ran off to his room to find the blocks. But two minutes later he was back. "I'm bored," he whined. "What can I do?" Jack's mother sighed. She knew she would spend most of her morning trying to entertain him and only dream of all the things she could have gotten done. Why couldn't he be more like Molly?

Individual differences become very pronounced during the early childhood years. Some children have trouble developing the capacity to regulate their feelings and behavior or adapting to their environment. These are the irritable children, the anxious or withdrawn children, and the many learning-disabled or hyperactive children. As a parent you can help such a child learn to self-regulate by providing a more structured, routinized environment.

Moody, irritable children—often called "difficult children"—seem to prosper in a well-structured, predictable family environment. These children seem to have little capacity for regulating any emotional stimulation. This difficulty of theirs is apparent even during infancy. These are the babies and toddlers who show very intense and changeable feelings. When they laugh or cry, glass could shatter. They also tend to switch from one feeling to another very quickly. They can go from fear to intense anger to nasty laughter in the blink of an eye. Whenever they are surprised, their reaction is unpredictable. If given a special surprise, they are as likely to have a temper tantrum as they are to squeal with delight. They seem to thrive when events are very predictable and surprises are unlikely. They appear to have more difficulty in unstructured environments and do much better once they know the rules, routines, and schedules. Consider this child:

When Justin was taken to Nursery 'Nastics, a disaster was a heartbeat away. The gym was large and noisy and full of bouncing balls, scooter boards, trampolines, things to climb and hand off of, screaming and running children, diligently pursuing mothers, and daydreaming fathers. Justin would run into the middle of the room, start screaming, hit a child, and take something away from another child. Within minutes, he had to be removed from the gym, kicking and flailing, his face beet red and sweaty. Moreover, he was getting a bad reputation. Parents did not want their children playing with Justin, because he was aggressive and, at times, downright mean. Eventually, the parents voluntarily withdrew him from the program and, on the advice of a friend, enrolled him in a more structured program. This one had a very quiet atmosphere and a set sequence of daily activities that were outlined during an initial meeting. Discipline problems were dealt with effectively with an immediate, mechanical time-out routine. Transitions between activities were ritualized through special songs or behaviors. After an initial and vigorous testing, Justin settled into the routine and seemed to thrive.

Children who have trouble adapting to change, regulating their feelings, or coping with uncertainty seem to settle down in orderly, routinized environments. Some such children may seem drawn to stimulation and may, in fact, crave it. But once they get it, they behave almost as though they are allergic to it. Highly noisy and stimulating places have a disorganizing effect on these children. They lose control and act out. Anxious, introverted children may withdraw in tears.

When the world is more certain, it feels safer to these children and they are able to cope.

While some children have a hard time regulating their feelings, other children have trouble organizing their thinking and behavior. They have not yet developed certain concepts that will help them do this. These developmental delays and difficulties take many forms. Some children have sensorimotor coordination problems, while others show more difficulty with language development. Often these children have difficulty learning time sequences such as the days of the week or the months of the year. They may have difficulty understanding directions that involve time concepts, like "before you do this . . ." or "after you do that . . ." They often have trouble understanding spatial relationships and telling their right from their left, and so have a problem with directions that involve spatial directions, such as "behind," "to the left of," or "next to." While it is hard for them to understand directions from others, they also have trouble directing themselves. It is often very difficult for these children to plan out their behavior and to think from cause to effect. They may have trouble thinking in sequences—they don't see that if they do Behavior A, it will lead to Consequence F. They may be able to think only from A to B. This often gives their behavior a random, helter-skelter quality. Sometimes they are called hyperactive. Such children will have trouble coping in unstructured situations in which the demands are unclear and they are unable to predict what is expected of them. Consider the following example:

> By the time Seamus was eight years old, it was apparent that he was not able to keep up with the other children in third grade. His speech was difficult to understand and he had clear coordination problems. He had a lot of difficulty in arithmetic. He had a lot of trouble playing group games in gym class.
>
> To his parents, he was an enigma and a source of great frustration. His room was an absolute nightmare and he was constantly losing or breaking his toys. Seamus always seemed to be wandering around the house, bored and irritable. When his parents tried to entertain him or involve him in some family games, he seemed to lose interest quickly. The parents thought he needed stimulation. After all, he would constantly ask, "What are we going to do next?" His mother and father thought he was asking for more stimulation. They thought he was a sensation seeker. In fact, his questions were genuine. He was an anxious

little boy who had a lot of trouble thinking through the sequence of daily activities.

Finally, enough was enough. The parents took the boy to a therapist. But the therapist began working with the parents on their lifestyle! The goal was to make Seamus's daily routine more predictable. This was a very hard adjustment for the parents to make, because they had enjoyed a certain notoriety in the neighborhood for spontaneity and spunk. But they found that when they were more scheduled and routinized, their son's excitement seeking vanished. He seemed much more calm. They also began to teach him to keep his room in order so he could be more responsible for himself. He learned better spatial organization. He stopped losing things. They began to do certain activities on specific days: yard work on Saturday, church on Sunday, laundry on Monday and Friday, etc. At night and in the morning they developed rituals to review the day's sequence of activities. He went to bed more readily at night and got through the morning routine more easily the next day. He also learned the days of the week in order.

Now, by using more structure, the family did not make Seamus's learning disabilities go away. The school provided a comprehensive special-education program to help with that. But the boy did learn some stable routines for daily living, showed a lot less anxiety, and became able to control himself in public.

Most children enjoy well-practiced routines in family living. While many children do not require a rigidly scheduled daily routine and are able to handle novelty and spontaneity, others need more routine in their lives. There are a few rules of thumb by which you can gauge your own child's need. In my clinical experience I have found that rigid, nonadapting children seem to do better with more structure and more routine. This helps keep their level of stimulation lower. Children who display chronic organization problems also do better in a well-organized routine. Like the boy in the example above, these are children who have difficulty with space and time concepts, who have trouble with organization at school, and who can't follow directions. They may look hyperactive because of their inability to think through to the consequences of their behavior. Very sensitive, anxious children also seem to need more structure. It helps them to soothe and settle themselves more easily. For these types of children, routine is essential to coping.

ROUTINE MAY BE ESSENTIAL TO YOUR OWN MENTAL HEALTH

Children do not live in a vacuum. When we provide discipline it is not only to teach *them* a lesson. It is also to make life more bearable for ourselves and for everyone else in the family. A structured daily routine not only may help your child, but can also do wonders for your own mental health. Problems can often seem overwhelming, especially if you think of them as lasting throughout a sixteen-hour day. How many times have I heard parents moan, "How am I going to make it through today?" By providing daily structure you will enhance a child's sense of prediction and control. But don't underestimate the effect of such anticipatory planning on your own mental health. Imagine yourself in this situation:

It's 6:15 A.M. and already you know it is going to be one of *those* days. A hot, humid night has just passed into a hot, humid morning. The kids didn't settle down until past 11:00. He is awake first, the three-year-old, and calling you in a toneless chant to come get him up. "Get yourself up," you call back as softly as possible so you won't wake up the other one. No way. Now he is yelling louder, more insistent. He wants you to carry him to your bed as you do every morning. But it is 6:20 A.M. and you don't feel like lugging forty pounds of irritable flesh down the long hall to your room. So you try coaxing him to walk on his own and he goes off like a bomb, stamping on the floors, screaming something unintelligible in a voice like fingernails on a blackboard.

"All right, all right!" You haul him up and the tears stop like magic. But as you come out of his room—boom!—*her* door flies open and there she stands, the six-year-old, rigid and glowering. "He woke me up." "Did not." "Did too." Now they are hitting one another. You break them apart and continue on into your room. He sits on the bed frowning at his sister, sucking his thumb. "Stop looking at me," she screams. She turns to you. "He's looking at me," she whines, and starts to cry. "Go get dressed," you tell her, but she can't think of anything to wear. Everything you suggest is wrong.

Now he tugs at you. "I need to go potty." "Fine," you reply, "go ahead." "No, be by me," he insists. You tell him he had better go on his own or you will take his toy pony away. He scurries down the hall sputtering. Meanwhile, nothing feels right to her. She can't pull her shorts up high enough and her shirt is too tight. Now her socks feel all wrong. She lies on the floor kicking and throws her shoes behind her dresser. At this point he calls from the bathroom, "I need h-e-e-l-l-p." "I'll be right back," you tell her and she crumples on the floor.

When you enter the bathroom you find everything is quietly dripping. He has hit the walls, the toilet paper roll, even a towel, but not a drop seems to have landed in the toilet bowl. What was he doing, shooting at flies? Big eyes now. "Who, me?" "Just go eat your cereal," and you turn to start mopping up. But now she comes down in her special party dress. "No, you're not going to wear that on the playground," you tell her, and she goes off like a rocket. He pokes her as he goes by, so she whacks him three times on the head. He gives a bloodcurdling cry and comes after her with fangs and claws bared. He bites her, she screams and pulls his hair. He screams and . . .

It's 6:40 A.M. Both of them are in their rooms. They'll stay there because you have their favorite toys and you just might burn them if anyone sets foot outside their door. You may keep them there until adolescence is over. It's 84 degrees and the humidity feels like 300 percent. Now it is 6:41 A.M. "The Today Show" won't be on for another nineteen minutes and they are already in their rooms. By all odds, they will be awake and at it for another fourteen or fifteen hours. How will you make it? You are beginning to understand why some people become alcoholics. You know what the day will be like. Fifteen hours. How will you ever get through? Maybe Valium?

Most parents have had days like this, when the children wake up with their self-control in flames. On school days, you may be able to save yourself. Let the teacher worry about it for a while. But certainly during weekends, holidays, and those long summer months, sixteen hours of residential treatment are more than most of us can bear.

Structuring the day, however, allows you to think about it in more manageable units. It is less taxing for you to plan how to move your child through short blocks of time than through the day as a whole, making the situation much easier to control. There are some periods in the day that are more naturally structured than others. Some children take naps. There are also certain times when a child can watch television, play outside, or go visit a friend. You may find you have to concentrate on getting through a few specific blocks of time. As you think through each block, you can feel some accomplishment in your ability to cope. The day is not so overwhelming after all. Who knows, you might even be able to turn the situation around.

Sixteen hours is an enormous amount of time, and if things are going badly, it can seem like purgatory. By breaking up the day into smaller time periods, though, you may find at what specific points your children are more likely to have difficulty. It is not the whole day that is difficult, after all, only specific activities or transitions. Daily structure allows you to encapsulate these problems and deal with them in isolation. When you focus on a specific problem, you can work out a plan to solve it.

Schedules, routines, and rituals not only help a child learn to self-regulate but can also help a war-weary mom and dad make it through the day. Schedules and routines will not make children into angels, but at least you can limit the spread of misbehavior and feel more confident that you can cope.

BLOCKING OUT THE DAY

What follows are some suggestions for developing a daily structure. Many times parents will say their lifestyle is simply too hectic for them to think about schedules. Certainly there may be some amount of uncertainty or variability in every family's life. Families, after all, are not automated assembly lines. But days usually have some measure of natural structure. There are usually a beginning and an end point. There are usually meals spaced at intervals throughout the day. These create natural time blocks. In addition, parents can develop routines to cope with fixed events such as bedtime as well as with more flexible periods such as free-play times. Not every schedule has to be carved in stone. But if there is some flexibility in your daily schedule, it is wise to think about some way of coping with uncertainty and transitions.

As you work to structure your child's day, here are some steps you might employ:

1. *Divide the day into time blocks.* You may use the natural structure of the day, taking meals, school, nap time, time with the sitter, and bedtime as your time markers. For most children, this is usually the most effective route. The day usually has five or more time blocks.

There is a morning routine that lasts until after breakfast. Next may come a large block in which children are away at day-care or school. If you are at home with your very young child, you may have a morning time block, a lunch time block, and one or two blocks of time in the afternoon depending on naps. For most families there is a special late-afternoon block which includes that awful time when everyone comes home and drums their fingers until dinner is ready. You may want to include dinner as a separate time block, especially if this is a difficult time for the family. Then there is usually some type of after-dinner block and, finally, a bedtime routine. With very difficult children you may want to subdivide time blocks into smaller units. I have known some parents who have gone on an hourly schedule not only to structure their children but also for their own emotional well-being.

2. *Consider which units are fixed and which are flexible.* Some of these time blocks have a very stable, fixed routine. On most weekday mornings, for example, family members get up in a certain order. Some parents bring the baby to bed with them for a morning bottle. There is usually a pecking order for using the bathroom. There is usually some order for washing, dressing, and eating breakfast.

Other time periods are less structured. These would include free-play periods. Some children need very little structure for these, while other, more difficult children may need considerable supervision. Often these are the time periods in which many of the family chore activities get carried out. Laundry, shopping, and other errands can take place during these flexible time periods.

3. *Develop routines to help you get through the fixed units of the day.* Routines are fairly stable sequences of activities in any one time block. As you evaluate your day, you may find your life is a lot more routinized than you had thought. That is fine. But in families in which confusion reigns during stressful times, such as the morning, some orderly routine may go a long way toward solving the problem.

4. *Develop some control over the flexible units.* During free-play periods, you may want to narrow the range of choices. For example, you might tell your child he may play either in the backyard or in his room. The child may watch TV for half an hour before his morning snack and then go outside. As you look over your own chores, you may find certain ones fit better into some time slots than others, and that shopping works out better on some days of the week and laundry better on others.

5. *Identify the important transitions between time blocks.* Transitions are a major source of behavior problems in every family. Children have difficulty getting up in the morning and then getting off to school. They have trouble coming home in the late afternoon and settling down to do their homework. Often there are difficulties when they come in from play to get ready for dinner. Children are notorious for having difficulty settling down to go to sleep at night. Many are able to make it easily through some transitions but not others. Some children have no difficulty with the morning routine but have trouble in the afternoon settling down to do homework. Other children have difficulty coming in from play or settling down at night. It is very helpful to identify specific problem points so you can begin to work on them.

6. *Consider different schedules for different days.* In every family there are bound to be variations from day to day. Children go to day-care some days but not others. Some parents have unusual work shifts in which they work mornings on some days and afternoons on others. Older children are involved in extracurricular activities such as sports, clubs, band, etc.

There are also daily variations which create special problems. In divorced families children often have to move from one home to the other. This type of schedule difference is of great importance because children often have difficulty with the transition. It is not uncommon for one parent to complain that their child has temper tantrums every time a visitation with the other parent is scheduled. They also note that when the child returns from a visit, a similar tantrum occurs. These, for the most part, are fairly natural responses and are not usually indicators of psychopathology. The transition from one home to another is extremely difficult for most children, even well-adjusted older children. Identifying these schedule variations allows you to focus on a specific problem and solve it.

7. *Work out schedules for "easy days" and "hard days."* Every parent has those mornings like the one described in the earlier example. *He* is irritable and crabby and wants to be carried everywhere; *she* is glowering and all of her clothes feel funny. Not every day is going to be an "Ozzie and Harriet" day: some days will be straight out of "The Twilight Zone." Consider scheduling your day differently depending on the tone and the mood. You may want to break hard days down into smaller units. This will afford you greater control and the added

structure might help the children settle. On easy days, you can relax the structure, allow for more free time and a greater range of choice in their activities.

WORKING OUT ROUTINES

During many portions of the day you may find you need to follow fairly fixed routines. Often, by observing how your family functions, you will discover many such routines are already in place. Some routines are less obvious than others. For example, on Saturday mornings the routine may be that the children get up and get themselves cereal, and that once they are done, they can watch TV until their eyes fall out. The parents may rise somewhat later and enjoy breakfast by themselves. Once breakfast is finished, the paper has been read, and the cartoons are over, everyone gets dressed and cleaned up. This seems like a fairly easygoing structure, but if this is the way the weekend goes, it is a *routine*. A routine does not mean that everyone marches in a straight line, each person in step with the other. Routines can be loosely structured. The point is that by using routines, you are more likely to control the difficult points of the day. What follows below is a series of routines for dealing with many common family problems. These are intended to be examples only and are by no means presented as the one *right way* to carry out any of the activities.

In looking at your own family's functioning, carefully observe the normal sequence of events. Also be aware of any daily variations. If you need to change a routine, be sure to work out the changes in advance and to let everyone know that it needs to be changed. It is only fair to the other people in the family. Consider the following examples:

The Morning Routine: The routine for the morning is usually fairly fixed. Children rise at a regular time and usually go through a certain sequence of activities in order to get ready for the day: going to the bathroom, cleaning up, getting dressed, and eating breakfast. Some families have morning chores that need to be done. These may include certain activities in the house or on the farm. In some cases they may involve picking up toys, making the bed, and putting clothes away.

Some families allow children to watch television before they go to school.

It is not uncommon for many children to be irritable in the morning. This is true especially of children with difficult temperaments. A child storms into a sunny kitchen and immediately rain and hail appear. Parents will need to have a hard-day routine and an easy-day routine to cope with these emotional changes. On hard days, for example, the parents want to be much more directive in helping the child get ready in the morning, and this may involve more concrete, specific directions on what the child has to do and when. Her choices for clothes and breakfast foods may need to be narrowed considerably: "Do you want to wear your green pants or your red pants?" "Do you want to get dressed in your bedroom or the bathroom?" Limits should be very clearly set, and it may be necessary to use short time-outs to help the child soothe and settle herself when she becomes frustrated. In essence, you are telling the child that she has to get herself ready emotionally as well as physically. Naturally, you will help her do this.

Other parents find their children dawdle excessively in the morning. The children may get up late, get dressed only with repeated threats, or try to watch TV before they eat breakfast. You might try getting these poky horses to pull their own carts. If your child likes to watch television, a rule can be made that her morning routine (rising, washing, dressing, etc.) needs to be completed before the TV goes on. A standard kitchen timer can be used to set a specific limit. If the child *really* wants to watch TV, then the morning routine will be completed quickly.

Of course, the child may set the parents up a couple of times just to see if they will follow through. Remember, the child only wants to see what you will do so she can find out if she can trust you. Show her that she can. But don't get stuck on the idea of taking TV away. Many children enjoy TV when it is on but are willing to give it up when push comes to shove. You want to find out what children are willing to work for, what will make doing something disagreeable important to them. You need to find the dessert that they are willing to eat their broccoli to get.

Chores: Many parents experience difficulty getting their children to perform certain chores. They are forever nagging their children to clean their rooms, pick up their toys, cut the grass, walk the dog, take

out the garbage, etc. The parents carry all the urgency and responsibility for remembering; the children couldn't care less.

What chores do you want your children to carry out? Even very
young children can do simple tasks around the house. When are these
chores to be completed? It is important to establish time limits and to
stick to them. Many parents allow their children tremendous latitude
in getting their chores done. I suppose these parents think they are
being nice to their children or are helping them be responsible for
themselves. But if a child keeps putting off doing a chore and the
parents have to do all the work to remind the child, who is being
responsible?

Finally, what makes it worthwhile to complete the chores on time?
Do you depend on the force of your relationship? If you do, you are
likely to be disappointed. There are very few young children who are
able to work for any length of time out of concern for another person.
Most young children need tangible reasons to work. Some children
will work for an allowance. If that is so, you might consider making
the blade cut both ways. You will gladly pay them to do their chores,
but if they fail to do them, then they have to pay you. If they run out
of money, they can always pay you with their time or their labor. For
many children this is a very effective approach to the problem.

Homework: The problems with homework are similar to those with
chores. In many families there is no clear routine for getting the
homework done. Children come home from school and immediately go
out to play. When their mother asks about their homework, they reply
that they have very little and will do it later. Then "later" comes and
they want to watch TV. Finally they go to bed without having gotten
their homework done at all.

If you have young children, start them off with a stable homework
routine. It is much easier to teach them a routine initially than to try
to get them to change some irresponsible behavior later on. I have had
the most success by having parents follow the "broccoli-before-dessert"
approach. When children come home from school, you discuss their
day and give them a snack, then they start their homework. Once they
have completed their homework they can go out and play before dinner.

Please note that this section does not deal with the other major
problems surrounding homework: whining and crying for help or simply
not bringing it home. Here we are dealing only with setting up a clear

homework routine. When routines clearly don't work, you need to approach them as special behavior problems (discussed in Chapter 11).

Before Dinner: As I discussed in the previous chapter, there is a time before dinner when all semblance of rationality dissolves. This is especially true in families with toddlers and preschoolers. The parents are usually in a rush to get dinner made and the children have hit the low ebb of their energy and resources. It is usually very helpful to develop some specific routine to keep the children occupied so you can make dinner. Having the children watch TV, play quietly in their room, listen to tapes, or watch a videotape is very helpful. If the children can play outside without your direct supervision and without hurting one another, you may want to try that. But usually a more structured routine will get you through a more chaotic time. Clear limits on behavior need to be set.

Dinnertime Routine: Families often experience a lot of confusion and catastrophes during dinner. Children have poor manners, eat with their fingers, make messes, fight with one another, leave the table, and run around. There are certainly some behavioral consequences which can help eliminate most of these problems, but some—perhaps most—of them can be dealt with through the use of an orderly dinner routine. You should think of dinner as a train of events that you must go through in sequence. The sequence may consist of washing up, helping to set the table, bringing in the food, sitting down and saying grace, eating the dinner, clearing the dishes, and getting dessert. Children have to wash up before they can come in to dinner. They can choose not to wash up, but then guess what happens. Children must stay in their chairs in order to finish dinner. Children can choose to get down from their chairs, but then they are done with dinner. If they are done with dinner, they are telling you they do not want dessert. If they do not want dessert, they may be telling you they are ready to go to bed.

The Bedtime Routine: Bedtime is a very difficult hour in many families. Some children are fearful at night, as evidenced by their need for night-lights, open doors, and the magical rituals necessary to induce sleep. Some children do not like the feeling of falling asleep and fight it. Before bedtime it is not a good idea to show children horror movies or anything that is likely to arouse them emotionally. Many times I have heard families complain that their eight-year-old won't go to sleep after watching *Friday the Thirteenth*. What were they doing showing their child a movie like that before bed! A stable bedtime routine can not only decide the sequence of activities to follow and their time limits, but can also help isolate specific behavior problems. Usually it is best to begin the bedtime routine an hour or two in advance, to have some quieting activity, not rough-and-tumble play. This will help soothe and settle children. Stories and quiet TV shows are also helpful.

If children do not settle down during the quiet time, you can develop a specific plan to deal with the behavior problem. This may involve setting limits, giving them a warning, and imposing a logical consequence.

Children who get up at night need to be taught that the proper routine is for them to go to bed and put themselves to sleep. When little Gunther calls, "Daddy, Daddy!" and claims there are monsters in the closet, Dad might try to reassure the child by conducting an elaborate search of the room. But all Dad is doing is validating the fear that monsters really might be in the closet. If they weren't, why would Dad be rummaging in the dirty laundry and talking in his funny voice? Children need to learn that they are competent to put themselves to sleep and that their rooms are basically safe places. It is up to you to ensure that the room is safe from any physical danger. But once you pronounce it safe, you can confidently say to your little Gunther, "There aren't any monsters. Go to sleep."

If the child gets up, gently but firmly guide him back to bed. Once you decide you are not going to lie down with the child, don't give in. You may have to go through a week or so of gradually diminishing crying, but eventually the child will put himself to sleep.

These are just a few examples of using routines to deal with some fairly common behavior problems. You will notice most of them use a sequence of events in which some desired activity follows some chore or other undesirable task. First broccoli and then dessert.

Sometimes creating routines can have other benefits than merely solving behavior problems. I once saw a mother whose bright three-and-a-half-year-old suffered from daily headaches. These usually occurred in the front of her head and did not follow a classic migraine pattern. She was a very bright, active little girl who did not nap and slept only eight hours a night. A spunky child who was on the go throughout the day, she seemed to be quite driven and concerned about achievement, even at three and a half. As we discussed the headaches, I learned they came every afternoon at about three o'clock. She would come into the kitchen and complain to her mother that her head hurt. Her mother would give her some Tylenol and have her lie down on the couch. Within forty-five minutes, her headache would be better.

I suggested to the mother that perhaps the girl's body was telling her it was time for a break. If that was the case, it might be a good idea to have a rest period as part of her afternoon routine. Then every day at 2:30, the child was helped to enjoy a quiet time. She did not have to go to sleep, only to lie down and rest. She was told this would help keep the headaches away. Usually she would rest for forty-five minutes to an hour. Sometimes she listened to a tape, sometimes her mother read to her, and sometimes she preferred to lie by herself. But whenever she carried out this routine, the headache monster stayed away.

RITUALS

Rituals are a kind of magic we use every day to sail through routines and to guide us through difficult transitions. They are especially important to use during times when children are afraid. They are good magic.

As you look through your schedule and through your routines for the day, be very aware of how you make transitions from one activity to another. Small rituals can be of enormous benefit in making these transitions flow more smoothly. Many children, for example, have difficulty moving from a free-play time to a more structured time. Families may have a routine in which children need to pick up their toys and put them away before they come in and have a snack. With very young children (toddlers and preschoolers) a simple pickup song or rhyme can make the transition easier.

PARENT: Play is done and snack is set for all the girls and boys, but
   first we have to do our work—
CHILDREN: It's time to pick up toys.

Or sing to a simple melody:

Oh, do you know what time it is,
what time it is, what time it is?
Do you know what time it is?
It's time to pick up toys.*

Another example of the function of ritual is saying grace. In many families this is a brief period of silence and meditation in which thanks is given for the daily meal. But it is also a quieting time that levels out the tension and activity before the meal, helping children get ready to enjoy their food in peace. Some form of grace or meditation is conducive to setting a mood in which the meal can be eaten calmly and behavior problems can be avoided. This grace may be religious or it may involve a simple reflection on the family and their well-being. At any rate, it is a nice moment for everyone to share.

Transitions that involve leaving the house are often difficult for many families. Adults scramble to get children into their overclothes and to get them out the door on time. Children dawdle, drag their feet, or have temper tantrums at the most inopportune times. Again, specific rituals can help children through these difficult moments. These rituals can involve quietly sitting, receiving directions, getting clothes on, and waiting to go out the door. With some extremely hyperactive or developmentally delayed children this may be a difficult time even under the best of circumstances. But most children are capable of restraining their behavior and following the format of a ritual. If it is difficult to think what sort of a ritual to use, observe a nursery school or elementary school classroom. Most teachers have rituals that help with these sorts of transitions.

Another difficult transition occurs at bedtime. As noted above, specific bedtime routines can help make the sequence of activities much more predictable. However, bedtime rituals can provide that extra dose of magic which will make those things that go bump in the night stay away. This is one of the functions of prayer. Granted, the primary function of prayer is religious, but most prayers, especially those for young children, have soothing rhymes and rhythms. They are also often repeated and well known. They can be shared between parent and child. If you do not like the idea of using prayers, then poems or

*This is the pickup song of the Tenny Nursery and Parent Center in Madison, Wisconsin.

lullabies can serve the same soothing purpose. It is also helpful to have some way to bridge the transition between night and morning. A brief review of the day's events plus a discussion about tomorrow will often help the child think her way through the night. We must remember that for many children, sleep is a perplexing and frightening experience. It does not feel good to be tired, and that brief space between night and morning can be full of nightmares. If children need rituals to help them get through the night, there is no reason to deny them. When children do not need these, they will give them up.

To Sum Up: The Value of Anticipatory Planning

So much of our thinking about discipline is reactive. We wonder whether spanking will be effective or whether it will damage the child for life; whether we should offer a reward if the child stops some obnoxious behavior or whether that is bribery. Granted, we need to think about ways to deal with special problems—how to teach our eight-year-old to come home on time or to act appropriately in the supermarket. But most of the behavior problems we face are those low-grade, nagging problems that interrupt the flow of daily living. We argue with our children constantly over petty issues. They whine and bug us, dawdle when we need them to hurry, and refuse to go to sleep when we put them to bed. These are not disasters and it seems inappropriate to use rewards or spanking to cope with these problems. But planning, structuring, and routinizing many of these activities can be a benefit both to your children and to your own mental health.

The importance of rituals and routines cannot be overemphasized. There is a regularity and rhythm that is soothing and reassuring to most small children. Look, for example, at children's songs and games. The melodies and rhythms are simple and predictable, and there is repetition. Children never seem to tire of favorite books, songs, or games. How many parents thought they would vaporize if they had to read *Goodnight Moon* one more time at bedtime? But the children always seem to enjoy their favorites. In art, they delight in symmetry and show much more interest in regular patterns than in random ones. While children are aroused and made curious by the novel, they are not comforted. Comfort comes from the expected, the predictable.

Furthermore, rituals and routines derive their power not simply because children enjoy predictability, but also because it shapes their sense of safety in the world. They are able to figure out what will happen next and can regulate their behavior accordingly. They do not have to remain on alert since there is no uncertainty. They can relax and be soothed. Think about how important that is to the way children think about their world! Their day has an orderly flow. They do certain activities at specific times. They know when their meals will be served, when their parents will come home from work, and how to prepare for sleep.

We have discussed the use of structure, routines, and rituals to ease some problems of daily living. While these help a child develop a sense of predictability, they are certainly not going to solve all of the behavior problems that will arise in a family. Some form of active intervention is going to be needed to deal with most daily problems. In the next chapter, we will look at a routine form of discipline to deal with them, which will focus on developing appropriate expectations for your child, setting limits, giving warnings, meting out consequences, and making amends.

9

The Routine of Discipline

All of a parent's energy shouldn't be drained away by mundane but nagging discipline problems. There are so many memorable moments and good feelings to share in a family: the lively, excited chatter at dinnertime; play at the beach or the park; quiet times in front of the fire. Too often parents complain that they seem to spend all their time punishing children for little things, one after another. Children fuss at breakfast, fight with their siblings, make messes, and bother their parents when they are on the phone. Parents say they feel irritated all the time, but that nothing really awful has happened.

We discussed earlier how daily structure and routine can alleviate many of the above problems and help you to think about the day in a more constructive way. Despite your best efforts to schedule and routinize your children, however, there are many problems that will require your direct intervention. Your children will fight with one another, leave toys scattered about, and bother you at inappropriate times. They need to do these things because it is how they assert themselves, test their strength, and learn about their relationship with you. It may be necessary for them, but it is still an awful nuisance for you. You need a way to respond to most of these nuisances that leaves you with some energy and your sense of self-control intact. This is what is meant by a *discipline routine.*

Most forms of misbehavior are predictable. When little Jennifer finishes playing with her crayons, she sprints out of the room and the mess remains all over the bedroom floor. When you need a quiet moment to think about or plan something, guess who starts to bother you or to fight with his sister. But if these problems are so predictable, you can also plan a predictable response. You can develop family rules and a mechanical process for dealing with most forms of noncompliance.

Why are these chronic problems so irritating? Often it is because we want our children to respond to us on the basis of our *relationship.* "If you value my friendship," we appeal to our adult friends, "you will respond to me in a certain way." But when we say this to our five-year-old, the message may be entirely lost on him. Certainly many young children respond to appeals to relationship some of the time. But if these appeals fall on deaf ears, you are wise to have an alternate approach ready. Your child may be using a situation to deal with an individual problem of his and you need to be able to respond to this. Your child may be saying to you, "I really don't want an equal relationship right now. I happen to be working on some developmental issues related to my independence. I need to understand how much control I have right now and what your response is likely to be." But of course a child of five can't say these things, so instead he leaves a mess in the living room, turns up the volume on the TV until glass shatters, and eats ice cream before lunch.

Mundane problems demand mundane solutions. A discipline routine that is mechanical allows you to take the excitement out of misbehavior. Remember that many children cannot tell the difference between positive and negative stimulation. Excitement is simply excitement. It is as stimulating to be chased around the house by a beet-faced parent as it is to play tag with friends. Why waste your energy! You have much more enjoyable things to do with your child. Use your discipline routine to say in a bored but understanding tone, "We could be having so much more fun doing other things, but I see you need to work on some ordinary old behavior problems. Well, if that is what you need I will certainly help you. Once again, then, let's go through the routine . . ."

A planned discipline routine will save you mental energy. It is exhausting to try to think up meaningful consequences on the spot:

> "Johna, because you fought with your sister in the car, I am going to . . . to . . . take away your bicycle for a day—no, three days—because, well, a car is *transportation* and your bike is *transportation*, too . . . and if you can't handle it in the car, then maybe you shouldn't have a bike for a few days . . ."

The other advantage of a discipline routine is that it allows you to place the burden of responsibility for self-control on the child. Why should you feel the urgency to contain each successive crisis—all these teapot tempests! Let the child understand that your behavior is predictable and then let the child learn to think ahead. In a sense these are safe emergencies. The child creates a problem and can learn how to predict consequences and to control them as well. If we let children anticipate the consequences of their own behavior, they can learn self-control. What better method of teaching is there?

A GENERAL PLAN FOR A DISCIPLINE ROUTINE

Certainly, it is inviting to suggest that an ironclad routine would work with all children at all times. How nice if the world were that simple! Unfortunately, this is not the case. As you consider how you will develop your own discipline routine, you need to think of ways to build in some flexibility. There are four factors you must consider as you shape a discipline routine for *your* particular children in *your* particular family. These include: 1) your child's developmental level; 2) your child's particular temperament; 3) daily variations in your child's behavior; and 4) your own capacity to cope with stress.

1. *Your child's developmental level:* Certainly the child's developmental level is going to be an important consideration whenever you develop a discipline routine. Younger children need much more direct supervision than older children. They also have a more limited capacity to understand cause-and-effect sequences and to plan ahead. Some young children may be able to think of only the next direct step. Older

children or developmentally advanced children may be able to think three or four steps down the line. Very young children also need extremely concrete limits and warnings. Older children who understand time and space concepts may not require such concrete limits. Your child may also be unlike other children of a similar age. This means you may need to set up different rules, limits, and consequences than other parents.

2. *Your child's particular temperament:* Children with very easy temperaments may require less structure than children with very difficult temperaments. Very anxious, introverted children may do better with a softer tone, while more extraverted children may do better with greater stimulation. Children who have learning or organizational problems may require more repetition and may need directions to be broken down into smaller steps. Some children also tend to be very rigid in their interpretation of rules and you will need to make some allowances for this. Whatever the case, you must develop a discipline routine that is suitable to your own child's personality.

3. *Daily variations in your child's behavior:* Some children don't show much variation in mood, but the variations are still there. All parents know when a child is having a good day or a bad day. For some children, though, variations are much more extreme. Children with difficult temperaments may be very irritable one day and very lethargic the next. For part of the day they may be very high-strung and noncompliant, while during the next part of the day they are pleasant and cooperative. A good daily routine needs to take into account easy days and difficult days.

4. *Your own capacity to cope with stress:* Every adult has some days when it is more difficult to cope. Anticipate this and plan it into the discipline routine. Suppose you are feeling alive, full of energy, and able to deal with most crises. How do you respond to limit-testing behavior on the part of your children? On the other hand, if you are feeling burdened by stress and tension, how do you respond then? How do you let your children know what your feelings are so they can predict your response and regulate their behavior accordingly?

No, you do not need to have radically different plans to cope with every conceivable variation in development, temperament, or mood. That would be impossible. But understand that these differences will occur and give some thought to how you will respond to them. Many of these issues will be incorporated into the discussion below.

What follows is a general plan for developing a discipline routine to cope with the mundane problems of day-to-day living. As you develop your routine, you should address the following issues:

1. Setting family rules and expectations
2. Defining limits
3. Giving warnings
4. Controlling the tone of your response
5. Imposing consequences
6. Making amends

THE MECHANICS OF A DISCIPLINE ROUTINE

1. Setting Family Rules and Expectations

Every family has rules. Sometimes these are stated openly. At other times they are simply understood. But if you think about your own family, you will probably find your rules fit into two classes: specific rules of conduct and general precepts of social behavior. The specific rules of conduct might include such behaviors as expecting the child to sit at the table until he is finished with the meal, or flushing the toilet and putting down the seat. These are very specific rules, tied to specific situations. In contrast, the general rules tend to be more pervasive and also more loosely defined guidelines of appropriate social behavior. When our three-year-old son grabs a toy away from our neighbor's two-year-old daughter, we intercede with "No, honey, *be nice*." This is a general rule of social conduct that goes along with many others. We caution our children: "be nice," "don't hurt," "don't bug," "don't mess," "be gentle." We would like our children to use these general rules to gauge their behavior in many settings. They are not tied to any one situation. They are also very difficult to define.

The first step in setting up a discipline routine is to define your rules. First start with the specific rules. Block out the day and decide which periods are fixed and which are flexible. Describe the rules of behavior for all the fixed schedule points. Below is an example of the specific dinnertime rules for a six-year-old girl:

   a. Wash hands.
   b. Help set table.
   c. Sit down quietly.
   d. Join hands and bow head for grace.
   e. Use utensils, not fingers (with cuing).
   f. Chew with mouth closed (with cuing).
   g. Say "please" and "thank you" when requesting food.
   h. Stay seated until dinner is completed.
   i. Say "May I please be excused" when leaving the table.

Notice there are two rules that are followed by "with cuing." When you establish expectations, you must take into account the child's developmental ability. Many six-year-old children still have some difficulty using knives and forks and so it may not be appropriate to expect perfect table manners. Often children need to learn how to chew with their mouth closed and not to gulp and gag on their milk. But other rules can be followed without reminders or cues.

Next describe specific rules for different situations. What do you expect your child to do when you are shopping at the supermarket? How do you expect your child to behave when you are visiting neighbors? What is appropriate behavior in the car? As you think about these specific rules, you will also become more aware of the need to structure the child's time. For example, we may expect our four-year-old to sit quietly in the shopping cart for our forty-five-minute trip through the supermarket. Then again, it may be a lot easier if the child has some specific activities to do while in the shopping cart. One of the values of examining family rules is that you can think about activities which will make it easier for the child to follow your rules. You will also find there are certain problem areas in which you really don't have very well defined rules and in which there are few activities to structure your child's time. An example of this type of problem is finding something for a child to do in the doctor's waiting room, especially if the appointment is for another child.

The general rules are much tougher to define because they are usually so abstract. What, after all, does "be nice" mean to a five-year-old? Most preschoolers will respond by giving very specific, concrete examples of "nice" behavior. They may say, for example, that "being nice" means giving another child a piece of their candy. But when parents use the term "be nice," they may mean a general mode of behavior in which a person extends herself to another without regard to her own personal feelings or aims. Unfortunately, if our expectations are abstract, we will never be able to communicate with the inquisitive but concrete minds of very young children.

As children grow and develop, they learn to understand abstract principles and are able to use them to regulate their behavior. But first they need to learn the abstract rules through specific, concrete examples. Abstract principles are like algebra; first a child needs to learn how to add, subtract, and do times tables. Consider this: Most families have a general rule called "get along with others." As an abstract rule, there is also a negative side to this. We admonish our children, "Don't hurt." But when we use these general rules, we use them in highly specific situations. We use very specific examples of behavior to define the rules. Consider the following table, showing abstract positive and negative rules and their concrete examples in day-to-day living.

When deciding on general rules of behavior, keep them as simple as possible and use as few as possible. For most children, three to five general rules are sufficient. Don't make the mistake of overdefining rules. That simply makes a child's universe too complicated to understand. But when you use general rules of conduct, be sure *you* understand them and can back them up with specific examples.

As you set up your general and specific rules, you will also have to set up your expectations for the child's responses. You need to establish two types of expectations.

The first type of expectation is an ideal: how you think your child should behave in a particular situation. These expectations are aspirations, what you want your child to learn to do or to become. So, for example, we expect that our child, when visiting an elderly neighbor, will smile, be polite, and behave well. We have specific behaviors in mind that make up "politeness" or "good behavior." We hope that our child will suppress the urge to say, "Boy, are you old—look at all those wrinkles!" When the child deviates from these expectations, then she is breaking a rule and we impose a specific consequence. Simple mechanics.

But we also need to keep in mind another level of expectations. It is the child's purpose in life to test limits and to learn firsthand whether her behavior will lead to specific consequences. It is her duty to do so. Of course, you should not lower your standards because of the fear that your child will test limits. No, quite to the contrary, you should

Some Possible Family Rules with Concrete Examples

Positive General Rule	Negative General Rule	Positive Concrete Example	Negative Concrete Example
"Get along with others" (Be nice!)	No hurting	1. Sharing toys or food 2. Comforting another	Hitting, fighting, name-calling, and taking things
"Respect your elders" (Be good!)	No bugging	1. Using polite speech 2. Doing what you are told 3. Quietly waiting for others to stop talking	Saying no, ignoring adults' directions, and interrupting others
"Take care of yourself and your things" (Be responsible!)	No messing	1. Washing 2. Brushing teeth 3. Putting toys away 4. Cleaning up	Staying dirty, not brushing teeth, and leaving messes

maintain your standards, but don't be surprised when your child challenges you. You should expect this. While you maintain some ideal expectations for your child's behavior, you should also expect you will have to impose some very real consequences during the learning process. One of the purposes of setting up a discipline routine, after all, is to keep you from being upset by the mundane nuisance of your child's noncompliance.

2. Defining Limits

At what point is a family rule broken? How is your child to know when he has pushed things too far? When has he crossed that great imaginary line? This is the business of setting limits. Setting limits is not the same thing as giving warnings. When you give a warning, you are merely letting your child know at what point you will respond and how you will respond. You tell your child exactly what you will do if he crosses that imaginary line. This makes your behavior predictable. When you set limits, though, you are merely establishing exactly *where the line is*. The limits need to be clearly understood by both you and your child. Often parents have trouble deciding what the limits should be. If they don't know, how is a small child to understand? Consider the following situation:

Jean Marie knew she was in trouble. The social committee from her church was due to arrive at her house any minute. This was her first meeting as chairperson of the committee and she wanted everything to go smoothly. The house was cleaned, there were freshly cut flowers, the coffee was ready, and the petits fours and tea cookies were set out in neat arrangements. Her ten-year-old was away at camp. The only pea in the mattress was her youngest son, Collin. He was a cheerful red-haired and freckled boy who was fond of riding his tricycle down the front steps. He was chronically bored and had an attention span that died within seconds. He would also do anything on a dare and he never felt pain.

Just before the committee arrived, she caught Collin stealing cookies and took the opportunity to lay down the law—such as it was. She told him that Mommy really expected him to be good today because this meeting was so important to Mommy. She looked into his eyes for some sign of empathy. She found herself staring into empty rooms. Then she tried bribery: "If Collin is really good while Mommy's guests are here, she will give him lots of cookies once they are gone." He seemed to brighten at this and looked very excited. Then the doorbell rang.

Things went well for the first thirty seconds. Jean Marie was able to greet her guests and Collin was nowhere in sight. After thirty-three seconds, however, he said he was bored and wanted her to read to him. She reminded him that he was supposed to be good. He stalked away. A minute later there was a crash from the next room. Collin, reaching for the petits fours in the middle of the dining room table, had knocked the Noritaki coffeepot onto the floor. While Jean Marie mopped up, Collin again whined that he didn't have anything to do. "Just go play," said Jean Marie forcefully, trying to contain her irritation and embarrassment. She looked at the others for sympathy. She got plenty. After a few minutes, Collin was again at her sleeve. She attempted to ignore him, so he threw himself on her lap. Papers flew everywhere, into the flowers, under the couch. Groaning and muttering, the ladies impatiently cleaned up the mess. "When can you play with me?" asked Collin. "When this is all over, maybe later . . . we will see," snapped his mother. "But Mommy," whined Collin, turning the screws a little tighter. "Look, do you want to make me mad? If you keep this up, I am really going to get angry!" hissed Jean Marie. Now this looked promising and brought a sparkle to Collin's eyes. Still, he played his cards close to his chest. "I am going to play Space Warriors," he huffed and stomped out of the room.

Just as the ladies composed themselves and returned to their agenda, the proceedings were shattered by a horrible scream from Muffin, the cat. The terrified animal flew through the room as if she were burning rocket fuel, fur poofed out and claws extended. Teacups dropped, old Mrs. Blossom fainted, and then came the Space Warrior in hot pursuit, firing a barrage of rubber-tipped arrows. Ladies moved in all directions, darting for cover. Poor Mrs. Blossom, just reviving, was struck in the forehead. Out she went again with a miniature plumber's helper stuck to her head. Jean Marie tackled Collin as he jumped on the yet-to-be-paid-for Ethan Allen sofa and dragged him from the room by his left foot. "Now you have really done it, mister—now you have really made me mad," she sputtered. *Now,* thought Collin, looks like a good time to settle down and "be good."

This situation illustrates several important problems that many parents experience with limit setting. Poor Jean Marie feels caught between a rock and a hard place and has trouble establishing clear guidelines that her young Collin can follow. Under pressure, Jean Marie makes an appeal to Collin: "Be good." Unfortunately, this is too abstract for Collin, as it is for most young children. Collin may know how to play quietly in his room, to say "please" and "thank you," or to stay in the rec room until he hears the timer go off. But "be good" does not tell him *how* he is to regulate his behavior. Remember that young children are terribly concrete in their thinking. Therefore, when we set limits on behavior, the limits need to be established in very concrete terms. *Tell the child exactly what you expect him to do, where you expect him to do it, and for how long.*

When Collin comes to his mother and pesters her to spend some time with him, she responds, "Maybe later . . . we will see." This is a very common response that we have all made to our children at one time or another. Unfortunately, it does not help them regulate their behavior either. In this type of situation, a child is asking for a clear limit. The response is too vague. In fact, it is no limit at all. This leaves the child dangling in uncertainty and it encourages him to act out more strongly. Maybe you didn't hear me, Dad—I said I want you to set a limit on my behavior.

The final trap most of us fall into is the use of empty emotional threats. Sometimes this takes the form of "If you get me mad, you will be sorry." At other times, we may appeal to relationship and say in effect, "If you love me, you won't behave this way." Certainly, there are many people (adults, not just children!) who are susceptible to this type of blackmail. But for the most part, appeals which threaten emotional fireworks fail. In the first place, "If you get me mad" doesn't tell the child *what* gets you mad or *how much* of it will push you over the line. You will probably find your child keeps misbehaving until you get angry. This makes sense because your anger is the only guidepost he has to stop his misbehavior. Collin pushes Jean Marie until she grabs him by the ankle and drags him from the room. *Then* he knows it is time to stop. Clearly, though, this is not where you want *your* child to stop! Also, many children actively seek to make their parents angry. Attention is attention, even if it hurts.

If there is one general rule that can be applied to setting limits for a young child, it is this: Be concrete. Children cannot understand abstract rules or relationships. They cannot think in vague terms. They do not respond to subtlety or nuance. You need to give the child very concrete boundaries in terms of time, space, and behavior.

Most children need very specific time markers. Telling the child "Wait until later" is like waving a red flag in front of a bull. Older children can be taught to watch a clock and to look for specific times. Younger children need more specific time markers. A simple mechanical solution is to use a common kitchen timer. Teach the child to listen for the bell.

> Jeannie was going to the beach. But first, she had to wait until her mother made the beds upstairs. Jeannie's typical pattern was to pester her mother every two minutes about whether it was time to go. Jeannie's mother knew from experience that it would take her approximately twenty minutes to make up the beds. She made a deal with Jeannie that the child would play in the rec room until she heard the bell. When she heard the bell, she could tell her mother it was time to go. If she bothered her mother before the bell went off, then the trip to the beach was off. Jeannie was told it was up to her whether or not she wanted to go to the beach. If she really wanted to go, she would listen for the bell.

There are other natural time markers as well. TV presents an excellent marker. Taped music lasting fifteen to twenty minutes also provides a natural time boundary. Many parents who are fortunate enough to have VCR's can use taped half-hour programs to provide time boundaries as well. As you consider your own family, you will find you have many such concrete ways to measure time for your children. If all else fails, remember the kitchen timer.

Spatial boundaries also need to be clearly spelled out for most children. If you tell them to play in their room, does that mean they are able to play in the whole upstairs? If as a punishment you have your child sit on a chair in the corner, does that mean he can sit on the floor by the chair? Spatial boundaries are usually fairly easy to define since everyone can see them. The only problem many parents have is in enforcing the limits consistently.

Brian was a little boy who had difficulty staying in his room during time-outs. If he was placed in his room, within a moment he would be hanging out the doorway. Soon, he was lying on the floor. Finally, he would be in his brother's room, playing with his toys. Though Brian's father did not like to close the door to his room for these short time-outs, he was concerned about the problem. His solution one day was to tell Brian to sit in his room for one minute, adding, "If you come out of your room, then I will put you back in the room with the door closed for three minutes." Brian could not tell time but it sounded to him like that meant things got worse. Brian's father also made it clear what it meant to "come out of your room." He showed Brian by example that even stepping briefly outside his door was coming out of his room. He made it very clear that he was going to be strict in his interpretation of the rule. Brian was told that he certainly could come out of his room, but that he needed to think about what would happen if he did. Immediately, Brian's toe crossed the threshold of his door. His father stated that Brian had apparently decided to stay in his room and abruptly closed the door. Brian squawked in horror and dismay. But from then on, his parents had little trouble with getting him to stay in his room.

The third and most difficult type of limit setting concerns establishing firm behavioral boundaries. It is not enough to tell most children to "go play," "be good," or "be polite." Certainly there are many children who are very sensitive and responsive to their parents' behavior, but most children require more concrete cues. Children need to be taught to monitor their own specific behavior. A child may have a snack when *all* of the toys are picked up off the floor. A child can have dessert once she eats three more bites of broccoli. Bathtime is over when you count down from five to zero.

Children also need to be careful to monitor your behavior. Here is an example of how a five-year-old learns to pay attention to her mother's cues:

> Katelyn was a five-year-old who seemed unable to tolerate her mother being on the phone. Whenever the phone would ring, there would be Katelyn, tugging at her mother's dress, demanding snacks, asking to be played with, or simply wanting to be picked up. She would whine and complain. Once she bit through the phone cord. Her mother set up a simple behavioral program. Whenever Mother was on the phone, Katelyn was to play with her toys or watch TV. She was not allowed to bother Mother while she was on the phone. If she did bother her, she would be given a time-out and her favorite doll would be put away for an hour. For Katelyn, this was the worst of all consequences! Katelyn was to listen for her mother to say, "I am off the phone now." If she was able to play or watch TV until she heard her mother say this, she could earn some sugarless gum. The program was not presented as a punishment. It was presented as a challenge, as a game between the two of them. Only once did Katelyn test the routine. She hung on her mother's leg and whined at her. Her mother hung up the phone immediately and said Katelyn had apparently decided to take a time-out and Mimi would have to go too. Mother's attitude was cool and mechanical. From then on the child was able to wait for her mother's "I am off the phone now."

Parents are often confronted with situations in which there are no clear time, space, or behavioral limits. Children often ask to do something later and the parents aren't sure how to answer. Parents can still define limits even in these uncertain situations. Suppose your child asks if you could all go to the playground after dinner. If it's early on in the day, a lot of things can happen between now and dinnertime. You need to stall the child, but you know that if you say, "Well, we will see," you will be pestered every ten minutes until dinner. You can still be fairly concrete about limits, even if you won't know the answer until much later. You can tell children the exact conditions under which you will know the answer:

> "That is not something I can answer right now. You will have to wait until dinner is over before I can answer that question. We will talk

about it after dinner. If you really want to go, you will have to wait
until then. If you bother me about it before then, the answer will be
no."

This type of response is not as callous as it sounds. It can be done
in a fairly warm tone of voice. You are simply telling the child when
you will have the answer to the question and what will happen if she
pesters you further. You are simply making your behavior predictable.

Many parents have no difficulty establishing limits for their children.
In fact, I have known some very lucky parents who are able to say,
"We will see" or "Be good" and, like magic, their children *respond*.
Most of the time, though, these sorts of limits are completely worthless.
When setting limits, remember to be as concrete as possible. Be very
clear about time limits, spatial limits, and behavioral limits. Teach
the child to monitor her own behavior and also to watch yours. In a
sense, limits are a contract between parent and child. If you abide by
a contract, you reap certain rewards; break a contract, and certain
consequences follow.

3. Giving Warnings

No child is able to always regulate his behavior, even if he understands the rules and limits. All children, at some point, will need to
be warned that they have crossed the imaginary line and are now in
jeopardy of losing their privileges and freedom. Warnings give a child
a chance to pull it together and get things under control. This is
especially important for small children who have difficulty watching
their own behavior. Let's go over some of the essentials about giving
warnings.

It is a snowy Friday afternoon. School has been canceled and nothing
is moving outside. You have been trapped indoors with the six-year-old
twins, Billy and Bobby, all day long. It is 1:15 in the afternoon and
there is nothing on TV except soap operas. They can't think of anything
to do and have used up all their energy whining at you since breakfast.
To kill time, they tease each other and fight. You are trying to talk on
the phone but you can't hear because of their racket. You cover the
mouthpiece and call to them, "Settle it down, guys, I am warning
you . . ." Silence for thirty seconds. Then you hear them giggle and they
start it up again. They come into the room where you are still talking

on the phone and renew their bickering. The silliness is getting out of hand. Now it is tickling, screaming, and throwing things.

"Okay. This is your second warning." You try to look angry and hope that will impress them. It doesn't. Within a few minutes they are running around the dining room table, throwing blocks at one another. You apologize to the person you are talking to, cover the receiver, and stare at the twins. You have got to think of something that will make them stop. Tomorrow is the big family outing into the city. You have looked forward to this for a long time and so have the kids. Maybe that is your bargaining chip! "You know if you keep this up, we are not going into town tomorrow. That means no train ride, no movie, nothing."

"Can we play outside then?" asks Billy.

"No, you will stay inside . . . all day."

What are you saying? You have just painted yourself into a corner! You can't stand to be trapped inside the house *now;* how will you feel all day tomorrow? You have been looking forward to this trip more than they have. You watch their eyes to see if your bluff has worked. They are quiet; perhaps you have caught them off their guard. Then Billy looks at Bobby. Bobby looks at Billy. They are sending their telepathic messages to one another. They smile. The mighty fortress of your threat is quickly turning to ashes. You read Bobby's face. Look, Billy, it says, Mom is full of it. Now the real fun can begin.

Now, down to the business about warnings. Rule number one is, *Mean what you say.* If you can't follow through, don't threaten. Warnings, after all, are not threats. When you threaten, you are trying to intimidate someone into behaving in a particular way. You rely on the emotional impact of the threat to do the dirty work. As I have said before, this leaves you feeling all the emotional urgency. Will your threat have impact or not? But children are rarely cowed by threats of emotions. Often it is to their advantage to push you past the limit just to see if you will follow through. A warning doesn't rely on emotional impact. It is merely a statement about the situation. If the child does throw the toy, you will respond by taking all the toys away. You do not need to carry the urgency. Let the child do that. But be ready to follow through. The second working rule is, *Make the process predictable.* If you give a warning, make sure your consequences will follow just as you say. There are three aspects to predictability and we need to consider each in turn.

1. *Give one warning.* Many parents have told me they give their acting-out children three or four warnings. Why do they do this? Most parents want to avoid having to punish their child. After all, it is an awful process; who enjoys it? Parents who give multiple warnings may be asking their children, "Please cooperate with me and don't make me punish you." But children are working on an entirely different agenda. They don't expect you to hurt them, just to let them know they can trust you. How can they know what to do if they get three warnings one time, five warnings the next? Give one warning, tell the child what is coming next, then follow through.

2. *Be prompt.* When you give a child a warning, be ready to respond immediately if the child further challenges your limits. After they have given a warning, some parents make the mistake of hesitating before they impose a consequence. Perhaps they feel they are giving the child one last chance. But the power of the warning is that it gives the child a sense of immediacy, and the urgency to change her behavior quickly. Hesitation only serves to weaken the power of the warning. After all, if you don't respond when you say you will, how is a child to know *when* you will respond? The urgency is gone. Instead, the child will tend to look for the actual consequence itself. Hesitate enough times and children will cease to listen to your warnings at all.

3. *Be exact.* If you say, "One more time," be sure you react after one more time. In actual practice I have found it is better to be strict than lenient in the interpretation of rules. If anything, respond when a child nudges the line rather than after the line has been crossed. Remember, children learn rules by pushing limits and discovering the consequences. Once a child finds the limit to a rule and can trust its consistency, she will take one step back and keep her behavior within bounds. If you don't respond as you say you will, you are inviting your children to push limits even more. Again, they will not listen to your warning but will simply push until you react with the consequence. This is not helpful to them. It encourages acting-out behavior and may stimulate their feelings of uncertainty.

In this chapter, we are dealing with predictable, minor behavior problems such as squabbling, bugging, and making messes. Clearly you do not want to be wasting a lot of energy and emotion thinking of novel ways to warn children. Warnings, after all, are simply a way of letting a child know what will happen next. Make the warning process mechanical and unexciting. The more mechanical or ritualized the warnings are, the more predictable they are.

MOTHER: Pick up your shoes.

CHILD: No.

MOTHER (*rapidly, in a flat tone*): I am going to count to three . . .

CHILD (*scurrying to pick up his shoes*): I will, I will!

MOTHER: If by the time I say "three," you have not picked up your shoes, I will put you in your room for two minutes. One, two . . .

Speaking from personal experience, I can assure you that you rarely have to get through the first sentence. Once the child hears that first phrase and the flat tone of your voice, she knows what will come next. This is the function of a ritualized warning. It is a cue to act *now*. Of course, it helps if the child has been taught the process since toddlerhood. Teaching any such process to older children is more difficult because their negative behavior is more firmly entrenched. But if you always use the same phrases to set up your warnings, they will learn the sequence more quickly. Once they mock you by finishing the warning in a singsong voice or say, "I know, I know," you know you have got them.

Many children will threaten noncompliance with a command or threaten to escalate their own behavior. Parents often will react to this resistance by saying, "You better not . . ." At other times, parents are drawn into power struggles with children. They squat down, establish eye contact, and in an earnest voice say, "I am not going to let you behave this way." Again, who is taking the responsibility for the behavior? Who feels the urgency to control the situation?

The real power in behavior management is determined by the selection of consequences. You cannot control the child's behavior. You cannot crawl into your child's brain and chew her food, use the toilet correctly, or make her stay in bed. You cannot control her thoughts. The child must learn to control those herself. The function of the warning is to cue the child that she has to get herself under control. What we want the child to do is to think about what will happen next if she continues her inappropriate behavior. She certainly has the choice of whether to misbehave or not. She merely needs to understand the consequences. Consider the following bit of dialogue:

FATHER: Billy, dinner is not ready yet. I want you out of the kitchen until I call you.

BILLY: I not going.

FATHER: I said go right now.

BILLY: No, and I gonna break all these glasses.

FATHER: You can certainly do that, Billy. But if you do, what will happen?

BILLY (*pouting, thinking*): Nothing.

FATHER: Good, Billy, you are thinking, aren't you. Now, I am going to give you to the count of three to get into the playroom. If—

BILLY: I going, I going.

A warning is merely a cue; it is not a threat. It is a simple signal to the child to stop doing one thing and to do some other thing. It is the child who is responsible for his behavior and the child who must feel the urgency to change.

4. Controlling the Tone of Your Response

Remember, we are discussing routine discipline here. It is very important to keep this in mind, both for ourselves and for our children. A calm attitude in dealing with these chronic minor infractions is important because it helps us maintain our mental energy and emotional well-being. It is also important because it communicates to our children the true nature of these problems. For the most part, they are trivial irritations, not worthy of an adult's concern. We are much more concerned with having warm, enjoyable experiences with our children than with wasting effort over mundane irritations.

Too often we tend to concentrate on what we say, on the words themselves. Yet verbal language makes up only a fraction of our total communication. Certainly our words convey a specific message, but what gives our communication life and importance is the way we say things. This is especially true when we communicate with our children. Small children move instinctively toward stimulation and warmth. They move away from everything that is cold and boring. If you react to every misdemeanor with the same energy and zeal you show for positive behavior, how are they to tell the difference? In a sense, it is helpful to react to these behaviors with as little emotion as possible.

How can you react to a child's misbehavior without paying attention? If you can learn to monitor and to regulate your nonverbal behavior, you may be able to respond to the child without giving *satisfying* attention. You need to consider such things as your tone of voice, volume, rate of speech, body posture, and facial expression. When children are appropriate, it is fine to energize your behavior; talk loudly, with great inflection. Show a full range of feelings: surprise, delight, warm joy. Use your facial expression to convey your feelings. When children break the routine household rules, though, remove the energy and emotion from your nonverbal behavior. Relax your face, slow your movements, drop your tone, and flatten your vocal inflection. Use stereotyped phrases ("I am going to count to three," etc.). The goal is to make your response as unemotional as possible. This takes the fun out of misbehavior.

Some parents will ask, "But don't children need to understand how you feel?" Certainly they do, but the question here is, at what point should you discuss your feelings about a particular behavior? From a practical standpoint, when you are moving a child from a warning to a consequence, it is a hindrance to concentrate on your feelings or the child's. How many of us have been derailed in our efforts to get a child to his room because the child says, "You don't love me." The whole system breaks down as we sit on the stairs and try to explain: "Of course I love you, I just don't happen to like you—no, that's not it, I am just mad . . ." Once you do this, you have lost your focus. The issue is no longer whether little Paul whacked Ginny with his toy hammer. Now it is whether or not you love him. Is this the issue?

Many rules in a family are followed simply because they are family rules. "No hurting" is a blanket rule because it protects the physical safety of the family members. *If you do the crime, you do the time.* How you or your child feels does not enter into the situation, but many children learn that by questioning their parents' love, they are able to upset them and to maintain a hammerlock on their attention. The process is no longer mechanical and the rules are no longer automatic. The child discovers there is room to maneuver. Also, if he is able to get a rise out of you by questioning your love, he is likely to engage in the same behavior again. Is that what you want? Often there are situations in which we need to discuss why a child broke a particular rule. Little Paul hit Ginny because she took his truck and he felt angry at her. But the time to discuss feelings is not before the consequence. Reserve these discussions for when the consequence is over and it is time to make amends.

5. Imposing Consequences

What will motivate children to follow the family rules? Children must feel there is something to be gained by following the rules. There must be nothing for them to gain by breaking a rule. Perhaps they may even lose something. This is most important. Children follow rules because they *feel better* than when they choose not to follow rules. It is the consequences that help them discriminate these differences in their internal state. When little Paul hits Ginny over the head, he doesn't feel anything in particular except perhaps a tingle of pleasure. If he is removed, isolated, and hears Ginny getting attention, then he may feel different—certainly not pleased. He does not like feeling isolated. He does not like feeling jealous. When he is behaving appropriately, he feels the warm glow of his parents' attention. Consequences change how a child feels *on the inside*. This is the barometer a child uses in choosing whether or not to follow family rules.

What things in life are most important to your child? You need to list these and have a clear idea of what they are. The most important motivator, as I have said before, is probably your attention. To many children this has nothing to do with your *feelings,* only whether or not you are actively focused on *them.* They do not care whether you are angry or happy with them. They only care that you are paying attention to them. Every child enjoys being the center of the family universe. Most children will work very hard to be there. The loss of attention is very disagreeable and most children will work doubly hard to get it back.

Yet there are other bargaining chips in your child's life. Many children have special toys. Removing these toys creates a powerful emotional response. Some children find certain activities stimulating. They are willing to exert effort to maintain them. Finally, freedom is a powerful motivator, especially to older children. How many nine-year-olds enjoy spending the day in your line of sight?

Use language that will make it clear who is responsible for the consequence. Do you wish to take responsibility for the misbehavior? Is the child being sent to her room simply because you are annoyed with her? If this happens to be the case, you can tell the child, "I am too angry to talk with you right now. I want you away from me. Go to your room and close your door, now." But in this particular case, the feelings have clearly gotten out of hand. For most simple rule infractions, it is the *child* who has misbehaved and the *child* who is responsible for being sent to her room. What you want to reinforce is that the child has made a decision about her behavior that has resulted in a loss of freedom. You do not need to carry the urgency. She clearly has the choice as to whether she maintains her freedom or loses it. This particular time, perhaps, she has chosen to lose it. Let your language reflect that.

> "I see by your behavior you have decided to spend some time in your room. You may go to your room on your own or I will help you."

As noted earlier, it is important to plan out a series of steps to most consequences. Suppose a child balks at being sent to her room; what do you do then? Suppose once a child is in her room she comes out. For most minor behavior problems it is sufficient to think of a three-step time-out routine. There may be one or two instances in which a child will push the limits beyond that, but for most children, following household rules is not an emotionally charged issue. It is very important, however, to use a foreshadowing technique to describe the three steps in the process. You can build this in as part of your time-out routine.

> "Take thirty seconds on the stairs. If you get off the stairs before your thirty seconds is done, I will put you in your room for one minute. If you come out of your room, you will be placed back in there, with the door closed, for two minutes."

For most small children, especially those who can't tell time, the issue of the time is not very important. But they will get a sense that stopping their misbehavior will lead to a shorter time-out. They certainly may choose to push you, but they will get the idea that if they do so, they will feel worse.

When you impose a consequence on a child, be clear about the limits of the consequence, how the child is to behave while it is being imposed, and what the child must do to have it lifted. Again, you can work these points into a regular routine.

"Okay, you are in your room for two minutes. I have set the timer. When the bell of the timer goes off, I will come to check on you. If you are quiet, then I will let you come out. If, however, you are still having a tantrum, I will reset the timer for another two minutes. Use the time to settle yourself down."

Sometimes a child will threaten to destroy her room. Usually this is a ploy to get the parents to pay attention to her in some negative way. As with warnings, you can use these threats as a springboard to helping the child think about the consequences of her own impulsive behavior.

CHILD: I am going to tear up my room and break all my toys.
MOTHER: You can certainly do that, but what will I do with your broken toys?
CHILD: Throw them away.
MOTHER: That's right. And what about if you mess up the room?
CHILD: I have to clean it up?
MOTHER: That's right. You have two minutes in your room. It is up to you.

Many children will still throw their toys around—although in a limited, calculated way—just to see what you will do.

MOTHER: Two minutes are up. You have settled yourself down very nicely.
CHILD: Can I come out now?
MOTHER: Looks to me like you have got some picking up to do. As soon as that is done, give me a call and then you can come out.

For little children, you can use a simple five or ten count as a time-out. Remember, these short time-outs are mere interrupters so you can stop the momentum of some annoying behavior. The advantage of this type of brief consequence is that you can apply it almost anywhere. Children can be given brief ten-second time-outs in the supermarket, at the beach, or at church. It usually helps if you have some other child upon whom you can lavish attention while the offender is sitting with head bowed.

Consequences that involve removal of toys need to follow the same process. A child needs to know how long the toy is removed for and what she has to do to get it back.

6. Making Amends

After the consequence is over, there is still some work to be done. First, this is a time in which you can help your child integrate the experience. You have an opportunity to reinforce the mechanics of family rule violations: What did the child do? ("Paul whacked Ginny") What was the rule? ("no hurting") What happened? ("got a time-out"). You also have the opportunity to discuss specific circumstances which may have led to this particular problem. If Ginny took Paul's toy, discuss that now. This is the point at which you can discuss the child's feelings and also your own. Often it is helpful to have the child do something so this situation can truly be concluded. If the child has hurt someone, then saying "I am sorry" or doing some other act of repayment may be warranted. If the child has made a mess, then he has to clean it up. Making amends is a way of finishing with a particular problem so no one feels the need to carry it on as a burden. Paul apologizes to Ginny, then tells her that he didn't want her to take his truck. She wants to keep Mommy's favor, so she immediately gives it back; then they resume play.

Sometimes children who are still angry will refuse to make amends. There are several ways you can handle this issue that are beneficial to the child. I strongly recommend against trying to *make* a child say "I am sorry." Once you try to force a child to say anything, you are immediately taking on the urgency and you give the child something to struggle against. Instead of focusing on his own behavior, the child starts to struggle with you. This is clearly not the focus in simple family-rule infractions.

Instead, think of how you could set up the situation so it is more advantageous to the child to make amends than to refuse. You might tell the child he is all done with time-out but that he has to be alone to play, can't have friends over, and can't be outside because you are concerned that he is still angry and might hurt another child. For his own protection and the protection of other children, you need to watch over him more closely. Of course, if the child chooses to make amends, he is letting you know the issue is over and he is ready to move on. It is up to the child to decide. You can suggest these alternatives in a matter-of-fact way. Most children over the age of four know the simple social mechanics of saying "I am sorry" if they have hurt someone. They certainly do not need any lengthy explanations. In fact, lengthy explanations are counterproductive. Keep it simple, short, and matter-of-fact.

When the child makes amends or through some other bit of appropriate behavior is released from a consequence, you have a fine opportunity to display some positive attention. Again, watch the tone and keep the emotions somewhat restrained. The child, after all, is just being released from a punishment. But you do have the opportunity to let the child know that the issue is over, that he has done the right thing and can now get on with his day. As children come out of time-outs or other consequences, it is important to get them focused in a positive direction and not dwell on the negatives.

To Sum Up: A Discipline Routine for Routine Behavior Problems

We have been focusing on the mechanical routine of discipline. Certainly, structuring the day will alleviate many types of behavior problems. However, there are times when it is important for you to intervene in your child's behavior for the safety of the child and others and for the well-being of the home. Most of these problems are fairly predictable. You know how your child will react in certain situations. You know how he is jealous, for example, of his brother or sister. You know the problems that crop up at mealtime. You know how he responds when you ask him to clean up a mess or how he behaves when there is company. This means you can develop a general behavioral plan so you can intervene without making matters worse.

The whole purpose of a well-developed discipline routine is to deactivate the excitement of misbehavior. So many discipline problems are predictable, why should you waste your energy on them? Why should you be continually surprised by the obvious?

The purpose of a routinized, mechanical approach is threefold. First, it allows you to get through most of these minor annoyances with a minimum expense of energy. Second, it allows you to communicate to your child a certain sense of bored disdain at having to take time away from a rich, warm relationship to go over some uninteresting routine.

As a direct consequence, the third effect happens within the child. You help the child feel the difference between the warmth and energy of your positive attention and your cool, lifeless, mechanical response when he misbehaves. As children become able to discriminate between these internal feelings, they will learn to regulate their behavior.

The key to developing an effortless routine lies in anticipatory planning. Outline the family rules in advance. Translate fairly abstract rules into concrete terms so they will make sense to a very young child. Next, establish clear limits to help the child define the rules. You cannot describe these limits in terms of abstractions or emotional dynamics. With young children, you need to stick to concrete time limits, space limits, and behavioral limits. After all, the purpose is to teach a very concrete child something about the world. You must speak the child's language. Next, understand the functions of a warning. Warnings are not threats, they are cues. They impart a sense of urgency to the child to change behavior. They do not signal a sense of urgency in the adult. It is just as important to understand the workings of consequences. Please reread chapters 5, 6, and 7, on positive reinforcement, punishment, and attention, if you have any doubts about how these work. Finally, it is important for a child to have some way of repaying damages done and of atoning for hurts. This is the way issues are resolved so no one feels the burden of guilt.

Up to this point we have not dealt with any of the major disasters that seem to be of such concern to so many people. This is because in most cases it is the minor problems which cause the most wear and tear. Now we will turn to another issue that leads to many commonplace, though minor, behavior problems: how children differ in their capacity to tolerate stimulation. Most parents can tell you how their children go haywire when overstimulated. Often, though, they do not pay attention in advance to the child's tolerance for stimulation. Next, we will discuss how to evaluate your child's tolerance for stimulation and explore ways to use daily structure to pace children and restructuring to help them settle down. Finally, we will discuss the impact of the parents' behavior on the child's ability to self-regulate.

10

The Importance of Speed and Volume Control

Until now, we have focused on the willful behavior of children. We have explored the purposes of misbehavior and how parents can use daily schedules, rituals, and discipline routines to teach predictability and control. Certainly children use misbehavior to test the boundaries of their world, the limits of their independence. But there are also many times when children misbehave because they *can't* seem to regulate their behavior. They are simply out of whack and need your help to get back *into* whack.

It is easy to overlook these situations because they don't seem to be *discipline* problems. Imagine it is 3:30 on a rainy afternoon and your children have been bouncing around the living room like Superballs, their eyes are glazed over, and when you talk to them, they don't seem to listen. Clearly, they have gotten themselves overstimulated and can't settle down. Or think of the times when they have been frustrated or disappointed. Perhaps you had planned to go to the beach, but now you find the beach is closed because some environmentally hazardous yuck has washed up onshore. The children scream and cry and don't listen to your nice rational explanation. In each case, the children are so upset, can you really justify punishing them? Don't they just need a little sympathy and cuddling?

But discipline is much more than punishment. In fact, in these situations, discipline can be a great act of kindness. First of all, upset and overstimulated children have lost control and are more likely to fight with their siblings, be disrespectful to adults, or break things. When children are out of whack, they also don't listen to reason and are *unable* to follow rational problem solving. Finally, when children can't settle down, it has an impact on their relationship with the parents. Ten minutes of a child's squealing or crying is usually enough to push most parents over the edge. This is why discipline as a teaching process is so important in helping children settle down. Children need to learn how to settle themselves down *before* they get out of control.

Now let's explore ways to help children settle down when they are out of control. First, we must understand how children experience their feelings. As in other areas of learning, there are some striking individual differences in the ways children experience the world and cope with their own emotions. What "works" for your neighbor's children may not be effective with your own. It is also essential to recognize those situations which are most likely to cause problems for your children. It is possible to anticipate many of these situations and to develop plans in advance. But there are also times when something unexpected happens, so we need to consider ways to cope with overstimulated or upset children. Finally, we will discuss ways of teaching children to monitor themselves and to regulate the expression of their feelings.

HOW ADULTS HANDLE THEIR EMOTIONS

When you are upset, how do you settle yourself down? Most adults learn fairly adaptive ways to regulate the expression of their feelings. Granted, all parents argue, pout, or give each other the silent treatment, and one or the other usually spends more than a few nights sleeping on the living room couch. When four or five individuals share a common living space, this is bound to happen. But parents usually find stable ways of coping with the minor anxieties and disappointments which pop up in day-to-day living. We learn to take a break, to give ourselves a time-out, or to go for a walk. Most of us learn to calm ourselves down in a rational, evenhanded way. Many times we use words and phrases our parents used to repeat to us when we were little. I remember hearing the managing supervisor of a factory calm down by saying to himself, "Now, Douglas, you just settle yourself down and think for a minute, just think." We use words to interpret and tone down our raw feelings. We also learn to recognize our feeling states from our behavior. We know we are anxious when we pace, pull on our lip, bite our fingernails, or smoke too many cigarettes. We know we are depressed when we are irritable or sit in the living room in the dark. We can identify our feeling states with words, can communicate these to those we love, and can develop some type of plan for coping: "Some things happened at work today, honey, and I am feeling really down. I just want to sit here by myself for a while so I can think. I will be okay. I just need to think, and then I will be in to talk to you."

TODDLERS AND THEIR FEELINGS

Very young children under the age of three usually show a lot of ups and downs in their feelings. They squeal with excitement, stamp and shout with anger, and wail when they are upset. They also tend to express their feelings directly through their behavior. When their brother takes a toy, they don't say, "I am feeling angry that you took my toy without asking," they simply whack him on the head with their plastic light-saber. Toddlers need a lot of external control in order to regulate their behavior. These children are watched closely and allowed little independence. Toddlers also have a very limited capacity to differentiate their feelings and identify them with words. Sometimes they can tell you when they are happy, sad, or angry, but often they cannot do this unless they are directly asked. Toddlers spontaneously *behave,* they don't spontaneously explain.

As a three-year-old, Pamela had difficulty settling down at bedtime. After dinner, she and her father were accustomed to a period of rough play in the living room. At 7:00, though, he would abruptly try to stop the play and tell her it was time for her to go to bed. She would plead and beg with him to continue. Sometimes he would for a few more minutes if she would promise to go to bed then. However, after a few more minutes she would be more desperate in her attempts to keep him playing with her. Finally, she would run away and hide under the dining room table. Soon, Dad was getting mad and the scene would start to turn ugly. He would yell at her and threaten her; she would run away giggling, yet somehow oddly fearful. When he would grab her to take her up to bed, she would scratch at him and try to bite his arm. He would spank her and she would scream and cry. He would put her in her room, holding the door so she could not come out. After half an hour of intermittently tugging at the door and throwing her toys, she would fall asleep in a sweating heap on the floor. Dad would quietly come in, gently pick up his daughter, and put her in bed. Then he would go downstairs and pour himself a double scotch. Another day, another bedtime.

Toddlers cannot monitor their internal state. They have very little capacity to regulate their excitement, and as in the case of Pamela, it is very easy for fun experiences to quickly change into angry confrontations. Pamela also didn't have a way to explain or describe feelings. Instead, the expression was given directly over into behavior. She bit and kicked and threw her toys when she was angry. Clearly she needed a lot more help from Dad to settle down before she became overstimulated and lost control.

SCHOOL-AGE CHILDREN AND THEIR FEELINGS

While we may expect Pamela's type of behavior from toddlers, we usually expect older children to show more self-control. We expect them not only to understand our rational explanations, but also to be able to articulate their own feelings with accuracy. But many children, even eight- and nine-year-olds, have difficulty living up to these expectations. Many children continue to have trouble using words to express their feelings. They have trouble differentiating one feeling from another. Of course there are times when they can tell you they are "happy" or they are "sad." But what happens when they are simply "excited"? Young children still have a limited capacity to use language to regulate their feelings. When they are upset, they are still likely to vent their feelings through behavior.

Joshua was turning seven and his parents decided to have a party at the county fair. That morning Joshua, who was an excitable boy, acted as though his toe had been caught in an electrical outlet. Even though his parents kept telling him to "settle down," he seemed to move at a continual run and talk in a continual yell. He could not sit still for a second. His parents were sympathetic and didn't want to burden him with any responsibilities. But two hours before the party, black thunderclouds appeared on the horizon. The weather report said there was a 50 percent chance of severe weather. Joshua's parents were unsure whether or not they should have the party and communicated their uncertainty to the boy. For Joshua, who was scared to death of thunderstorms, this was too much. He screamed and cried. His parents tried to soothe him, but to no avail. To make matters worse, he followed them from room to room wailing until they could stand it no longer. When the children began to arrive for the party, Joshua was still bellowing. The clouds still hung overhead, threatening to zotz with a bolt of lightning anyone who dared ride the ferris wheel. His parents removed all of the birthday presents before Joshua could destroy them, and eventually removed him from the party altogether. The other children ate cake and ice cream and played a few party games, though no one went on any of the open rides.

Certainly school-age children can identify pure and simple emotional experiences and can often tell when they feel happy, angry, or sad. They can even identify these pure feelings in others. However, emotions are never pure and rarely ever simple. As in the case of Joshua, most problem situations usually result from the intermingling of complex or competing feelings. Joshua felt a happy excitement because it was his birthday. At the same time he was afraid because there were thunderstorms on the horizon. But the maraschino cherry on top of everything was the anxiety that was raised when it became uncertain whether the party would go on. The complexity and power of these feelings were too much for Joshua to understand or to regulate. They would be for most children.

HOW CHILDREN UNDERSTAND AND REGULATE THEIR FEELINGS

Often parents will credit children with being "more in touch" with their feelings than adults. Children seem to say what is on their mind and to express their feelings directly. But the emotions are expressed immediately, through behavior, not with words. Children laugh, cry, and stamp out their anger with big tears bursting from their eyes. They express their feelings and give in to their rage and then they are done. Perhaps a few toys are broken, a room is dismantled, or a little sister is bitten—but the feeling is done. However, this type of immediate emotional expression is not helpful to the child in the long run. In the first place, it is destructive. The child may later regret the special toys that were broken. People can be hurt. Acting-out behavior also doesn't allow the child to integrate and understand the emotions involved. The experience simply happens and the child learns nothing. This means similar destructive emotional expressions are likely to occur in the future. When the child feels, the child simply behaves and then the situation is over. If the child is unable to think about the experience, nothing will change the next time the child feels the same way. Even though the direct expression of emotion is appealing to adults, it is essential that children learn how to think about their emotional experience in a constructive way and to express what they feel in a more socially adaptive manner.

We must realize that children do not experience their feelings the same way most adults do. Most adults feel and can describe clearly identifiable mood states such as anxiety, depression, hostility, etc. When adults experience depression and seek help, they can usually describe a specific set of symptoms. In adults, depression is clearly distinguishable from other moods.

But this is not the case with children. Granted, some children may show clear depressive reactions in response to some specific trauma or loss. Most children also experience transient mood swings since they tend to be much more labile than adults. But these are usually short-lived. For the most part, children's various moods are very poorly differentiated. When children are upset, they show elements of anger, anxiety, and sadness—all at the same time. Irritable children or children with difficult temperaments, who are sometimes labeled "depressed," actually experience the full gamut of negative feelings. Often no single mood stands out. Before children are able to differentiate and articulate specific moods, they seem to go through a "blurp" of excitement. Sometimes this may take the form of a "positive emotional blurp" if the child feels happy, anxious, overexcited, and externally stimulated. Take a child to a county fair and this is what happens. Sometimes, though, it can take the form of a "negative emotional blurp." This is what happens when a child feels overexcited, irritable, scared, angry, and sad. Many times, a positive emotional blurp can turn into a negative emotional blurp in the wink of an eye. This is what happens when the child has to leave the county fair because it is bedtime.

While young children have the capacity to spontaneously express their feelings, they are unable to use language to explain and describe how they feel. Many times their feelings are too complex and over-whelming to articulate. Simple words such as "happy" or "mad" are inadequate to capture the intensity of their emotional experience. When that blurp of excitement is ignited, they have no way to un-derstand what they are feeling or to regulate their behavior in an adaptive way. Joshua saw black storm clouds and erupted into a fit of crying and destructive behavior. Children not only need you to help them pace and structure their behavior, they also need to hear you talk about how they feel so they can better understand their emotions. You not only make the outside world more controlled and predictable, you also help them to understand and regulate their inner experience.

INDIVIDUAL DIFFERENCES IN EMOTIONAL EXPERIENCE

Children exhibit a broad variety of moods and behaviors and are responsive to an equally broad variety of teaching approaches from parents.

Some children have a much more difficult time regulating their irritability. Their moods tend to be more negative. Often these children have difficulty sustaining easy, light behavior. They become quickly overstimulated and can turn aggressive and nasty. In their fantasy play they seem to obsess on themes of violence and may be easily over-stimulated by violent cartoons and movies.

Other children tend to exhibit very happy moods and show little if any irritability. However, they may also show a tremendous craving for external stimulation and excitement. Turn your back and the boy is hanging from the curtain rod. Blink your eye and the girl is riding her tricycle down the stairs. Unfortunately they don't respond at all to punishment and seem to have trouble developing a "conscience." These children learn about their feelings in a very different way from irritable, moody children.

Then there are those children who seem to internalize everything. Often they are susceptible to a broad array of psychosomatic complaints such as headaches and stomachaches. It is easier for them to describe physical pain than it is for them to sort out their emotions.

Watch how your own children behave in very stimulating, emotionally laden situations. Take them to a video arcade at a local mall, a county fair, or even a busy department store. How do they respond to the noise level? Do they cling to you and seem upset by the high level of stimulation? Some children are able to tolerate these noisy and confusing places very well. Others, though, may seem to crave this level of stimulation but soon become very disorganized by it. They appear hyperactive and behave without regard for people or objects around them. When you attempt to restrain their behavior, they become irritable and almost frantic. Try to understand just how your children tolerate stimulation and regulate emotion. This will be your best measure of how they can learn self-control.

ANTICIPATING PROBLEMS: KEEPING A POSITIVE MENTAL ATTITUDE

I am sure everyone would agree that the best way to cope with a behavior problem is to keep it from happening in the first place. If it doesn't occur, then it isn't a problem. Of course, you have to be realistic about the limits of your own crystal ball. After all, you are not all-seeing and all-knowing. You can't keep children happy or even placid all the time. For many problem situations that you *can* anticipate, though, there are things you can do that will help your child cope.

As with so many aspects of discipline, the first adjustment is *yours*, the parents'. The job of settling down an upset child is a lot easier if you can maintain your cool and think about the situation in a positive, constructive way. To do this, you have to understand that your child's tolerance for stimulation is different from other types of behavior problems. Your child is not just testing limits to learn the family rule system, your child is *out of control*. She can't regulate her behavior and she probably feels irritable as well. But she doesn't just need sympathy or "a little space." She needs someone who can give her some direction and supervision. She needs your help.

Often the distinction between overstimulation and willful limit testing is a difficult one to make. For one thing, if you miss all of the early warning signals and your child starts spiraling out of control, she is probably going to start acting out and testing all sorts of limits. Then when you try to intercede, she is more likely to be defiant and disobedient. As a parent of two small children, I have come across this situation many times. I have also encountered it professionally. So many times parents will say to me, "I can't tell whether she *can't* control herself or simply *won't* control herself." For some reason the difference between "can't" and "won't" is important. Why?

Apparently the distinction is important because it legitimizes a specific emotional response from the parents. If your child really "can't" do something, then you sympathize, reassure, and make soft cooing noises. But if your child simply refuses to behave or willfully misbehaves, then you are right to be angry and increase your demands for compliance.

But the distinction between "can't" and "won't" is a false one. When your child is out of control, she simply *isn't* behaving. It is usually very difficult, if not impossible, to really understand how much is willful and how much is involuntary. Besides, when your child gets upset, your own emotional response is no longer important. Your child probably isn't going to pay attention to your feelings, since she is too caught up in her own. To get a child to attend to your feelings at this point, you would have to turn up your own speed and volume past the point of reason. So you yell, threaten, and perhaps swat your child in anger. Your child probably doesn't learn anything from this and feels angry at you, and you feel angry for losing control. This is why it is important to anticipate trouble spots or to respond to ticklish situations before the feelings get out of control.

But positive, constructive attitudes don't *just happen*—they need to be actively shaped and worked on. You have the great gifts of thought and language, and you need to consciously use these as instruments of self-control. Try to lead yourself through a mental process to construct a positive attitude:

1. *Allow yourself to recognize potential problem situations.* This will give you the chance to work on them while your child is still feeling relatively happy and receptive to your rational thinking.

2. *Separate your problems from your child's problems.* All of us are prone to stress either at certain points in our lives or in response to

some situations. If you have had a bad day at work and find you are screaming at your five-year-old because his shoelace is untied, then you probably have some feelings of your own you need to take care of. For now, though, try to be as fair to yourself and your child as you can.

3. *Focus in on the child's problem*. What is likely to set your child off? How is he likely to go out of control?

4. *Think about what your child needs to learn*. You are now in a situation in which your child can learn some necessary skills for living. What is it you want to teach?

5. *How can you help your child*? This is a critical question, one you might allow yourself to keep in mind: "You are out of control, how can I help you?"

6. *Always remember that your child is fortunate to have someone like you to teach him*.

IDENTIFYING PROBLEM SITUATIONS IN ADVANCE

As with so many aspects of your child's behavior, you are probably well aware what sorts of experiences will be most upsetting to her. Most of the trouble spots are predictable. So many times, though, I have had parents come to me who say, "I just dread taking her to a store. Why, just last night my husband and I had to pick out new flooring. We couldn't even talk to the store manager because she was behaving so horribly." It's like a self-fulfilling prophecy: our children misbehave just the way we expect them to. We can help our children by doing some advance planning. The first step is to identify the problem situations ahead of time.

Time of Day: Certain times of day are more stressful than others to our children. For many children, the late afternoon is the time when their adaptive abilities are at a low ebb and their irritability is high. Other children have problems just before bedtime. Again, they are often fighting sleep and appear hyperactive. They move at a continual run and squeal away in a voice that could shatter glass. They can shift from a screaming laugh to an angry temper tantrum in the blink of an eye. Finally, there are some children who have difficulties in the morning. They wake up grumpy and irritable. It is not until nearly lunchtime that they are able to settle down. As you think about your own children, consider the times of day when they seem to have more difficulties with self-control.

Easy Days and Hard Days: Many children show marked variations in behavior from day to day. One day the child will wake up sunny and bright, and sing merrily through the morning. But the next day he is Mr. Hyde and every minor nuisance is a major catastrophe. As a result, when you first look into that face and see that pout of unconditional grumpiness, you need to be prepared with a "hard day" routine.

Holidays: We usually think of holidays and other special times as being filled with joy and a sense of family togetherness. Birthdays, Thanksgiving, Easter or Passover, Christmas or Hanukkah—these are normally times of great warmth and sharing. But they are also very stimulating times, full of excitement and apprehension for all. In many families, these are very stressful times. There are all of the preparations, the visits from parents or in-laws, and the emotional impact of the event itself, which can make even well-adjusted adults frayed around the edges. Many adults also experience considerable anxiety or depression around holiday times. For children, these special times can act like a powerful stimulant to their nervous system. Some children become wild and overexcited. They seem unable to slow themselves down, identify their feelings, or express them appropriately. The surprises of Christmas or a birthday party can be as likely to set off a temper tantrum as a squeal of joy. Most children need a lot of external pacing and structure during these special times. They also need much more feedback about their feelings and help soothing and settling themselves when they are upset.

Major Disappointments: Children have difficulty handling frustrations and major disappointments. This was certainly the case with little Joshua in the previous section. Not only was he excited about his birthday, but he was afraid of the impending storm clouds and worried that he might not have his party at all. Young children as a rule have trouble coping with uncertainty or disappointment. Children like to see the world in black and white. When they are told to wait, they usually find it unbearable: "Are we going to the beach? Good, let's go now!"Even though we try hard to make our children understand our clear, rational explanations, even though they seem to understand exactly what we say, they continue to pout, whine, and cry. This can be very frustrating for adults, especially if you are also irritated by a delay or some other uncertainty. But what their behavior is telling us is that they need some help soothing and settling themselves, help that goes beyond mere rational explanations.

Certainly there are many times, events, and special circumstances that are going to make it more difficult for children to calm down and settle themselves. Consider your own children. Do they have particular times of the day when they are more irritable and more out of control? Are there special outings or holidays that are more difficult for them to handle? Are there certain places, either overstimulating or under-stimulating, in which they are more likely to be irritated or upset? Do they have easy days and hard days? What happens when they are frustrated, disappointed, or uncertain? It is important to identify those times and circumstances with which your children have difficulty coping. These are the times when they need your special help and guidance. To help your children get through them and learn to understand their own feelings, you need to consider three approaches. First of all, you can anticipate some of the problem situations before they arise—often you know what is likely to set your child off. How can you handle the situation to minimize both the emotional upset and the problem behavior? Certainly you can use the daily structure discussed earlier. But you also need to think about pacing your child through certain activities. Don't forget to consider your own behavior, how you will relate to your child so he will be less likely to go over the edge. The second approach concerns coping with overstimulated or upset children. You certainly can't anticipate every problem situation. After all, you do not live on "The Cosby Show." Still, there are some things you might try in order to soothe and settle the hurt feelings and contain the behavior. Finally, you can teach your children to keep watch over their own behavior, to understand their own feelings, and to exert some self-control. Let's discuss some ways you can implement these ideas.

ANTICIPATING PROBLEMS: A RATIONAL APPROACH

If you know a difficult situation is just around the corner, how can you prepare a child so he will not become overstimulated? The first thing you can do is identify the problems and begin to talk about them with the child in an up-front and evenhanded way.

Suppose we give Joshua's parents another crack at handling the birthday fiasco. All of us have experienced similar disasters and we have all lain awake at night wishing we had another chance. Let's give Joshua's parents that chance.

Now, what is clear about this situation is that it is probably not much of a surprise. Joshua is a very excitable boy and has probably given ample clues throughout his development that he is likely to become electrified during his birthday. So when he gets up at 6:00 A.M. he will look excited but is probably not yet out of control. His parents, realizing today is a special day, do not conduct "business as usual." Instead, they sit down and talk with him about how they are going to help him cope with his excitement so he can have the best birthday party ever. They might say something like the following:

> "Joshua, today is your birthday. You are seven years old! Such a big boy! This afternoon you are going to have a party and lots of your friends will be here. They are going to give you presents and we are going to go to the fair. That will be lots of fun, won't it?" (The parents wait for Joshua to respond about how much fun his birthday party will be.)
>
> "We want to do everything we can to help you have fun at your party. This is your special day and there will be lots of people, presents, things to eat. It will be fun and very exciting. You know what exciting means, right? It means that you are going to feel really jumpy inside. It may be hard to settle down and to keep your feelings under control. But if you get out of control, then you might get in trouble, and that wouldn't be much fun, would it?" (Again the parents allow some time for Joshua to talk about how it would feel if he got in trouble on his birthday.)
>
> "Your father and I are going to help you. We are going to help you to have fun on your whole birthday without getting into trouble."

At this point Joshua's parents can reinforce the family rules. A term like "out of control" is all right as a general topic of discussion, but it doesn't tell Joshua (or your child either, for that matter) *what* he has to do and *how* he has to behave. So the parents go over their general expectations, such as him talking with his "indoor voice," sharing toys with his little sister, following the "polite" rules, and doing what he is told. They also let Joshua know how they will be monitoring his behavior. This will include not only warnings when he breaks a rule, but also letting him know when he is doing a *good job*. In essence, what the parents are doing is reinforcing the normal rules of family living. Just because it is Joshua's birthday, normal family law and order is not suspended. In fact, because Joshua is so excitable, the rules are reinforced. But please note the tone that is used in communicating this to the boy. The rules are not there to punish him or to "make him be good." The rules are there to help him regulate his feelings and his behavior.

The parents also realize that Joshua has five or six hours to get through before his party starts. The first time around they did not structure him and took away all of his daily responsibilities. Apparently they thought that such responsibilities were drudgery and so he shouldn't be burdened with them on his birthday. The second time around, though, they see that five or six hours of unstructured time is simply too much uncertainty for Joshua to handle. Because he is the type of boy who needs a very predictable daily structure, the parents actually help him by providing one. They reinforce the normal routines that occur during the fixed time periods of the day. The breakfast routine is to be carried out as usual. So is the lunch routine. The time immediately after lunch will be structured since Joshua has to get himself ready for the party. The difficult period will be between 8:30 and 11:30 in the morning. During this time there is not much for Joshua to do and the parents have to prepare for the party.

By the time they are seven or eight years old, many children are able to keep themselves busy for lengthy periods of time. They can shift from one activity to the next and need minimal supervision from their parents. However, many children, such as Joshua, seem to have difficulty organizing their own behavior. They prefer more supervision from their parents. When there is excitement in the air, as there normally is on a birthday, it is even harder for these children to occupy themselves without adult guidance. Joshua is a child who clearly has trouble regulating his excitement, and he is not able to pull himself together when his parents give him vague cues to "settle down."

Because this is likely to be a difficult day, the parents help Joshua structure his flexible time. Since three hours is too long a free period for any young child, they decide to give him a snack at 10:00 in the morning. This breaks the morning time into two shorter, more manageable time periods. The parents decide that after his snack, Joshua can help with many of the party preparations. He can help set the table, fold napkins, and put out party favors. Joshua, like many children, likes not only structure but also responsibility. He starts to take ownership of his own party. The time period before his snack is left for free play, though the parents are careful to have Joshua choose a sequence of activities. On exciting days like their birthdays, children will often need to play outside, where there aren't so many restrictions on their behavior. However, sometimes children will surprise their parents by choosing to remain indoors just so they can watch all the preparations being made. This is the case with Joshua. His parents make it clear, however, that if he wants to remain inside, he will have to come up with three activities to occupy himself until snack time. He decides he wants to watch a cartoon on TV, play with his Legos, and make a picture with his art materials. Actually he watches two cartoons on TV and becomes so involved with his Legos that his mother has to go and get him to have a snack. It isn't important whether or not he completes the three activities he planned; he just needs some way to structure his free time and it has to be spelled out in advance.

It is vital to give children accurate feedback about how they are doing. This helps keep them on-task and encourages them to monitor their own behavior. Now, most of us do the same sort of thing Joshua's parents did in the first example. We caution our children to "settle down" or "cool your jets," well-intentioned advice but not very helpful to the child. Instead, it is more helpful to let the child know what he is doing *right*. Joshua's parents comment on how quietly he is sitting when he is watching TV. Later they may say to him, "Look at how you are keeping yourself settled down," or "You are playing with your Legos so quietly," and "We are really proud of you!" Many children like Joshua need very frequent, specific positive feedback in order to stay on a positive track.

Suppose, though, that your child is not as pleasant or compliant as Joshua on his second chance. Even with careful structuring and consistent positive feedback, many children are not able to regulate their response to stimulation. In these cases, the parents can try several additional approaches. Start by giving frequent feedback about the *pacing* of your child's behavior. Children may need extra help to monitor their tone of voice ("Use your indoor voice") or their speed of movement ("Slow it down, Joshua—walk"). Parents can also try *regrouping*. If two siblings cannot play together in a cooperative way, perhaps they need to play by themselves in their rooms for a while. You can also try *restructuring* activities. If Joshua could not play quietly with his Legos, his mother could intercede by saying, "You're having some trouble playing with your Legos and keeping yourself settled down. Looks like it is time to move on to your art project." Finally, parents can use brief time-outs to help children settle down. If Joshua was unable to sit quietly and watch TV, his father could intercede by saying, "You're having some trouble sitting quietly. You need to take thirty seconds on the stairs . . ." Very brief time-outs can help stabilize the situation. If you catch the child before he has spiraled out of control, he is often more compliant and sometimes even willingly co-operative.

As I am sure you can see, the actual behavioral mechanics are fairly simple and straightforward. Always identify the problem you are addressing and then agree on some method to work things out. If you can, make the consequences for noncompliance clear from the beginning. Then you know what you are going to do and the child knows as well. By focusing on structure and accurate feedback you can often avoid having to intercede. If you do have to intervene, you can grade your responses, from cuing, to restructuring, to removal.

One final phase in the process which must not be overlooked is evaluation. Once the situation is ended, sit down with the child and review how well he did. Most small children do not spontaneously evaluate their own behavior and often they do not immediately know whether their parents think they did well or not. It is important to tell children what they did well. The praise does not have to be loud and noisy, since that would probably be overstimulating. Instead, the parents' tone can be quiet and respectful as they emphasize the child's demonstration of skill. Joshua's father might say:

"Joshua, I am really proud of how you handled yourself this morning. You figured out things to do while we were getting things ready for your party. You were able to keep yourself busy, and when we told you to do something, you did it immediately. I don't think it was easy for you.

Birthdays are so exciting and it is hard for any kid to stay settled down. But you did it today and that tells me what a big boy you really are."

An evaluation and praise session at the end of a difficult situation is essential for most children. It helps them integrate their experience and be more aware of their own behavior. After all, we want children to see themselves as rational and capable of coping with challenging situations. By evaluating their behavior, we give them new and positive things to say to themselves *about* themselves. They will begin to see themselves as more competent and will gain confidence in their coping skills. The more they are able to see themselves in this way, the more likely they will be to act appropriately in the future. Like all aspects of discipline, the more the process can be positive and constructive, the better.

COPING WITH OVERSTIMULATED CHILDREN

Of course, you cannot anticipate all problems. Joshua's parents, for one reason or another, did not anticipate the worsening weather forecast. All of us at some point have had disappointments or unpleasant surprises we did not foresee. These letdowns have a terrific impact on children. Sometimes special activities have to be canceled at the last minute. At other times, problems just seem to add up. This might occur when we have to take a child who has just had an awful day at school to the doctor or dentist. Other children who have more unpredictable temperaments simply unravel without warning. Many children are easily disorganized and upset, and unfortunately for us, their behavior can't always be foreseen.

How do you cope when your child goes off like this? Many of us, taken by surprise, are often frozen in our tracks. After all, the child is not willfully misbehaving or trying to manipulate us—the disappointment and the pain are all too real. Certainly you want to sympathize with how your child feels and to give comfort where you can. But as the child continues to act out his overstimulation or disappointment, you will probably begin to wonder what will get him to stop. If simple sympathy and support won't help your child cope, what will? The difficulty here is that the behavior is no longer just the child's problem; it is yours as well. When children act out their overstimulation or disappointment, it is often irritating to the parents and sometimes embarrassing.

The first step in coping with the situation is to separate *your* problem from the *child's*. This is easier said than done. But before you can actively help your child you must be able to cope yourself. Settle yourself down as best you can. Try to recognize your own feelings in the situation. Are you disappointed? Do you feel embarrassed that your child is acting foolish and that others are staring at you? Is the sheer noise level getting on your nerves? Consciously identify your own feelings and actively talk to yourself about them. Active self-talk will give you that extra bit of distance between your thinking and your feelings so you can keep the situation under control. Self-talk is much more rational and quieting than explosive screaming or hitting. If there is another adult present, then you can use that person to talk out your own feelings as well. Sometimes this takes no more than a phrase or two: "Boy, this is really getting on my nerves. I better step in and help this little guy settle himself down." It is important to recognize your own feelings in any situation. Don't simply act out your feelings or, at the other extreme, pretend you don't have any at all.

When you are able to, begin to focus on the *child's problem*. Unfortunately, children do not have speed and volume knobs on the backs of their heads that you can simply turn to adjust. You cannot *make* them settle down. Instead, you need to think what you can do to help them settle themselves. How capable are they of controlling themselves? Can they quiet themselves in the current situation or do they need to leave? These are clearly some of the questions that Joshua's parents need to ask as his birthday party starts.

Unfortunately, in the first scenario, Joshua's parents make the same mistake all of us do—they don't recognize the problem until it is too late. When Joshua's friends begin arriving for the party, he is already out of control. He is not going to listen to reason and has no capacity to settle himself down. In this case all the parents can do is save the presents, protect the children, and remove the boy from his own party. If, once again, we gave Joshua's parents a second chance at this, they would certainly try to cope with the problem several hours earlier, when the threat of bad weather was just appearing and Joshua was more in control. Aside from anticipating the situation, probably the most effective way of coping with overstimulation is to be sensitive to your child's low-level cues. Parents need to build in an early warning system that sounds when their child feels excitement but is still capable of thinking, self-monitoring, and following directions. If you can pick up the early warning signals, then you can identify feelings, develop a plan, and help pace the child through the situation. In Joshua's case, it would be very important to cope with his fear of thunderstorms and the uncertainty of whether his party was going to go on as scheduled. As noted earlier, there are ways to make uncertain situations seem more predictable. For example, the parents can tell him when they will know whether or not they will go to the fair, the specific circumstances under which they would cancel the trip to the fair, and what they would do instead of going to the fair.

The parents' *nonverbal behavior* is as important as the words they use. Children pay a lot of attention to facial expression, physical tension, and body posture, gestures, and tone of voice. Often they don't interpret this type of behavior accurately, although they pick up our tension like sponges. If we want our children to settle down, then we must settle down first. The child runs from room to room squealing. This gets on our nerves, so we scream, "Shut up and sit down!" To our surprise, the child simply runs faster and screams louder. When you see your child getting more out of control, try to *work against the impulse*. Instead of screaming or threatening, soften your tone. Talk in a soft voice, just above a whisper. Slow your movements down. Get hold of your child gently and firmly and establish eye contact. Relax your body as much as possible and pay special attention to the expression on your face. Start to teach the child that when you are quiet, relaxed, and serious, you mean business. It is the contrast between your behavior and the child's that is the important signal. He is loud and raucous, diffuse in his behavior. You are quiet, well measured, and focused. Your behavior is novel, contrasting with his. This will draw his attention. In addition, he will have to stop his uncontrolled behavior in order to pay attention to you. This will naturally make it more difficult for him to start up again, and for the moment it gives you the advantage.

Now that you have his attention, you need to come up with a behavior-management plan. It is helpful if you have some rudimentary plans worked out in advance. You should have some idea of which approaches are more effective and which are less effective in certain situations. Generally, though, there are two routes you need to consider. The decision you have to make is whether or not your child can remain in the situation or needs to be removed. Once you get the child's attention, set your limits and foreshadow consequences right away. The child needs to know what in his behavior will lead you to make certain decisions.

If you decide the child can remain in the situation, then you have to be clear on what your rules are. What you are telling the child is that he is capable of keeping himself settled down. You will have to give a lot of feedback about his behavior, cuing him to do some things and warning him not to do others. You may need to give a lot of cues to help the child pace himself and help him pay attention to his speed of movement, tone of voice, etc. You may need to regroup children by separating quarreling siblings or making one of the children hold your hand. You may also choose to restructure the activity by giving a child something different to do. But if you opt to keep the child in the situation, you are accepting the responsibility for monitoring his behavior. You have to be very clear in your own mind as to how much of this responsibility you are agreeing to take on yourself. Remember, the more responsibility you choose, the less responsibility the child will voluntarily assume. If your child continues to act up, don't get mad. Realize, though, what he is telling you through his behavior! If he cannot soothe and settle himself in a difficult situation, even with your responsible guidance, he may be saying to you that he needs to leave the situation until he can settle down and a more concrete behavior plan can be made. This is not *your* problem, this is *his* problem, and he needs you to help him.

If you have to remove your child from a situation, the basic mechanics are still pretty much the same. All you are doing is allowing your child an opportunity to settle down so you can work out a more controlled behavior plan. The time you need will vary depending on the situation. I have had a child sit for ten seconds on the supermarket floor by the charcoal briquettes. I have also put a child in a car seat for two minutes, waiting behind the car so I was out of her line of sight but could watch over her. Once the behavior is settled, it is time to deal with the feelings. This may involve sorting and organizing both your feelings and the child's. The main thing is not to let your respective emotions become obstacles to thinking and acting responsibly. Once you talk about the feelings, move on to developing a plan of behavior, review your rules, set your limits, and foreshadow consequences. Before you go back into the situation, make sure you have a commitment from your child to follow the plan. Make sure also that he understands the consequences for noncompliance. Don't go back to work without a contract!

To Sum Up: Teaching Children about Their Feelings, Learning about Your Own

When your child has one of those "awful days"—refusing to eat peas or get dressed, picking on her brother, or acting up in the supermarket—it is easy to become consumed with the task of keeping her behavior under control. As if she were some wild beast caught in your net, you can become so occupied by all of the naughty things she is *doing* that you forget to teach her how to regulate what she is *feeling*. Emotions are not simply a by-product of misbehavior; they are a vital form of energy, necessary for self-understanding, communication, and relationships. We all want our children to control their behavior, but it is just as important for them to learn how to identify their feelings, understand them, and express them in acceptable ways. Since children will learn best by the models their parents set for them, it is crucial for you, the parent/teacher, to be able to read and regulate your own emotions.

Children's feelings are more changeable and often more volatile than those of their parents. Some children, of course, are more reactive than others and so their emotional learning is likely to occupy a more central role throughout their growth and development. It is dangerous to assume that just because children do not express their feelings outwardly, they do not *feel* them at all. Many children, like their parents, internalize their emotions. But all children, both internalizers and externalizers, need to learn how to understand their feelings as part of the larger task of understanding themselves.

Parents play a most critical role in a child's emotional learning, not only by reacting to displays of emotional fireworks with stability and soothing, but also by teaching children to regulate themselves *before* they lose control. This means that parents must help children identify troublesome situations before they walk into them. Children also need to work on ways to keep themselves in control and to recognize when they are doing a good job. Parents accomplish the most important goals in teaching emotional discipline *before* the child acts out.

The task of teaching children about their feelings is much easier if you can regulate your own. Your child may listen to what you say about self-control, but he is also watching to see how *you* manage problem situations. In the long run, your personal demonstrations of "crisis management" will probably have a more lasting impact than anything you say. This doesn't mean you are supposed to be placid and serene like some Yogi master. How many of us are wired for bliss? But you need to show your children how you sort out your feelings, settle yourself down when you are upset, and recognize when you cope successfully. Your working on your own emotional issues provides your children with a powerful model which will encourage them to learn self-control. It certainly can't hurt you, either.

But despite our wishes, we cannot anticipate all of the problems that will arise. Sometimes situations get out of control and our normal routines and teaching practices are not sufficient to meet our child's needs. Then we require a practical problem-solving approach to help our children learn and to get these nasty problems under control. Next, let us at least address some of these major catastrophes of child rearing.

11

Pearl Harbor and After

We all have television images of the Good American Family engraved in our minds in concise half-hour formats. The Nelsons, Andersons, and Bradys: cheerful families with Anglo-Saxon names who looked as if they stepped from the pages of the L. L. Bean catalogue, with lifestyles as simple and well managed as their hairstyles. Every week some unforeseen problem would disrupt the cheerful clip-clop of family life. But you could be as certain as you were of the "oh-oh" on some of the laugh tracks that they would have things back in order by the time the theme song swelled and the credits rolled. They did not bear their problems from week to week. Moreover, the parents seemed to possess a serene wisdom about their families—they saw their children in a clear light and understood their motives and actions. Of course they could—they had read the script.

But we don't have the benefit of scriptwriters, or perhaps ours don't let us see the scripts in advance. We knew the families we saw on television were not like our own, but they still stood as powerful models. They were indelible images of the "ideal family." But this "ideal" can do more harm than good to a parent's self-concept.

Real families are not always harmonious, and our problems are not resolved by the end of a weekly episode. Nor should they be! Parents and children struggle to know one another, to control and adapt to one another. Parents do not see their children in any clear light. Often it is more like a fog, with parents and children making uncertain movements toward or away from one another. We proceed by hunches, by best guesses. All children experience some problems in their lives that require some extra-special effort on the part of the parents. Granted, the majority of problems can be dealt with through scheduling, a discipline routine, and speed and volume control. The more you front-load your discipline and plan in anticipation of events, the less likely it is that many problems will arise. But this is not a panacea. Do not think that if you just do such and such you can avoid *problems*—that you can keep your child from emotional pain. Conflicts are a natural part of life, and when we learn from them, we can emerge stronger. When children learn to cope with problems, they improve both their competence and their confidence. It is important for our children to experience conflict so they can be tested. It is important for us to exert that special effort to help them through.

Many parents I see in brief therapy have questions about their own ability to handle these special problems. Often, as we discuss what they have done by following their instincts and hunches, they are able to see they have solved the problem in a reasonable, rational way. Then why all the self-doubt? Because in the Age of Good Managers, we have become obsessed with the idea that for every behavior problem, there is a correct technique to solve it. If you know the right technique you can live as in a dream, bathed in apricot- and rose-colored light. This of course is rubbish. The psychologist sitting across from you has probably experienced the same difficulties with her children that you have with yours. Now, when problems become chronic or serious, it is not because you don't know some simple technique which everyone else, including the psychologist, of course, takes for granted. What the psychologist may know, however, as a result of her experience, is how to follow a *process of rational problem solving*. She is also able to *use her feelings* in a constructive, adaptive way to help solve the problem. Finally, she *sees herself as someone who is competent* to solve it. Once again it is the process, not the technique, that is important. If the psychologist can learn the process, you can learn it too.

Before we can discuss the basic problem-solving processes that can be applied to a wide variety of special problems, we must first understand what constitutes a special or chronic problem. It is surprising how many parents have trouble recognizing problems when they occur. Next, it is important to be able to stabilize disastrous situations. As will be shown, the most important work to be done is on your own attitude toward the situation. To borrow from an old mental health saw, "There is no behavioral emergency except when the parent panics." Finally, we will outline a fairly straightforward problem-solving process and see how it applies through case studies.

WHEN DO YOU NEED TO TRY "PLAN B"?

A child throws a temper tantrum in the supermarket.

There is nothing unusual about this. Almost all children at some time or other will try a little emotional blackmail in order to get you to buy the cereal that sponsors their favorite Saturday morning cartoon. Some parents will respond with a scolding or a swat on the bottom. Some will simply ignore the behavior, while others will give in and buy the cereal. But happily, most of the time the tantrum stage is short-lived. Instead of flailing on some supermarket floor, children learn more socially acceptable ways to manipulate you into giving them what they want.

But sometimes they don't. Some children are more reactive, less inhibited, and absolutely unresponsive to reason. The parents may have tried to make the shopping trip highly routinized, but the child won't follow the plan. Simple discipline procedures don't seem to have any effect. The parents report they have tried scolding, spanking, ignoring—all to no avail. Some will simply arrange for a baby-sitter to watch the "problem child" or will drop the child off at Grandma's house before heading to the supermarket. There are a very few extremely hyperactive and usually developmentally delayed children who are simply too disorganized to go to the supermarket. Sometimes these children need special teaching programs and perhaps some medication to help them self-regulate. But these are exceptional cases. All other children can and do *need* to learn how to control their behavior in public. The question is, how do you teach them? When the usual and customary family discipline routines don't help, then "Plan A" has failed. Time to switch to "Plan B."

Many parents resist the idea that they need to develop a special "Plan B" to cope with a problem behavior. Sometimes, on the advice of a friend, they may try something in a piecemeal, halfhearted way. As soon as the child resists, the parents give up. It is not unusual for parents to claim they have tried everything and that "nothing works." They are not resigned or complacent about the problem. In fact, they may be very upset and irritated. But they talk about the problem as though it simply cannot be solved. Then they ignore it.

Other parents simply refuse to recognize problems from the start. I recall one mother who brought her child in for psychotherapy because his first-grade teacher had said he was a "handful." Now the mother, who had a degree in medical technology, was intelligent, alert, and reasonable in her thinking. Yet she denied having any problems at home and expressed wonder that her little boy could be causing such trouble at school. As she talked, though, the boy emptied her purse on the floor and tore her driver's license in half. No response. He climbed on the arm of her chair and began hitting her on the side of her head. She bounced as he hit her but, like some inflated Joe Palooka doll, seemed oblivious. When I pointed out what he was doing to her and asked if he did that sort of obnoxious thing all the time, she replied, "Well, he's just a boy, you know. Maybe he is a little tired."

Before you can switch to "Plan B," you have to recognize that "Plan A" isn't working. You have to acknowledge the problem. Why should this be so difficult? Because how our children behave has a tremendous effect on how we think and feel. Our children do not misbehave in a vacuum. Examine this for yourself. How do you feel when your child acts up in a public place? You may feel self-conscious, angry, sad, scared, and vulnerable all at the same time. We all carry hopes and expectations for our children that can be either confirmed or threatened by the way they behave. We may want a child to be socially competent and may feel shocked when she acts like a fool in front of others. We may be angry at the behavior, but we also worry about whether this is a sign of things to come. How our children behave provides a powerful emotional stimulant that makes it very difficult for us to keep our perceptions and thinking clear. Emotionalism interferes with rationality. It is no wonder that many parents will ignore or deny problem behavior clearly evident to others. Let's face it, if you don't see it, maybe it really isn't there.

Of course, if you do see it, then you have to do something about it. Not only do you have to relieve your own emotional indigestion, you also have to come up with a plan that makes sense. How do you begin?

You look at other people's children and you don't see the problems which your child is showing. You may get a lot of advice to spank the child, be easy on her and understand her feelings, offer some reward as an incentive, just ignore her, etc. None of the advice, though, seems to apply to your particular child in your particular situation. Again, the feelings of helplessness and confusion arise. It is not surprising that so many parents are unwilling to recognize problems, or that when they do, they simply throw up their hands and say nothing works.

Nonetheless, it is crucial that parents be aware when their routine discipline approach, "Plan A," is no longer effective. The process of solving problems is not really that difficult. The hard part is working through the feelings so you are able to address the problems with energy, remaining alert and flexible enough to consider different approaches.

WHAT DO YOU DO AFTER PEARL HARBOR?

Unexpectedly, your child loses all control. What should you do?

When it happens to you, it is the element of surprise that has the greatest impact. It doesn't make any difference where or when it happens. Whether it happens in the supermarket, at church, or at a friend's house, your response is still the same: dumbfounded shock. There you are, riding peacefully at anchor on that Sunday morning in Hawaii, when out of the dawn sky come the fighter bombers. What do you do? Often it may seem to you that you do very little. You are so flooded by shock, horror, and near-panic that it seems like an eternity before you respond. When you do, you feel as though you move through Jell-O, as in a dream. You are aware of everyone around you, the awful staring. Your child, still spinning out of control, wreaks more havoc and destruction before you can get to him. Your mind seems to be filled with static, and no quick, clever plans bubble to the surface. "I'm sorry, we're not at home now, but if you care to leave a message . . ." You make your escape, full of volcanic feelings, and your first question is, what was the right thing to do?

You probably did well if you managed to escape with minimal physical injury and destruction of property. You already did the right thing. Little Pearl Harbors are a part of every parent's life and must be accepted. In any situation a child can always surprise you. The next time, though, you will be ready. Given an example of what to expect, you can make a plan. Of course it is important to *recognize the problem* and take the opportunity to solve it. If it happened once, it very likely will happen again. Don't be surprised by the obvious.

But it is the feelings that are so difficult to reconcile. The initial flood of panic and shock gives way to frustration, anger, embarrassment, and despair in the aftermath. These little Pearl Harbors are to be expected, yet you feel so awful afterward. It doesn't seem fair and it isn't. No, the first question does not concern the right thing to do, but how you can take care of yourself and your feelings in the process. Try to notice what you go through, whether it is a major disaster or a tempest in a teapot. If you want a happier ending, pay attention to the process. You may not feel happy about what you go through, but you can at least learn to use your distress to your advantage. How you feel during these times of crisis can not only tell you about who you are but also reveal a great deal about your child and what he needs to learn.

Many parents will simply try to repress or deny their feelings of anguish. Maybe *good* parents aren't supposed to feel anything negative! If you are *really good,* maybe you just pay attention to your child and remain levelheaded and rational. So you want to tell your little girl to stop playing fort in the middle of the department store dress rack. You are polite. You say please. But your voice comes out like a cross between Mr. Rogers and an air raid siren. Who are you fooling? Certainly not the little homemaker. She knows just how you feel. All right, you feel distress, but if you don't organize it or acknowledge it, where does it go? If you don't deal with your feelings, they don't just disappear. Do you get headaches? How about stomachaches? If you plan to leave your feelings at home the next time you go shopping with the little darling, be sure to take along the Pepto-Bismol.

Of course, the other extreme is not helpful either and can even be destructive. Parents who mindlessly vent their anger and despair can scare their children and invite onlookers to intervene. This can create a nightmarish situation: children crying, adults arguing, and storekeepers wondering whether they should call the police. The odds are that neither the parent nor the child learns anything from the situation. The alternative to repression and denial is not unbridled expression. As always, the truest path is the most difficult one: you must search for the "happy medium."

Your own feelings not only present a powerful obstacle to problem solving, they also can give you a lot of useful information. In order to solve difficult problems effectively you have to be able to work through both the positive and negative aspects of your own feelings. Actually, there are three steps you probably need to go through in order to effectively utilize your feelings. The first step, though it may seem obvious, is to simply acknowledge the feelings you have. But more than this, try to get some sense of what these feelings are all about. Why do you have them? The second step is to use your thinking ability to help regulate your feelings. Granted, you may have a lot of very powerful feelings, but you must get them under control so you can solve the immediate problem. The best way to do this is to talk to yourself. The third step is to understand and use the types of feelings you have— they can tell you a lot about what needs to be done in the situation. Your feelings are both legitimate and instructive.

Initially you may not know what you feel besides shock. After all, the bombers coming out of the sunrise have taken you completely by surprise. As soon as possible, though, try to discern the feelings behind the shock. Are you afraid for your child because she might get hurt? Are you simply angry? Are you embarrassed by your child's display of inappropriate behavior? It is not helpful to deny these feelings or to criticize yourself for having them. Simply notice them when they occur and label them as best you can. Notice also that feelings are not usually simple, but are more often compound or complex. You may feel both anger and embarrassment, fear and irritation. Allow yourself to acknowledge the feelings when they occur. You can't stop them anyway.

Once you have identified your own feelings, try to get some sense of *why* you have them. Sometimes we can feel a strong shock simply because our child has done something completely unexpected. For a moment, we are speechless. Once the shock subsides, other feelings gradually begin to seep through, gathering in force. You may feel angry because of the blow to your expectations. You may expect your child to be capable of much more mature, organized behavior. Suddenly she behaves in some grossly disorganized fashion and you find you are furious.

Stephanie seemed very mature for a six-year-old. Her mother liked to have her around when her adult friends visited, and she was usually complimented on how smart Stephanie seemed to be. In the library one day, Stephanie began running around in the reference stacks chasing her three-year-old brother. Her mother, who was waiting in line to take out some books, cautioned her in a hoarse whisper to "please settle down." Stephanie took no notice and seemed only to squeal louder. Her mother felt a burst of fury overtake her. As though a demon had seized her, she slammed her books down on the desk and marched in a loud clip-clop over to where her daughter was climbing on top of a library table. She grabbed her forcibly by both shoulders and, shaking her, told her how angry she was. Stephanie was cold and defiant: "I don't care." The furious demon inside Mother again acted. She gave the girl a half turn and spanked her twice on the bottom with an open hand. Stephanie turned back to face her mother with a look of fury. "That didn't hurt me one bit," she snapped through her tears, "you dummy Mommy, dummy dummy dummy!" and off she ran.

In this case, the mother was overwhelmed with feelings of anger because her expectations had been dashed. But she was angry not only because of what the child did, but also because of the meaning it had for her own personal growth. The child was not behaving in a vacuum. Part of the mother's own identity was that she was able to raise a very intelligent, rational, and well behaved child. How her child behaved in public was very much tied up with the mother's own sense of well-being. This is not pathological or wrong. To some degree, we all hold expectations for our children as measures of our own self-worth. After all, our children are the products of our parenting skills. The mother was not at fault for having these feelings—we all have them. What the mother was unable to do, though, was to recognize the feelings when they occurred, so that she could regulate them. Instead, she simply acted before she thought things through.

Taking that extra moment to acknowledge your feelings and identify where they come from has two benefits. In the first place, it helps you to understand the situation and can lead you to personal growth. The second benefit is much more pragmatic. If you take that moment to identify your feelings and think them through, you are buying a little time. This moment will put some space between your feelings and your behavior and allows you the opportunity to get things under control.

The most effective way to regulate your feelings is to use verbal language. Talk to yourself. As you do this, consider some of the following points:

1. Your child is not *bad* for doing stupid things. All children do them. It is a part of being a child, and this is why it takes them twenty years to grow up and why they need someone like you to be their parent.

2. You are not *bad* because your child does stupid things. Misbehavior is the way children learn. They are presenting you with an opportunity to teach them.

3. The people around you probably do not think you are *bad* because your child is misbehaving. They are probably wondering where they put the coupon for the orange juice or how much check number 1604 was for, since it is not written down in the checkbook. If they have children of their own, they will probably sympathize with you. They've seen it all before. If they don't have any children, what do they know anyway?

4. It's time to focus in on your child. By misbehaving, your child is telling you she needs to learn something. Is now the time to teach it or do you need to make a simple, orderly retreat? Sometimes parents can think of clever things to do on the spot to teach the child.

> A father is waiting on the checkout line with a basket full of groceries. The baby is in the cart and the four-year-old boy is grabbing all the candy out of the rack. Dad looks at the baby and says, "You're being such a big girl, sitting there, that I am going to buy you an ice cream cone. But I only get ice cream for little kids who listen, help their dad, and don't make messes." Hearing this, the little boy shouts, "I will, I will!" and puts back all the candy and helps his father unload the cart.

Sometimes all the clever tricks just seem to backfire.

> A father is waiting on the checkout line with a basket full of groceries. The baby is in the cart and the four-year-old boy is grabbing all the candy out of the rack. Dad winks at the lady behind him and, turning to the boy, says, "I bet you can't put all of that candy back and help me unload this cart. I bet you can't count everything I've got here. Besides, I might have a treat for you." The boy looks up at his father and says, "Who cares? Keep your dumb old treat—I got this." He holds

up a Snickers bar and, right before his father's eyes, tears off the wrapper and begins to eat it.

When you get hit by a surprise attack, don't put too much pressure on yourself to be perfect. Sometimes a simple intervention such as a brief time-out, a shift of attention to a well-behaved sibling, or a threatened removal of some reward may solve the problem. In cases of the true surprise attack, though, it usually doesn't work. When the child does something awful or goes over the edge, there isn't much you can do. The child may be too uncontrolled and you may be too angry or exhausted. In an emergency, your goal is to stabilize the situation so you can get through it in one piece. Finish doing what you need to do as efficiently and quietly as you can. Help contain the child's behavior, perhaps by grabbing a couple of limbs or a few articles of clothing—whatever you can get hold of without hurting the child. Make whatever apologies you feel are necessary. These are usually more effective if your tone is quiet and your statements are simple and straightforward: "Looks like this little guy is really out of control. I need to get him home so I can help him settle down." Then make an orderly, quiet retreat.

Once you are away from the situation, the raw emotions of the emergency will diminish. This will allow you to reflect on what happened. Again, it is important to think about your own feelings as well as the child's behavior. Be sure to acknowledge what you did well in handling the situation, even if you simply managed to blunt the effects of the disaster. If you managed to get yourself and your child away from the situation without a great deal of destruction and bloodletting, you probably did your job well. Now it is time to concentrate on the next step. Your child has shown you he needs to learn something and has provided you with an opportunity to teach it. Allow "Pearl Harbor" to go by the boards. You were surprised, caught off guard; no one under the same circumstances would have done any better. Now you have the opportunity to think about what happened and to make a plan. The next time, you will be ready.

SOLVING SPECIAL PROBLEMS

Before you can attack these special problems you need a method or a strategy. In this section we will outline a straightforward approach to dealing with those special behavior problems. The process involves a sequence of steps:

1. Identifying the problem
2. Evaluating what you have tried before
3. Generating a new plan
4. Troubleshooting
5. Giving the plan a fair test
6. Making adjustments

You will notice there are no real surprises here, no innovative or clever techniques. Frankly, I don't trust them. This problem-solving process is one that is commonly used by many practicing therapists. It is not flashy, but it works. If you are able to apply this approach to many of the special problems that arise in family living, you may find you are able to cope with most of them. First we will examine each part of the process in greater detail, and subsequently, using case studies, we will see how the process can be applied to various problems.

1. Identifying the Problem

What exactly is the problem? Sometimes it is very hard for parents to describe it in concrete terms. Instead, they will often describe the impact of the child's behavior on their feelings. They may describe their own frustration. But the problem needs to be defined in very clear, concrete terms. What does the child do? When and where does the child exhibit this behavior? When you define the problem in terms of specific behaviors, you are helping yourself in three ways. In the first place, you are giving yourself something very concrete to work on. By focusing on specific behaviors, you will see the problem can be contained. This makes it seem less overwhelming, more psychologically manageable. As always, it is important to maintain a positive mind-set about discipline. Finally, concrete definitions afford you the opportunity to define the new skill you want your child to learn.

Consider this situation:

> The boy's mother was very upset with him. "This one," she said with a disdainful flip of the hand, "just never listens to me."
>
> "Is that what you want to work on?" asked the psychologist. He immediately began to think about ways to strengthen behavior that would help the child's interpersonal communication. He started to think of ways to improve the child's eye contact. He also thought of having the child repeat back requests and directions so the mother could be sure he had heard them.
>
> As they talked on, it became apparent that the boy had no trouble paying attention in most situations. The only time it seemed he "never" listened was when his mother would ask him to clean up his room or put his toys away.

The problem in this example is very common in many families. The parents will say the child "never listens" or "is very rude." Their definition is vague, overgeneralized, and couched in the terms of their own frustration. It is hard to address a "rudeness" problem, especially if it occurs "all the time" and "everywhere." Fortunately, the actual problems the parents want to work on are much more specific. In the example, the actual problem has nothing to do with the child's auditory process, but concerns his willingness to comply with demands and requests under very specific conditions. As it turns out, the mother does not want to work on a *listening problem* at all. She wants him to comply with some very specific requests.

If I ever did come across a child who "never" listens or is "always" rude, I would feel pretty overwhelmed and hopeless right from the start. If I were in that parent's shoes, I would be inclined to see what is on television and forget about the problem until tomorrow—maybe. But in this example the problem doesn't occur "always." For the most part, the boy is very compliant, especially if he has to do something to get something he wants. He is noncompliant only when he is asked to pick up his toys or clean his room. Now the problem is not so overwhelming. The parent can make a plan and through a trial-and-error process eventually solve the problem.

Our own feelings can have a powerful influence on the way we see problems and choose to work on them. A mother who is very frustrated with her child may feel he never listens to her. Is there a parent who has never felt frustration because a child is defiant or refuses to follow a request or direction? Sometimes parents and children can get locked into an intense, stalemated power struggle over these household rules. Actually, there may be two problems this parent needs to work on. The first is not so much the child's behavior as the mother's feelings. The child's behavior has repercussions. When he ignores requests to clean his room, the mother feels a powerful surge of frustration and anger. She may be bothered by all sorts of unreasonable thoughts. She may think that her child doesn't love her, that she is a bad parent, or that she is simply too stupid to solve the problem. None of these are true, but her powerful feelings of frustration are clearly blocking her ability to see the problem from the child's point of view. Therefore, before she can even begin to work on the child's behavior, she has to find some way to settle her own feelings of anger and frustration.

The second problem in this situation must be defined from the child's point of view. What do you want the child to learn? Often, parents will state they want the child to stop hitting his sister, to stop running away in stores, or to stop getting down from the table at mealtime. But look at how this phrasing shapes your approach to discipline. The most obvious approach to stopping a behavior is through punishment. What you have already found is that even in cases where punishment is effective, it will usually stop the behavior only for a short period. So the child stops being rude to his sister for an hour or two. So what? The main problem is to get the child to learn a more appropriate behavior that will take the place of "rudeness."

When you define the problem you are working on, try to think in terms of behaviors you want to strengthen. The little boy in the preceding example has trouble being responsible for himself. He needs to look after his own toys and other belongings. When you encounter one of these difficult problems, be careful how you define it in the first place. What is it about the child's behavior you want to change? Under what conditions does the problem occur? What is it you want the child to learn?

2. Evaluating What You Have Tried Before

Before you can actively solve the problem you are working on, you must think about all the things you have tried in the past and how well they've worked. The first step is to make a list of all the different approaches. It is important at this stage not to be too critical. Then you need to evaluate what you have tried. Going through a process such as this will give you some clues as to what you might try next.

> As the mother thought about what she had tried, she was able to generate an impressive list of failed strategies. She had of course tried reminding, then nagging. The parents had tried a sticker chart on the refrigerator and they had also tried giving an allowance. If the boy didn't put his toys away, they would confiscate them for a week. Finally, once they even tried grounding him. The mother found this intolerable because he spent the whole day following her from room to room, whining unmercifully.

As in our ongoing example, when you encounter difficulties with your own child you will be surprised at how many approaches you have tried. When you generate your list, be sure to be fair to yourself. Think of all the ways you have tried, even if some of them seem trivial, unsystematic, or inconsistent. The important first step is simply to generate a list.

At this point also pay attention to your own thoughts and feelings. Do you criticize yourself for not being strong or consistent enough? Do you find you are becoming angry and critical of your child? These thoughts and feelings are not bad! Try not to repress or deny them when they occur. Any parent who has been frustrated in her attempt to help her child will feel anger both at herself and toward the noncompliant little tyke. But these feelings can exert a powerful influence on your ability to think about the problem and to solve the problem in the future. So as you evaluate what you have tried in the past, listen to your own inner responses.

Once you have put together a list of all the things you have tried, it is time to evaluate how well each has worked.

> Mother found that she was giving too many reminders and that the nagging didn't seem to work at all. Eventually she would pick up his room because she found the mess intolerable. The sticker chart worked for one week but then mysteriously disappeared from the fridge. Even though the boy was very excited about getting an allowance, he was never able to organize his behavior enough to make it to the first payday. His parents discontinued this after two weeks. The mother stated that she and her husband were most frustrated when they tried to confiscate

his favorite toys. The boy's response was impassive. He said he didn't care if they took his toys, that he had others to play with. Of course Mother tried grounding him that once but didn't think she could handle that again without Valium.

In this example, the family has tried most of the stock approaches to discipline problems. Clearly none of them have worked very effectively. But when the therapist and the mother sift through the rubble, they find a number of very important clues that will help them develop a new plan. In the first place, it is the parents who are clearly feeling all of the frustration. They are carrying all of the urgency to solve the problem. The boy sits quietly and waits to see what the parents will come up with next. He does not feel any urgency to solve the problem and is therefore not going to take on any responsibility. Why should he? The parents are feeling enough anger and urgency for all concerned.

In the second place, each plan has been tried out for only a short period of time. Once the parents have encountered failure, they have immediately switched to a radical new approach. The novelty of a new behavioral program usually wears off fairly quickly. Even though the boy may comply for a couple of days or even a week, his behavior soon returns to normal. When the parents see this, they immediately drop the program and switch to something else. Even though they have tried a lot of different approaches, they haven't given each of them a fair test. What the boy has learned from all this is that he is much more persistent than his parents. If he simply holds out, the parents will give up and try something new.

Finally, the boy has found out his persistence pays off in a single important way. If he simply leaves the mess, it is intolerable to his mother. If he waits long enough, it is very likely that she will clean it up. Now, note that the mother does not clean up the mess every single day. In fact, the boy is not even sure when or if she will clean up his mess. But she has done this often enough that he is willing to take the gamble.

Some people have trouble giving a fair critique because of the hard-and-fast notions they hold of "correct discipline." Some parents *believe* in spanking even though their child has never learned a thing from it. Actually, some are not so much concerned with whether the child learns as with whether the child sees them as strong-willed. They don't want him to think he is getting away with something. Other parents refuse to give reinforcement strategies a try because they feel rewards are simply *bribes*. It is very important to discover your own biases about rewarding and punishing. Your attitudes can color what you will allow yourself to see. When you are trying to help your child learn a new skill, it is important to see as clearly as possible.

When you evaluate what you have tried before, look closely at your own behavior and the child's. How does your child respond to punishments? Does the effect carry over for a day? A week? Will your child work for positive rewards? What happens to you when the child does not respond at all? Who feels the urgency? Who feels the responsibility? Were there some approaches that seemed to work very well initially but lost their effectiveness over time? Did the child simply lose interest? Were you inconsistent in following through? These and other questions can help you as you proceed to the next stage.

3. Generating a New Plan

Once you have defined the problem clearly and have examined everything you have tried previously, you must attempt to construct a new plan. You do this by building on what you have learned from your prior experience. Eliminate outright those approaches that have had no effect. Start building on those approaches that have had some marginal impact on the problem. How did things break down before? How can you combine elements so that the approach is more cohesive? What sorts of things motivate the child? How can you keep the plan interesting enough for the child to continue? How can you discourage regressive, limit-testing behavior? How does this problem situation affect you? How does the child use the situation to manipulate your behavior? How can you adjust your own behavior so the child is more likely to learn from the situation?

The mother began to focus on the question of how she would teach her son to be more responsible for his own belongings. The first step was to set some clear goals. What did she want him to do? She decided that "being responsible for his belongings" meant that her son must:

1. make sure his bicycle and other "outside toys" were put away before dinner

2. properly pick up and organize his room every Saturday morning before he could watch cartoons
3. pick up his toys when she told him to
4. clear his bedroom floor of toys and clothes before bedtime

Now, the boy liked his Saturday morning cartoons and he also liked to eat. By simply adjusting the schedule, problems one and two were easily dealt with. The major difficulties came with the other two responsibilities. He did not generally respond when he was told to do something. He also did not like going to bed at night and didn't mind if his toys were on the floor. However, his mother was already relieved to be able to focus on two very specific problems and didn't feel so overwhelmed anymore. A rational problem-solving approach dictates that you deal with the simple problems first. Isolate the ones that are more difficult, more resistant to scrutiny. Again, the most important issue is not merely finding something that works, but also being able to see that the problem is manageable. Once the easier problems are taken care of, it is time to focus on the more difficult ones.

The mother now began to look at ways to teach the boy to pick up his toys on demand. As she examined her own behavior, she found she was fairly inconsistent and unpredictable in her demands. Sometimes she would let the boy play all day, and by dinnertime, the whole bottom floor of the house would be covered with toys. On other days when she was feeling more irritable, she felt as though she badgered him every few minutes to pick up this sock or that truck. She decided to be more systematic and predictable and looked at the naturally occurring daily schedule for the optimal pick-up times. She decided she would have better compliance if she had him pick up his toys at transition times before some other desired activity. These activities included snacks, lunch, TV, and playing with a friend. The mother developed a specific pick-up routine. This seemed to take care of the third problem.

Without even having to resort to extravagant or complex reinforcement schemes, the mother is able to deal with three of the four problems. Notice how she uses the naturally occurring schedule of the day. Do you want your dessert, little boy? First eat your broccoli. Now it was time to move in on the last, the most difficult problem.

The mother then thought about how to get the boy to tidy up his room before bedtime. All the nagging and threats of punishment had had no effect. They simply made her feel all the anger. The boy was fairly passive. She decided she had been focusing too much on the negative aspect of his behavior and had not been building up the positive side enough. She then thought about what she wanted him to learn and how to sell him on it. She decided to define picking up his room as part of "big boy" behavior and to contrast that with the behavior of his little brother, who needed help with dressing and using the toilet. She talked about some privileges and freedoms that were associated with being a big boy. Big boys, for example, got to go to bed half an hour later than their little brothers. They were also allowed to go over to their friend's house and to cross the street by themselves. They were also allowed to choose some movies at the video store. They were also their dad's special helper on the weekend. Now, there were a number of ways he could show his parents he was a "big boy." One way was to take care of himself. Little boys certainly couldn't do that, but he could. When he took care of his things, then his parents would know he was ready for these privileges and freedoms. His mother decided to put some stars on his calendar whenever he showed them he could take care of his things. She decided for the time being not to be any more systematic than that. She didn't want to make the process too mechanical. But she did want to keep it very positive and to focus on building the child's concept of himself as the "responsible older brother."

The stars on the calendar will probably have a reinforcing effect. The little boy may actually like to see more stars on his calendar and may not like it when one of the squares is empty. But the mother presents the charting as "a way of keeping track." The boy may place some reinforcing value in the stars, but Mother is careful to keep her own feelings separate. This is very important because often when parents use a charting system to reinforce behavior, they find it means a lot more to them than it does to the child.

Mother also decides to monitor her own emotional behavior. Up to this point she has found that the child's passivity and noncompliance make her very angry. She has been the one who has carried all the urgency and has felt all the responsibility for him to change. Now she has set up a system which should be able to take care of itself. If the child wants B, he has to do A first. The mother is very careful to watch her own verbal and nonverbal behavior so she does not communicate a lot of tension or urgency to the child. In order to pull this off, though, she needs to actively watch herself and to talk to herself. She works out a way so she and her husband can monitor each other and mutually support one another.

4. Troubleshooting

Simply coming up with a new plan may not be enough; after all, you have tried these plans before and how well have they worked? Before you actually try the new plan out, think it through carefully to anticipate any obvious trouble spots.

> The mother knew from previous experience that these sorts of plans would work for perhaps one week. The boy was intrigued by shiny new things and especially if there were stars and charts. This would be a "honeymoon." She knew the real test of the program wouldn't come until the second week. Therefore she decided to give the plan a good two weeks before making any adjustments. She also tried to think about what types of problems would arise. How would the boy test the limits? Suppose he simply forgot? On three of the four problems there were naturally occurring consequences to take care of that. After all, if the boy wanted to eat, play with a friend, or watch cartoons, certain things had to happen first. Suppose something came up unexpectedly that required the family to leave before his toys and clothes were picked up? Mother decided she would define that as an "emergency" and that as soon as possible life would get back to normal. She would be very careful, though, to make sure "emergencies" did not happen too often. Suppose he simply refused . . .

When you troubleshoot a program, try to anticipate what problems are likely to occur. Don't expect you are going to anticipate all possible problems; just try to think about the more obvious ones. Some of the issues that are easiest to deal with are the clear black-and-white ones. The child refuses or forgets. How do you deal with these? It is much more difficult to anticipate and come up with plans for the more grey-area problems. Suppose the child only does a marginal job. At what point do you impose a consequence? Suppose you are simply tired and you start to let things slide. How are you going to safeguard against that? If you can identify some holes in the plan, try to plug them up as best you can. Don't expect you are going to have a perfect plan on your first try. You want to plan for the types of difficulties that might arise but allow yourself some margin of error. When you have completed your troubleshooting, get ready to take the plan out for a trial run.

5. Giving the Plan a Fair Test

The only way you will know whether the plan actually works is to give it a fair test. This means you have to give the plan enough time to get through the honeymoon period. Also give the child a chance to poke a few holes in it, to see how badly it leaks. Sometimes you may be very lucky and the child will be perfectly cooperative. He will go along with the program quite agreeably and you will never experience another troublesome day in your life. Normal children, though, being inquisitive and devious, won't let you get by that easily.

Before you take the plan out for a test run, be sure you have a way to present it to the child. With most children, you will be more successful if the behavior plan is presented positively—even if it involves a punishment. You have a special plan that is going to help your child grow and develop. You are going to teach him a whole new way to behave so he is more competent, more able to stand on his own two feet.

> The mother tells the boy she has been very concerned about the way things have been going. She feels she and his father have not been helping him to learn how to take care of himself. They have been thinking about this and they have come up with a way that will really help him. She then presents the plan in considerable detail; she gives him a new calendar and shows him how she is going to put stars on it to keep track. He asks a few technical questions about the consequences. After this, much to the mother's surprise, the boy seems to accept the plan in a very matter-of-fact way. But the mother also knows that deep inside the boy's mind, in the war room, the computers are already working.

You can anticipate that within a couple of weeks the child will find most of the weak spots in the plan. Sometimes children will simply dig in their heels and refuse to comply. When consequences are imposed, they say they don't care. If this happens, refer back to the previous chapters. Remember, don't look for immediate impact. A child may be willing to accept consequences in the short term, especially if he believes you will give up at the first sign of failure. Look for a gradual change in behavior over the full course of the trial period. Sometimes children will hold out for a week until they sense you are really not going to give up. Then their behavior will turn around.

Before you test the plan, you have to believe in it. It is not enough simply to try something on the advice of some expert. In my own practice, when I hear the words "I'll try it, but I don't think it will work," I know the plan is doomed to failure. Usually I stop everything right there and start from scratch again. You are the only one who can make the plan work. If you don't believe that it can succeed, don't waste your time with it. Why set yourself up to fail?

Before you try out the plan, be sure your mental attitude is positive and constructive. Certainly things may not go perfectly. They may not even go well. What the child is going to show you during the first couple of weeks is what she needs to learn and how well your plan will teach her. She will show you all the flaws and, through her behavior, will tell you what you need to do to correct them. Failure is not bad, it is instructive. Let your child teach you.

6. Making Adjustments

The course of true parenting never did run smoothly. Nobody's perfect and nobody can come up with a perfect plan that will work for all situations. We may have a nice blueprint on the drawing board, but our children are clever enough to reacquaint us with the demands of the real world. Therefore, after the trial period has ended, it is important to make whatever adjustments are necessary.

Think of this process as "tightening up." Unless there is some major disaster, it may be unwise to radically change the whole plan. Remember, your child has probably been through this type of experience before. If he pokes a hole in your new battleship, everyone abandons ship. Children learn very quickly that if they are persistent, you will give up. They come to expect it. I am very concerned when parents tell me they have tried *everything* to deal with a problem and can list off ten or twelve approaches they have used in the past month. Clearly, none of them have been given a fair test.

Granted, there may be some situations in which a totally unexpected disaster occurs. Remember the earlier story about Thaddeus, who liked to poke his classmates. Certainly in this case, the behavior plan taught the boy to be more aggressive in order to get attention. The psychologist was correct in stopping the plan before any further damage was done.

But usually this is not the case. Some children may test limits severely. They may throw temper tantrums or use other types of bullying tactics to make you back down. They simply want to see if you will stand by your word. Do you really mean what you say? Although you must stick to your guns, you will usually need to make some adjustments to deal with loopholes or other unforeseen problems.

On the whole, the behavior program went very well. The boy did try the usual sorts of tests: forgetting, dawdling, and several days of out-and-out refusal. The parents stuck by the program, and once the boy saw they meant business, he happily complied for the most part. He cleaned his room before his Saturday morning cartoons and turned this into a Saturday morning ritual. After several skirmishes he began getting his outside toys put away before dinner. He did, though, miss dinner a couple of nights before he realized his parents were going to hold to their limits. Now the boy was abundantly well fed. They had more difficulty getting him to pick up his toys on demand. Here he did refuse several times and seemed willing to give up his snack, a chance to play with a friend, and even his lunch in order to test out the situation. He had chosen his ground and decided to fight his battle here.

At this point the parents have found their first real obstacle. This is not uncommon in working through behavior problems with children. Children tend to be fairly fixed and inflexible in their approaches to problem solving. Their strategy is straightforward: refuse to comply and tell the parents anything they do won't hurt. Most very young children behave this way. If you really look at their behavior they are not as devious as they may seem. They usually have a limited number of behavioral strategies that they will try.

As adults we have the mental capacity to be a lot more flexible than our children. But this means we have to take that step back from the problem, examine it from a distance, and think about new approaches.

When the mother saw this refusal was in earnest, she recognized a familiar ploy. The boy would be unmoved no matter what consequences were threatened. But she was surprised to see how easily she fell into an old automatic pattern in response. She tried an escalating series of threats, and when none of these had any effect, she began to assume more of the responsibility for solving the problem. The boy in turn felt less of the burden and also less of the urgency. She decided the most important thing to do was to keep from getting into the power struggle. She would not take on his anger no matter how he taunted her with his "I don't care." To this she responded with "You don't have to care, that's all right. But it's lunchtime. Before you can eat, the toys have to go away." She left it at that and went into the kitchen. She was surprised and bothered by the fact that he chose to skip his lunch and to leave his toys on the floor.

She decided to resist the temptation to throw up her hands, and to hold out through snack time. Again the toys stayed on the floor, but this time the boy was not so passive. He cried and whined at her about how hungry he was and accused her of starving him. At this point she turned very sympathetic. "Of course you can eat, honey. I want you to eat. But you know the rule. Your snack is waiting for you and you can have it as soon as you pick up the toys. Why do you want to make yourself miserable?"

Once again, he tried to shift the burden to her by saying it was not he who was making *himself* miserable but his mother. Again she offered sympathetic support but held firm to the limit. He quickly threw his toys into the box but left a few scattered by a chair. She reminded him gently that all the toys needed to be off the floor. With great declamations and beating of breast, he threw the toys into the box and stomped into the kitchen to eat his snack. She allowed him the time on his own. She did not gloat. She did not rub salt into his wound. As before, she was gentle, sympathetic, and matter-of-fact. The battle over the toy box had been won. So he shifted his energy to bedtime.

When you consider changing strategies, you have to evaluate where things break down. Sometimes the reinforcements or the incentives to behave are not sufficient to help the child change. Sometimes, as in this particular case, it becomes a battle of attitudes. If the child can get you to see the problem in a certain light, you may be less willing to persist. Here the child was very skillful at making the parent feel responsible for his hunger. Fortunately the mother was levelheaded enough to realize that her child was not starved, was in fact well fed, and that the strategy was a fairly old mechanical one. But still the tug was strong. When the behavior did change, the mother was very careful not to humiliate the child. She might have chosen to go right in and lecture the boy about being more responsible while he was eating his snack. Instead of graham crackers and nectarine, he would have been eating crow. However, this only would have served to frustrate and anger the boy and possibly to elicit another power struggle. Instead, the mother downplayed the whole effect of the power struggle and concentrated only on the responsible behavior the child showed. But she did this in a muted, toned-down way.

Sometimes, though, the behavior plan contains a hole big enough to drive a truck through. When this happens, the necessary adjustments must be made to close the gap. Consider the next phase of the problem.

The boy complied with the nightly room cleanup plan for one week. After that, he stated that he wasn't really interested. His toys and clothes were on the floor at bedtime and the parents started to lapse back into nagging him to pick things up. He was not especially fond of going to bed, so he didn't really care about having a power struggle at nighttime. Both the mother and the father could feel the mercury of their anger rising rapidly. With each power struggle it felt as though the boy were handing them a large ball of emotional yuck: "Here, Mom and Dad, you take it, it's yours." He liked being a big boy and liked the privileges and freedoms he got from this. But he was clearly having some trouble connecting those privileges and freedoms to the immediate power struggle over cleaning his room. The mother and father also knew that for some reason he was baiting them to get them angry. They needed to decline that gambit but still make it more worthwhile to him to be responsible.

Often our problem solving breaks down because we think of only one step at a time. If a child resists or breaks through, we have no backup plan. This is what often happens when parents try a very simple time-out. Most parents find that a graded time-out, one with several levels, is usually more successful.

Some resistance can be dealt with through troubleshooting, but you should always be ready for the likelihood that the child will find a weak area of the plan and you will need to come up with some alternate strategies.

Again it is important not to panic. The child has simply shown you that what you have come up with is not sufficient to teach him. He is also exercising his creativity and showing you he has the capacity for complex thought. Children can also use the element of surprise, as the little boy with the Snickers bar showed us at the beginning of the chapter. However, remember: they can always get you once, but the next time you will be ready.

Whenever a child learns a new skill, you have to not only encourage the new behavior but also discourage attempts to return to immature, disorganized, or inappropriate types of behavior. In the current example, the mother developed a plan based solely on encouragement. She worked very hard to define the new behavior in a very positive light and attempted to sell the child on all the advantages of carrying out the new behavior. However, change is difficult, not only for adults but also for children. In part, the boy's sense of himself and his relationship with his parents was based around the anger everyone felt when they tried to make him do something. If he was going to change his behavior and become more responsible on his own, he was going to have to change the way he thought about himself and the way he got along with his parents. That's pretty scary for a little child. Most children will not take on a new self-concept without a good test. This little boy is no different. It is not enough for the parents simply to encourage him to try something new; they also have to show him that returning to the old way of behaving will no longer be satisfying. The child will be more likely to move toward warmth and light if his old resting place is cold and dark.

The mother decided she had to actively discourage the child from his irresponsible behavior, but she also knew he was looking for any sign that she was becoming angry or frustrated. She told him she and his father were going to change the nighttime routine a little bit; they knew they were encouraging him to be a big boy, but sometimes boys his age just weren't ready. He said he was ready, but she reminded him that he told them things by both his words and his behavior. Sometimes his behavior told them he wasn't ready.

She then gave him quite a list of the privileges and freedoms he enjoyed as a big boy. She told him if he was not ready to be a big boy, she could certainly understand that and she would help him. She would be happy to come in and help pick up his toys and clean his room. But if she had to do that, she was also going to look after him in other ways as well. For one thing, he could not stay up as late as he did, and he probably shouldn't be playing with a lot of the toys he had, because they were only for big boys. If she had to come in and pick up his toys, she would have to look them over carefully to see if they were the sorts of things that a little boy should be playing with. They would also have to restrict his outside play because little boys needed much more supervision.

In all, she listed about a dozen ways in which his privileges and freedoms would be drastically curtailed. However, she was very careful not to threaten and watched her tone of voice very closely. That night, the boy immediately tested the new limit. Mother, though, followed through exactly as she had said and braced herself for a couple of awful days. They *were* awful, but the mother and father were careful to support each other through this and to provide each other with sufficient breaks so they could manage it better. At the end of the second day, they brought up the big-boy issue again in a very matter-of-fact tone. This time the boy said he was very ready to try the program. They said they weren't sure, but they would be happy to let him have another chance. He took great pride in proving they were wrong about him.

It would be foolish to assert that complex behavior problems can be solved immediately by simple strategies. There are a number of factors working against you. First of all, by the time you and your child are trying to solve a special behavior problem, you have already tried a number of different approaches. You have a history of trials and errors behind you and have accumulated a strong set of attitudes and expectations. The child believes he is a certain type of person and sees his relationship with you in a certain light. You have similar beliefs about the child. It is hard to change attitudes, not only in ourselves but also in our children. People tend to resist these sorts of changes, especially if they come from the outside. As you have probably found out, simple plans don't work. The type of problem solving outlined here will give you some more flexibility to cope with these difficult problems. But be alert to the fact that you are not just changing some behavioral mechanics. The behavior you are trying to change is rooted in and sustained by your relationship with the child. When you change behavior, you are also changing beliefs, expectations, and conceptions about that relationship.

To Sum Up: Changing Attitudes As Well As Behavior

In the Age of Good Managers we are led to expect that if we know the right techniques, we can solve almost any problem. This is a dream.

Life in your family is not rose-colored. It is not rose-colored in anyone else's either. Trust in that. Conflict is merely a normal part of living. It is a natural phenomenon that occurs whenever you get three or four people living under the same roof who are merging to form a family yet simultaneously pulling away to establish individual identities. So many of us are afraid of conflict, as if it were something awful and destructive. Yet conflict can be used constructively to define the boundaries and the relationships among the individuals in a family.

But while it is important to use conflict in a growth-producing way, it is also important not to be oppressed by it. While it is unhealthy to avoid conflict altogether, it is equally unhealthy to see your relationship with another member of the family as based only on conflict and stress. Yet if we see ourselves as constantly frustrated in our relationship with our children, that belief is exactly what we are supporting. Our power struggles are not isolated acts of behavior. They generate and nurture enduring attitudes, values, and beliefs. There is an old saying: "Some people have many different experiences; some have the same experience many times." It is very easy for parents to fall into self-defeating patterns of behavior. We are not so different from our children in this respect. We like reality to be predictable and controllable. If we think about our relationship with our children as having a certain quality, then we expect that this quality will be borne out through our interactions with the child.

So often we are led to expect that we should be child-centered in our parenting: we need to focus on what the child's experience is, what she needs to learn. Certainly this is very important, but we cannot forget ourselves in the process. We are not merely manipulating our child with mechanical arms from behind a glass shield. We grow through our interaction with our child, face to face, skin to skin. It is not sufficient to work on the tricks and techniques that make our child behave in a certain way. We need to first consider our own feelings and our relationship with the child. We need to be careful to separate our issues from those of the child.

As we discussed, how a parent feels can be both a powerful obstacle and a source of information in effective discipline. We can allow ourselves to be trapped by our own attitudes, values, and beliefs so that even though we may feel angry and desperate, we cannot allow ourselves ways to solve the problem. We try "new techniques" and give up the minute they fail. Like poor workmen, we blame our tools. We hear advice from Dr. Wizard and grudgingly accept it, knowing in our hearts that it will not work. What are we really saying to ourselves? Clearly, when we have this much resistance to new ideas or simply get stuck in self-defeating patterns of thinking, we have some work to do on our own before we can help the child.

This has nothing to do with blame. It is not "bad" for parents to feel angry and frustrated or to get stuck in their thinking. Most parents that I know of are very isolated in many ways. Granted, there may be a wealth of information on television and in magazines, but open, compassionate communication among parents is often missing. Parents often feel as though they are moving through a fog, never quite sure of their way or what lurks in their path. No, it is certainly not wrong for parents to have these feelings of frustration and anger, but it is very important for them to recognize these feelings and to work them through when they can.

Even the process of working through chronic problems is a difficult one. We looked at a fairly complex but flexible way to identify and work through these problems when they occur. This working-through process involves a number of steps: 1) correctly identifying the problem; 2) evaluating what you have tried in the past; 3) generating a new plan; 4) troubleshooting; 5) giving the plan a fair trial; and 6) making adjustments. The approach is based on a rational problem-solving technique. Pay careful attention to what your child needs to learn and how she learns best. No two children learn in quite the same way, so maintain some flexibility in the teaching process. Stay with programs and give them an adequate test, avoiding radical shifts that only serve to confuse the child.

Ultimately you are not just changing a set of simple behaviors. You are influencing how your child understands herself and her relationship with you. You are also affecting your self-concept as a rational, capable parent. Discipline problems can serve an important constructive purpose and that is why we must approach them carefully.

There are bound to be those times or situations in which we are simply not able to go it alone. Even though we have done all the right things, there may be issues between ourselves and our child which we cannot overcome on our own. There are many circumstances in which parents may need the help of other people. Your child may have a developmental problem that requires a radical approach to discipline. You simply may not have sufficient knowledge and may need the advice of an expert. There could also be issues in your personal life that make it more difficult for you to parent your child effectively. There may be strains in the marriage or problems at work. You may find you have a diminished capacity to tolerate stress or adjust to the demands of others. Finally, you may simply feel isolated and perplexed. Sometimes we just need the reassurance that comes through a helping relationship with another individual. We will next discuss when to seek the help of a therapist as well as some issues involved in developing and maintaining a therapeutic relationship.

12

When to Send
for the Cavalry

As much as we would like to be the masters of our own destiny, it is not always possible. Sometimes even the best of managers needs a consultant or two. It is no different for parents, especially those who have difficult children. Sometimes the problems are too distressing or we are too distressed to go it alone. Then, despite our best intentions or strongest resolutions, it is vital that we seek the help we need. The self-help books are no longer sufficient. We need another mind, another view, another source of energy. This source often comes in the form of therapy.

The first issue to deal with is how to tell when you need a therapist. It is important to understand who these therapists are and what they do. Therapy is a process of working through, not a set of pat answers. Therapy helps those who *seek* the help, who feel the urgency and the need for change.

Simply put, parents seek therapy because someone is distressed. Either they are distressed about their child's behavior or the child is personally distressed. Sometimes, though, the atmosphere at home is as placid as a fish pond, but the child's school life is in an uproar. Any of these situations *could* be sufficient to warrant some type of outside therapy. Whether or not it is necessary depends on the specifics of the situation.

ANXIOUS ANGELS

The most obvious and probably the least common scenario is when the child is distressed and directly asks for help.

Julie was an eight-year-old who midway through third grade began having severe headaches. Medical examinations could not determine any physical cause for the headaches. In addition, she was having trouble sleeping; her parents would find her pacing the floor at 10:00 at night, worrying about her schoolwork. Her appetite declined and she began to lose weight. She asked to see somebody at school, but because of budget cuts, there was no developmental guidance counselor at the elementary school. Her parents asked her if she would like to "talk to somebody" outside of the school and she agreed.

It is not very common for young children to ask for help on their own. Occasionally, though, some bright, usually anxious children will recognize her own distress and will ask for help. Often these are children who tend to internalize their feelings or who experience them through the body either in the form of headaches or stomachaches. In the above case, Julie was asking for help with her headaches and difficulty in sleeping. Therapy revolved around her immediate concerns and started with a fairly concrete behavioral approach to her problems. Julie was a highly motivated and very bright little girl who was willing to follow a relaxation program and a self-monitoring program. The therapy then moved to issues that were probably at the root of the headaches. Julie was a very rigid, perfectionistic child—and had been so since early on. She had always had difficulty adjusting to change and had never been able to adapt to failure. Unfortunately, through the luck of the draw, Julie had a third-grade teacher who seemed at first glance to be perfectionistic and demanding. Each day Julie went to school with her stomach tied in knots. Part of the therapy involved helping Julie to change how she thought about herself, especially in demanding situations. Another aspect of therapy was to try to work with the school to make appropriate adaptations as well. The teacher was surprisingly responsive to the child's needs, and by the spring of the year, the headaches were gone, Julie's sleep pattern had improved, and she was making excellent progress in school.

DISTRESSED PARENTS

More often than not, families come into therapy because the parents are the ones who are distressed by the child's behavior. Sometimes the child is exhibiting chronic behavior problems, which might be the direct outgrowth of some temperamental characteristics. Very impulsive, labile children who are prone to acting out often fall into this category. There is no acute distress as in the case of Julie. Usually parents are worn down by the never-ending defiance, temper tantrums, and power struggles.

When I first saw Alec he was nine years old. He marched into my office ahead of his mother and father, flopped into the largest and most comfortable chair, and threw his feet up onto my desk. The father, who was purpling with anger, entreated him in a hoarse whisper to please sit in the small chair. Throughout the interview, Alec moved about the room and did everything possible to irritate both his parents and me. He had apparently been a behavior problem since he was in the womb. He had been extremely active *in utero* and used to kick his mother repeatedly, making her irritable and uncomfortable. He had behaved in a similar way ever since. The parents first thought it was a stage that would pass. It didn't. They went through a period of feeling guilty because it must be *their* fault. It wasn't. Now they were simply fed up. Alec on the other hand was as happy as a clam. He saw no problem and, therefore, no reason to change.

In Alec's case I briefly clung to the idea that he really did feel some distress, way down there, someplace. After all, it was possible that his obnoxious behavior was simply being trotted out for my benefit. Some "bad boys" will do that. Unfortunately, in Alec's case this was not so. He was very oppositional and had learned to get attention by not paying attention. Therapy consisted of working very closely with the parents on setting ironclad rules and working up reinforcement systems. Alec never did become an easy child and I still see the family every year or so to work through a new problem. But he is holding his own at school and the relationships within the family are steadily moving from mutual nonaggression to peaceful coexistence.

LOSS OF EXPECTATIONS

Sometimes the parents feel distressed and seek therapy because the child, for some reason or other, is not living up to their expectations. Sometimes this can be because the parents have expectations or ideals the child is developmentally unable to meet.

> Laura's parents were coming in because they were very distressed about her lack of progress in nursery school. They had enrolled her in an academically oriented preschool in which she was systematically instructed in beginning reading, writing, and arithmetic skills. She was also exposed to French and BASIC computer language. Laura was not very interested in reading and would have temper tantrums when her parents would sit down with her at night to do her "homework." They also were distressed because she was still reversing many of her letters. She did not know her right from her left. She could not tie her shoes. They thought she had a learning disability.

All of us have expectations for our children that we have developed in the course of our own experience. Laura's parents were not harsh or overly demanding. Laura was their only child, and having had no prior experience with children, they had very little information upon which to base their expectations. When Laura was a baby, they had read a couple of paperbacks which informed them that they could raise the infant's IQ through intense and thorough stimulation. They believed what they read. They were shocked and distressed when she did not make the progress they hoped for, and so they came to therapy. Fortunately, they were very open to new ideas and a new perspective. Once they were able to adjust their expectations to Laura's developmental ability, the situation immediately improved. They learned that right-left confusion and letter reversals were very common in a child Laura's age. They relaxed their demands while still providing opportunities for exploration in an atmosphere of play. Now, Laura, like most children, loved to play, and she began to enjoy these more age-appropriate activities. The parents also switched preschools!

PROBLEMS IN PARTICULAR PLACES

Sometimes a child really does exhibit some significant problems outside the home. As long as the child is sheltered in the family she seems to do quite well. Unfortunately, when the child enters school and encounters a time-ordered, task-oriented routine, she may fall apart. When parents who don't "see" the problem come in to therapy, they may be confused about why they are there.

Ricki, a seven-year-old second grader, had just been identified by the school multidisciplinary team as needing a special-education placement. She was reading at a preprimer level and her spelling skills were at a similar level. She was also causing a lot of behavior problems in the classroom. Now the parents were doubly shocked by the findings of the "M-team." Not only had they thought that Ricki was a very bright little girl who was going to excel at her studies, they were also appalled by what the school team was recommending: because of her behavior problems in class, the school was recommending placement in a classroom for *emotionally disturbed* children. The school psychologist had told them that Ricki should be on some type of medication because she had a "biochemical imbalance." The school social worker had suggested that she be involved in counseling so she could "talk out her feelings." The parents had no idea what a "biochemical imbalance" was, nor did they think their daughter needed to talk out her feelings. Neither did Ricki. Nonetheless, here they were sitting in the psychologist's office waiting for him to say something that made sense.

When parents first find out their children are struggling in school they are beset by a host of conflicting emotional reactions. Naturally they worry because their child is struggling. It hurts to see their child in any sort of distress. But it is also a blow to their own expectations. In an instant all of their hopes for their child have disintegrated, with nothing new to replace them. What dreams can you have for your child if she is learning-disabled? How will you be able to guide her and inspire her if you have no idea how far she is capable of going? These are not trivial issues of vanity. They strike to the very core of the parent-child relationship. In this particular case, the treatment's focus was to help the parents understand Ricki's abilities so they could assume that guiding, inspiring role. This was accomplished in a few quick sessions. The therapist also worked closely with the school to develop a better behavior-management system, which centered on completing assignments, getting along with others, and following rules. Often the schools are very valuable in identifying children who have attention or mood problems that respond well to psychoactive medication. In this particular case, however, the girl's behavior problems were simply a manifestation of her frustration in school. Once her learning program was altered, the behavior problems disappeared. Medication was not necessary. After two sessions the therapist concluded the child was not interested in individual psychotherapy. Her distress was related strictly to her difficulties in school. It was decided that instead of becoming an additional helper in the child's life, the therapist would work behind the scenes with the child's naturally occurring environment. As it turned out, the social worker at school had been developing a "friendship group" to help children learn social skills. Ricki became a part of this group and seemed to thrive.

WHAT ARE THERAPISTS?

Therapists are people who are trained in special ways to help you deal with problems in living. They differ in their background, training, and orientation. Some are medical doctors who practice psychiatry. Others are doctors of psychology. Many social workers and counselors are accomplished therapists as well.

In choosing a therapist, it is important to consider the needs of your individual case. Some children require more medical management and therefore the involvement of a psychiatrist is necessary. Other children need more systematic behavior management. This usually falls within the psychologist's realm of expertise. Finally, other children or their families need very regular contact with a therapist for emotional support and to work on family communication skills. While a psychologist or psychiatrist may certainly be able to provide these services, often they are expertly managed by social workers or marriage and family therapists. When you think about seeing a therapist, do not allow yourself to be bound up by the notion that you can "only see a doctor." You need to consider the issues and concerns of your particular family.

Other than that, the important issue is working with someone you can get along with.

WHAT IS THERAPY?

Many of my patients, feeling self-conscious and vulnerable on their first visit, will remark, "Am I supposed to lie down? Where is the couch?" In many people's minds, psychotherapy is equated with psychoanalysis. But classical psychoanalysis probably plays a very little role in the actual therapy process. Most therapists are ordinary people who are trained to help you cope with problems in living. Therapy itself can come in many forms. These can vary according to the theoretical orientation of the therapist as well as the format of the therapy itself.

Some therapists concentrate exclusively on the behavior of the patient or client. Behavioral therapists will identify specific problems to work on, carefully define them, and develop an intervention strategy. This type of approach can be especially helpful when the goal is reducing aggressive behavior, improving compliance, increasing homework production, decreasing bed-wetting, or eliminating out-of-seat behavior at the table. When problems are easily defined, then specific behavioral strategies can be developed to solve them.

Many times families will come in seeking therapy because they are concerned about a child's self-concept or they sense he has some vague, ill-defined problems with relationships or communication. In some cases the child simply needs a friend. The child isn't the slightest bit motivated to work on specific behaviors. Does this mean therapy is not needed? No, only that a very strict behavioral approach to treatment will probably have little effect. Sometimes, simply developing a relationship outside the family will have a stabilizing influence on the child.

Rod was a twelve-year-old boy with an irritable bowel condition. He was brought into therapy by his mother, who was very concerned because Rod would not stay on his special diet and seemed to be distressed. At school he was a loner and his academic performance was poor. Unfortunately Rod could not think of anything to say. He was willing to acknowledge that his bowel condition was painful and that he would be willing to "try some things" to be rid of the pain. He met weekly with the therapist and they talked and played games together. They didn't really work on a "problem," they just got to know one another and developed a trusting relationship. Rod began to stick to his diet and practice his relaxation exercises, and his pain diminished. Then he and his therapist began talking about other aspects of his life, such as his family and school. Gradually his performance at school began to improve. He paid more attention to his grooming and hygiene. Soon he even had a girlfriend!

In Rod's case, I am not sure I could document specifically how the intervention was successful, though it clearly was. When he was given some emotional support and a structured outlet for his feelings, he was able to pull himself together and stabilize his physical condition, his academic functioning, and his social relationships. Even though therapy did not systematically solve his problems, it was an important catalyst to his growth and development.

Some therapists work mostly with the young children themselves. The focus of individual child treatment is to help the children organize and express their own thoughts and feelings. One of the limitations of this type of therapy has to do with the mental development of most children. Young children, often even very bright ones, are not usually able to talk about their experience in an accurate, effective way. Their natural medium for expression is play, and a skillful therapist uses play activities to help children express their thoughts and feelings. The therapist is then able to interpret the play experience into verbal language. Gradually, the child is able to move away from *acting out* to *talking out* the troublesome experiences.

While some therapists choose to work with individuals, others choose to work with the family as a whole unit. This is especially important if there are multiple problems within the family or if one of the contributing factors to the child's behavior problem is a breakdown in family communication. The goal of family therapy is to reconstruct the cohesive family unit.

Though there are many approaches to therapy, they are linked by a common set of characteristics.

1. The therapy setting itself is a structured time away from the arm-twisting and bullying of the real world. It is a safety zone, a

neutral arena, in which problems can be worked through without danger to any of the participants.

2. The therapist is able to provide a structured outlet for thoughts and feelings that would otherwise be bottled up or hidden away. Since the clients, whether they are adults or children, have an outlet, they are much less likely to become overwhelmed and crises can be averted.

3. The therapist can also provide an objective point of view. While the therapist cares for and supports each of the family members, she is not an active part of the family. She is much less likely to become enmeshed in the situation. Therapists provide a real-world view of the family situation. When a particular problem gets distorted, or if you feel you are being ganged up on by everyone else in the family, a good therapist can help clarify the situation and realign the power balance. Since the therapist provides an outsider's point of view, she can also support and validate your perceptions of the situation. Maybe it isn't "just you" after all.

One therapist had always considered his yellow-and-black-striped sweater his favorite, until he met Jeffrey. His mother, a single parent, brought the boy in for counseling because she simply couldn't manage him anymore. He was eight years old and had always been a handful. He had a history of setting fires and had destroyed her living room furniture, and their pets kept disappearing. The mother did not know how to discipline him. He had terrible temper tantrums and seemed to feel no pain. She had tried spanking ("Ha, that doesn't hurt!"), using time-outs, and taking away his bike ("I don't care, keep it if you want"). He had been grounded so much that he wouldn't get out of his room until he was eligible for Social Security benefits. Mother felt tired and defeated. She had tried to be both mother and father to the boy and it had clearly failed. She did not know what she had done wrong. The therapist sat there stroking his beard and looked into the boy's shallow, wolf-gray eyes. Jeffrey, a powerful kid, apparently decided to show the therapist what his mother was talking about. He abruptly stood up and stated, "I am leaving."

The therapist asked him to sit down and tell his side of the story. The boy turned on him and said, "I don't have any side-of-the-story. I am bored. I wanna go."

The mother turned to him and snapped with icy clarity, "Sit down . . . now."

The boy backed away toward the door. "You gonna make me?"

"If I have to."

The therapist, trying to intervene, said softly, "Jeffrey, why don't you come back in and—"

Jeffrey wheeled on the therapist. "Oh shut up. I don't got nothin' to say and I don't want to sit around here saying nothin' to"—he gestured at the therapist's sweater—"some damn bumblebee." He turned, tipped over a small bookshelf, and ran out of the office.

The therapist watched a cloud of loose papers settle gently to the floor. "Now I know what you are talking about," he said to the mother. "How have you been able to stand it?"

The relationship between the mother and the therapist, at least, was cemented.

WHOM DOES THERAPY HELP?

One of the main reasons for seeing a therapist is that he is a trained professional who can provide information to help clarify problem situations. Unfortunately, though, he may not have a ready answer for your particular problem. After all, you are probably a bright, resourceful person who has tried numerous approaches before seeking the help of an outside consultant.

It was the father who brought the slouching, sullen ten-year-old boy into the therapist's office. The boy flopped down in one of the easy chairs and stared at his unlaced high-tops. His mouth was open, but fortunately he did not drool. The father looked at the therapist.

"School counselor says I ought to bring him in here for some counseling. He has been in a lot of trouble at home and now at school. Lying, stealing—some rough stuff. God knows I have tried to talk to him, but he won't listen none to me. The boy is as stubborn as a mule."

The therapist looked at the boy. "Your father says you have been having some trouble at school. I am wondering if you have anything you would like to say about that?"

The boy sat silently, picking at his fingernails, still staring. He said nothing.

The therapist tried again. "Do you think you are having any trouble?"

The boy looked up at the therapist and held his gaze for a few seconds. The therapist was struck by the boy's expression, which was blank and untroubled.

"No," he said simply and quietly.

The therapist tried numerous times to see if the child felt any distress or discomfort, to see if there were any problems they could agree to work on. Each time, the boy declined, claiming he had nothing to say, no problems to work on, and was not concerned in the least. The boy felt his father had a problem. He felt the school had a problem too. He didn't see that he had any problems at all. At the end of the forty-five-minute session, the therapist was inclined to agree with him. The boy genuinely seemed to have no distress and no insight into his own situation. The therapist stood up.

"I don't think therapy with the boy would be very helpful," he said to the father.

"But the school," said the father, "they said he should have this therapy."

"I know, and their intentions were probably very good," the therapist remarked quietly. "But your boy clearly has no interest and doesn't seem to feel any responsibility to change."

"Well, maybe you could talk some sense into him, open him up a bit," offered the father.

"But haven't you already tried that?" asked the therapist.

"Well, yes," the father admitted.

"Then I don't think I would have much more to offer."

"What are we going to do?" asked the father, genuinely lost.

"Well, you seem to be very concerned and so does the school. I would be happy to meet with you and see if we could put our heads together to figure out something to do. I could also work with the school, to see if we couldn't work out some way to manage his behavior in the class-room."

The father and the therapist struck a bargain, and the real therapy began.

As much as we might like to, we cannot drop a child off at a therapist's office to have him "fixed." Therapists are not very good at "talking some sense" into children, especially if they have chronic behavior problems. If a child simply has an irritable temperament, a therapist will be no better than you at "opening him up." The child may not have anything to say in the first place. Besides, you have already tried this and found that it doesn't work. Therapists can be invaluable in providing fresh ideas, a systematic approach to problem solving, and real-world perspective on your family situation. No, they don't have magic, but they can help you and your family work through the nagging problems of daily living.

ALTERNATIVES TO THERAPY

When things get out of hand in the family, is therapy the only answer?

Of course not.

In addition to psychotherapists, there are many other types of professionals who can help your family cope with problems in development or daily living. Here are a few of the possibilities:

Skill-Building Groups: Many times children experience difficulty not because they have an inner conflict, but because they lack certain developmental skills. Some children, for various reasons, have very poor social skills. They don't know how to interact appropriately with adults, get along in a group of children, regulate their behavior in the classroom, take turns, or make and maintain friendships. What such children need is for someone to teach them some basic social skills. Social skills are best taught in group formats. Many school systems offer systematic training in social skills through courses in *skill-streaming*. These groups are often lead by the school social worker, though speech therapists and occupational therapists are sometimes involved.

Special Education: Many times children who exhibit behavioral problems in the classroom can be trying to cover up developmental delays or learning disorders. In fact, children with learning disorders frequently come to the attention of the special education teacher because of their acting-out behavior. If you consider the problem from the child's point of view, this makes sense. It does not take a child very long to realize he is not understanding the things which seem to be very clear to everyone else in the class. A child with a learning disability does not like the feeling of looking stupid in front of other children. If he doesn't understand what is happening in the classroom, he feels out of control and vulnerable to criticism. If he says he does not like school and purposely misbehaves, however, then he feels in control: it is not that he *can't* do something; he simply doesn't want to do something. Any child would rather be "bad" than "defective."

Therefore, when children are showing a lot of behavior problems, it is very important to find out how they are doing in school. If you find out they are at grade level in most of their subjects, then you probably need to focus on the behavior. However, if they are far behind in their academic work or are struggling with basic academic skills, then some consideration should be given to ruling out a learning disability.

Tutoring: Some children will be behind in their academic work but will not qualify for special education. Sometimes these children can be helped by a private tutor. Tutors provide valuable assistance in two ways. In the first place, a good tutor can help a child improve in schoolwork because of the intensive teaching. Often children will rebel against doing schoolwork with their parents. They may be much less rebellious when they work with a tutor. In the second place, the relationship between the child and the tutor is very special and personal. Sometimes this can have the same positive effect on the child as working with a psychotherapist. Therefore, if the child is not exhibiting severe behavior problems or if most of the problems center around completing schoolwork, some consideration should be given to private tutoring.

Speech Therapy: Some children may not need psychotherapy but may have developmental language problems. Often children are referred to the school speech therapist if there is an obvious articulation disorder. But sometimes children have trouble understanding language or using language effectively in social situations. These difficulties are just as handicapping as simple articulation problems. Such children may have difficulty understanding schoolwork, playing with other children, or asserting themselves in social groups. A good speech-and-language clinician can provide support and teaching in these areas. Children may not only improve in specific speech-related skills, but may show improvements in their classroom performance and their social functioning as well.

Occupational and Physical Therapy: Some children exhibit behavior problems which are not due to faulty learning. Some of these children have sensory integrative disorders. These children often show very difficult temperaments during infancy and toddlerhood. In addition, they may have trouble with fine and gross motor coordination. Many times these children have trouble with early childhood play activities such as riding a tricycle, swinging on a swing set, climbing, etc. Some children exhibit tactile defensiveness. When touched lightly, they show a startled response and brush away the touch. Often parents will interpret this behavior in terms of their personal emotional relationship with the child. They will feel the child does not love them. In fact, it may be that the child's sensory feedback system does not function properly. When they experience light touch or unexpected touch, it does not feel pleasurable. It also does not feel painful. More than likely, it gives them a queer, uncertain feeling, like a tickle. If a child exhibits unusual sensorimotor behavior, consider a pediatric medical evaluation and referral to a therapist trained in sensory integrative testing and therapy.

Other Support Services: Many times children do not need a special therapist or specific skill training. Sometimes they simply need a special relationship and some emotional support. This is true especially for some children in single-parent families. Some possible avenues to explore include Big Brother or Big Sister programs, Scouting, the YMCA, or church groups. There are no hard-and-fast rules that define when these special relationships are sufficient to meet a child's needs. Perhaps the best indicator is the type and severity of the problem in the first place. If the child is showing marked developmental difficulties in speech and language, sensorimotor behavior, or academic functioning, then some type of specialized therapy should be tried first. If the child is showing some fairly mild behavior problems but also seems to have a few friends, if he lacks some structured social activity, or if he is missing a special relationship with an adult, then involvement with a community organization may be enough. However, if the child exhibits more serious behavior problems and is unmanageable at school or at home, then it may be necessary to consider working with a therapist or counselor.

MAKING THE DECISION TO WORK
WITH A THERAPIST

Seeking help for children is a rational and good thing to do. It shows you are aware of your child's difficulties and are adapting to her special needs. It shows you have the strength of character to admit to problems and the wisdom to solve them.

There have been incredible advances in the treatment of many learning problems and developmental difficulties. Children with these problems are no longer sent to the corner with dunce caps on their heads. There are special teachers, therapists, and learning programs that can help these children adapt. There have been great advances in medical science to help children with mood or attention problems. There is much more accountability in society and in the classroom. Parents no longer just accept that their children are "slow learners." Indeed, there are programs within most schools to help these children learn. There have been therapeutic advances to help children control bed-wetting, soiling, eating problems, and even some types of tic disorders. Our notions about treatment have to change along with the changing world. Many of the behavior problems which children exhibit are not due to faulty learning or "bad parenting." This is the fear that many parents harbor and that must be dispelled. Children with very difficult temperaments, hyperactive children, or developmentally delayed children are naturally more prone to maladaptive behavior. They are not "this way" because the parents have failed. If you have such a child in your family, then seeking therapy shows you are trying to adapt to your child's unusual temperament or developmental problems. Far from suggesting that you are a "bad parent," it shows you are displaying love, assertiveness, and intelligence.

So if your child is driving you crazy at home and your family life is crumbling to dust around you, do what makes the most sense. Get the help you need and deserve. When you have guilty feelings about seeking this help, pay attention to them, don't deny them. But as you pay attention to them, try to realize where they are coming from. These are old-fashioned, outmoded notions. Remember the two most important questions that you can ask at this time: What does my child need to learn? How can I help? Then you will know the way.

CHOOSING A THERAPIST

Once you make the decision to get some help, how do you go about finding a therapist who is right for you or your child? There are a number of places to start. Perhaps the best first step is to seek the advice of your family doctor. Usually a family physician is aware of the therapists in the area and can help identify an appropriate resource. When you talk to your family doctor, though, try to be as specific as you can about the nature of the problem. Some types of therapist are better at working with specific behavior problems, while others are better at working through more complex problems with communication or family relationships.

Also bring up with your doctor any concerns you have about the child's development or the need for medical management. Although many families think that all therapists are psychiatrists, this is not so. Though psychiatrists are extremely important when there is a question of a severe developmental problem or a need for medical management, they do not always provide direct therapy. However, they usually supervise social workers or counselors who do provide it. Therefore, if your doctor recommends a nonpsychiatrist to work on family relationship problems, don't be offended. Increasingly family doctors will refer patients to psychologists, especially for learning and behavior problems or problems that require some type of testing. They can certainly provide treatment for most behavior problems and can work closely with a psychiatrist for management of medication. If your family doctor cannot identify an appropriate resource, he may refer you to another doctor who can help. Sometimes you will have to see two or three different doctors just to figure out what types of help are needed in your child's case. Even though you are seeing a number of doctors, this does not mean that no one knows what they are doing. It is simply a necessary part of the process of diagnosing your child's problem.

In addition to the family doctor, the special services team at your child's school can assist you in finding a therapist. Sometimes the school's social worker or psychologist can help with behavior or learning problems in the school setting. However, they will not be able to provide more extensive therapeutic support or family therapy. Usually they will know of good people in the community who can help you. Remember, the school's special services team devotes their time and energy to working with children with special needs. Your child is not the first one who has had trouble. Chances are, there have been many before you who have needed help for similar types of problems. Another advantage to working with the special services team is that they probably know which therapists work well with the school system. It is often essential to coordinate efforts among the therapists, parents, and school. This improves communication and the general treatment effort. For the child, it provides a perception of cohesiveness, the sense that everyone in his world is working together to help him. There is also less likelihood that the child will be able to manipulate or to play one person off against the other. Therefore, working with a therapist that the school recommends can be very beneficial.

In addition, there are many other possible sources of referral. You probably know other adults who have had children in some type of therapy or who can recommend a good therapist. Usually clergymen are acquainted with the therapists in your area. In the end, there are always the yellow pages.

WORKING WITH THE THERAPIST

When you work with the therapist, the most important thing to develop is a positive mental attitude toward the therapy process. Certainly, the major obstacles to that attitude are going to be your own feelings of guilt and anger and your resistance to getting outside help. You cannot avoid these or pretend they don't exist. As best you can, though, try to identify these feelings when they occur so you and your therapist can work them through.

It is very important that you see yourself as an equal partner in the therapy process. This also holds true if your child has other developmental handicaps and requires a lot of special services. Certainly parents can often feel overwhelmed and confused by the number of professionals who are treating their child. Some parents can be very intimidated by a whole treatment team. Work with the psychotherapist or with the case manager of the treatment team to develop some assertiveness. You are the child's parent and an important member of the treatment. You deserve respect and your ideas deserve consideration. If you are a part of the treatment team, then be sure that you understand what is going on. So often medical, psychological, or educational treatment teams can spew forth a lot of technical mumbo jumbo. You have the right to ask questions and to have the therapists define what they are talking about. You do not need to be aggressive or hostile. Assertiveness is not the same thing as anger.

If you are entering into some type of therapeutic relationship, understand the purposes and limits of the treatment. Work with the therapist to define specific problems. Usually a treatment plan is developed prior to starting therapy. This is true in most medical settings as well as in the school system. Try to get at least a verbal understanding of what is to be treated and how the problem is to be approached. Also try to get some sense of the estimated length of treatment. At least determine from the therapist if the treatment is to be a short-term process (under ten sessions) or a long-term process. Finally, note how you will evaluate the effects of treatment and at what points you will make decisions about whether or not to continue.

Make an effort to understand your role as a consumer of special help. Therapists do have an obligation to provide the most effective form of treatment in the most economical way.

To Sum Up: Therapy—a Partnership among Equals

Try as we might, we are not always capable of solving on our own all the problems we face in family living. If you follow the steps in this book, you may be well attuned to your child's developmental abilities and to her particular temperament. You may also carefully manage the daily schedule of making the most use of routines and rituals. You may have a well-established, balanced, disciplined routine to handle most of the rules of family life. Finally, you may have made every effort to work on specific behavior problems in a rational, levelheaded way. Still, for any of a number of reasons, you may find you need some outside help. It is important for parents to recognize when they need to seek help and to take appropriate steps to get it. So many times parents look at seeking help as a sign of failure, yet it is just the opposite. It shows they are perceptive, resourceful, and caring.

There are many reasons why a family will seek the help of a therapist. Usually it is because there is some distress on the part of the child or, more often, on the part of the parents. Sometimes this distress is due to a deviation from some ideal. Other times it is because the child's behavior deviates from some developmental or behavioral norm, though neither the parent nor the child is especially distressed. In some cases therapy is sought because of some acute problem or stress. In other cases, especially in children who have difficult temperaments, the problems are long-standing, although there may be "a straw that breaks the camel's back."

We have discussed a variety of options for therapy. To sum it up, certainly some problems need to be dealt with by a medical doctor. When medical management of a child's behavioral or developmental problems is an issue, a trained child psychiatrist should probably be involved. Many behavior problems, however, can be dealt with through formal psychotherapy or behavior modification. Sometimes in-depth psychological evaluations are necessary. These functions can all be carried out by a doctor of psychology. Many specific problems can be dealt with by well-trained social workers or counselors. Often these therapists are supervised by psychologists or psychiatrists. Your family doctor will certainly know what resources are available in your area. Also, the psychologist and social worker in your school system are probably aware of which therapists work best in the school setting.

Don't forget to pay attention to other types of problems which may not require a psychotherapist. Children who have specific skill deficiencies may do best in some type of skill-building group. Other children show specific learning problems and attempt to cover these over with negative behavior. If this is the case, then the special services team in the public school may be the appropriate resource. Some children have specific problems with communication and may need special therapy to help their understanding or use of language. Then a speech therapist may be the best person to see. Occupational and physical therapists can provide help to children who have sensory integrative disorders. Finally, under certain circumstances involvement in community organizations or with community volunteers may be all that is really necessary. Assess the situation before deciding immediately on a course of treatment. Here, the advice of a trusted doctor, teacher, or clergyman can be helpful.

It is very important to develop and maintain a positive mental attitude when entering into any therapeutic relationship. This is difficult because of some deeply ingrained attitudes and beliefs about psychotherapy. So many people feel that one goes to a therapist because of failure or weakness. Even though seeking the help of a therapist may be a clear sign of a parent's mental health, it is often tied up with archaic notions of mental illness. Deal with feelings of resistance when they arise and do not simply sweep them under the rug. After all, most of the behavior problems I see are not anyone's fault. The child may be developmentally delayed or have a peculiar temperament that makes it more difficult for her to regulate her behavior. In addition, there are many circumstances of modern living that may have an impact on the child, but these can be worked through. Divorce is one such problem area. Certainly it is important to acknowledge and attend to the feelings of guilt and anger when they occur. But families must get beyond these to tackle the real behavior problems they face.

Even though you may be seeking outside help, remember that you are still *the parent,* the one who is capable of competently dealing with the problem. Sometimes when problems get out of hand in a family, it is easy for parents to feel overwhelmed, incompetent, and ashamed. Often parents who seek therapy do so out of anger and frustration. Part of the process of therapy may need to be devoted to helping you regain a balanced, rational perspective not only on the problem but also on your role as a parent. A therapist is like a consultant, providing knowledge and some emotional support. But while the therapist can provide these, you are still the parent, the most important person in your child's life. You are the image your child emulates, the great teacher, the maker of rules. No therapist can take that from you and no good therapist would even want to.

Afterword

Where Has All the Goodness Gone?

In the musical *Bye-Bye, Birdie,* an irate father strides across the stage and angrily sings, "What's the matter with kids today?" It has been nearly thirty years since that show opened and yet we are still asking the same question. But many are also asking, "What's the matter with parents today?" Despite the fact that we are loaded down with magazine articles and self-help books, despite the fact that Phil and Oprah regularly have programs which focus on the problems of child rearing, we seem as lost and confused as ever. Are children really that much more difficult to raise nowadays?

Yes, child rearing is much more difficult, for a number of reasons, some more obvious than others.

Many people will immediately point to problems in contemporary American society. Our country, as wonderful as it may be, often doesn't seem to be a very *good* place to live anymore. That van which drives slowly through your neighborhood—is that a child molester stalking his prey? Those teenage boys with shaved heads and torn jeans—are they going to try to get your child started on drugs? Should you let your child walk to school? Suppose some PCP-crazed psychopath gets loose in your child's school. You even have to be careful about baby-sitters and day-care centers: the Little Lamb Nursery School could be a cover for a child pornography ring. It seems as though the dangers of the world have infiltrated all those places we used to assume were safe. The "friendly stranger" doesn't wear the black shirt and the white tie anymore. He might look like Grandma. He might *be* Grandma.

As frightened and hysterical as we can get about the decaying fabric of social order, there will always be those who pull us back toward a more stable (and somewhat repressed) perspective. Look, they will point out, these dangers always existed; it is simply that we are more aware of them now. The actual incidence of child sexual abuse may not be increasing; perhaps it is simply being reported and treated more openly. Certainly there is an epidemic of drug abuse and the violence that goes along with it, but is this any more of a social problem than alcoholism, which has been with us for centuries? People are the same and the problems are basically the same. It is simply that the labels are flashier and the images on TV more stunning. Whether or not our social structure is *really* crumbling is of little consequence. What is important, though, is that we think and feel that social problems are out of control. It is the psychological reality of a terrifying world that is most difficult to bear. Each of us swims about in our own personal sea of attitudes, values, and beliefs. Sometimes these may correspond to events out in the real world. Child sexual abuse *may* be increasing, the government *may* be losing the war against the drug kingpins, but it is not necessary for us to be *right* in order to be confused or frightened by the world around us. It is simply enough to *believe* the world is a confusing or frightening place.

What about today's children? Are they really so much more difficult? They are, of course, healthier than they have been in the past. That is, they are less susceptible to the types of infectious diseases that would regularly hew down a good proportion of children in generations past. Now we are made aware of disorders that have only recently been discovered—or invented. We are told of children having "attention deficit disorders." We have to worry about our children's cholesterol levels and need to worry about their level of stress. We are told there are epidemics of teenage suicides in various communities. Of course, there is the glassy-eyed spector of drug abuse nodding off in any child's room of the future.

Some of these fears have a basis in reality. There is a lot more violence, especially in inner-city schools, and there are more illicit drugs of many varieties available to children at younger and younger ages. The incidence of teenage pregnancy is on the rise, as is the incidence of sexually transmissible diseases among the adolescent population. These are very real problems and cannot be ignored.

Many of the problems which children seem to be experiencing may be either caused or influenced by changing social expectations. We certainly expect more quality assurance from our public education system, but we are told our public schools are getting "poor grades" or that they have gotten worse over successive decades. There is talk of requiring teachers to take a competency exam. One municipal judge receives media attention for jailing delinquents who do not achieve passing grades. Among middle- and upper-class families there are certainly changing expectations about achievement. In order to be *good* parents we are told we have to stimulate our children early to give them that competitive edge, so we expose them to formal instruction at earlier ages. At the same time, we are warned about the "hurried-child syndrome" and told that by giving them this early formal instruction, we are placing unreasonable burdens on them which may damage them later in life.

As we change our expectations about education and achievement, we also change our expectations about acceptable behavior. There is a tendency now to medicalize many problems that used to be thought of as purely social or moral in the past. The inattentive little boy who doesn't get his work done and talks out of turn used to be thought of as a nuisance and a behavior problem. Now he is likely to be "diagnosed" as having an "attention deficit disorder." Then the fun begins. One group of experts describes the syndrome and prescribes a stimulant medication that can miraculously improve attention and raise self-esteem. Another group of experts states that there is no such syndrome and that the medications are used only to achieve a kind of social control over unruly children. Parents are alarmed about the discovery of new problems and anxious to learn what to do about them, but they are distressed to find out that the "experts" don't seem to be able to agree and can't provide the answers. Instead, the confusion and uncertainty are increased. As in some chemistry experiment gone awry, the more information that is poured into us, the more we are blinded by bubbles and smoke.

Like the beleaguered experts, most parents find it impossible to discern the "right way" to raise their children. This seems oddly in step in a society in which the norms of social behavior keep being reinvented. In our lifetimes we have seen unprecedented scientific and technological changes. One of the by-products of change has been that the rules of social behavior are no longer clear. Women are no longer consigned to the drudgery of watching the crackling pork chops on the kitchen stove, and men are no longer assigned by virtue of their sex alone the job of bringing home the bacon. One of the by-products of feminism has been that women are given increasing freedom to choose what course their lives will take. What used to be automatic or assumed now must be carefully thought through and anguished over. Twenty years ago social roles were determined by sex, race, and economic class. This led to a constriction of choice to the point of social oppression—but social decisions were a lot easier to make. The baby in the stroller wears a cute T-shirt emblazoned with *Question Authority*. This may have been cool when we were eighteen, but now that we are settling into the girdles of our middle age we have to reckon with the fruits of our revolution.

The problem is this: we are confronted with the terrible responsibility of our own freedom. This includes not only the freedom to take on new social roles but also the freedom of choice in making many ethical decisions. This is what is involved when we make decisions about how to raise our children. There are no absolute standards of right and wrong to go by. What parents are shocked to find out after they have brought their soggy eight-pound bundle of possibilities home from the hospital is that they alone must make the decisions that will govern the child's growth and well-being. Freedom, which should be a liberating experience, can also be oppressive and terrifying. What is the right way to raise children so they will be *good* people? Against what yardstick do you measure whether you are a *good* parent?

As a society we have attempted to replace ethical decisions by turning to science and technology. Making a personal, moral decision is a lot like challenging someone to fight while you're wearing roller skates. It is very easy to get knocked off your feet. Science follows a logical and mathematical process involving reviewing the information, developing hypotheses, testing them, and evaluating results. It has been our most successful method of gathering the truth about the world around us in every field from agriculture to zoology. In the social sciences, there have been significant advances in our understanding about how children learn and develop, and how families interact, and we can derive general principles concerning the effectiveness of reward and punishment. All of this can tell us what works when we want to encourage some behaviors and discourage others. But behavioral technology cannot answer the question of how we should conduct our lives or how our children should conduct theirs. Instead, this overemphasis on behavioral technology has turned parents into managers and engineers laboring in fear of their own performance reviews. A "good" parent is determined by whether his children have "good" behavior out in public. This emphasis on the immediacy of behavior forces parents to be shortsighted and crisis-oriented. It is no wonder that parenting a difficult child or one who has developmental problems can be so exhausting. These parents are operating in a state of crisis most of their waking hours.

As I noted at the outset, this is not a "self-help" book. Although there are many technical and even practical suggestions about how to deal with behavior problems, the primary emphasis in this book has been on helping you, the parent, to get a better fix on where you are going through the long journey of the parenting process. The first step is not how to cope with whining, temper tantrums, or sibling rivalry, but to understand the function of misbehavior from the child's standpoint and the purpose of discipline as a teaching tool. If we are to bear the weighty responsibility of our freedom to make choices for our children, we must have some internal standards for making decisions.

Before we can proceed with a behavioral technology, we must understand the raw materials with which we are working: the children themselves. In the early chapters I suggested that if there is a throughline to a child's behavior throughout childhood, it is learning to regulate themselves and achieve social mastery. In other words, they need to be able to predict and control themselves in the world around them. Misbehavior serves a very valuable function for all children. It is the way they test the world and learn to trust the people they love. Viewed in this way, misbehavior has a positive purpose in a child's life. This does not mean we should condone or encourage children to misbehave—quite the contrary. We can seize these opportunities to teach our children important lessons about the world and about their relationship with us. We do not punish a child for "being bad" or reward another child for "being good." We use discipline to lead our children out of ignorance into more self-fulfilling and socially constructive behavior. Goodness has nothing to do with what we discipline children for, but by careful teaching, we can help a child learn to do good things in the world.

In order to accomplish this, though, we have to understand how our children learn. This is why it is important to take careful stock of your own child, noting what he moves toward and what he instinctively retreats from. Children at different ages are ready to work on different developmental tasks. Some children, despite normal intelligence, develop more slowly than others. There is considerable suggestion in the research literature that little boys learn somewhat differently from little girls. This has nothing to do with their potential, but it can influence how we go about the process of teaching them about the world. Finally, there are a number of personality and individual competency differences that can influence how children come to understand their world and regulate their behavior.

In addition to understanding your children, it is also vital for you to understand that you, the parent, are a participant in their journey. By placing so much emphasis on the technology of behavior, we have drawn our experts into the spotlight and seem to relegate parents to the role of spear carriers or walk-ons. This will never play well to the children. You, the parent, are the most important person in their lives and you alone are their best teacher. Experts may provide technical advice or directions but they will never replace you. This is why I have placed such an emphasis on parents as the teachers of their children.

It was only after covering a number of issues related to parents' attitude and orientation to parenting that we addressed the subject of behavior management. Quite typically, when I talk to parents, their concerns are whether a particular punishment is *bad* for the child or whether bribing a child with rewards is *good*. As we saw in the "Back to Basics" chapters, specific rewards and punishments have no moral value. The important questions are: "What do you want your child to learn?" and "What is the most effective way you can teach your child this particular lesson in living?" It is important, of course, to see how punishment works and the difference between rewards, positive reinforcement, and bribery. We must understand that when punishment works it has an immediate effect that is usually more gratifying to the parents when they are coping with misbehavior; but positive teaching practices, though they may take a longer time to take hold, will be more beneficial to the child in the long run. It is always easier to teach a child to *do* something than to *not do* something. In any case, the motivational technique, whether reward or punishment, must always be framed from the child's point of view. The child must feel the sense of urgency to learn and to change. As a parent you cannot make him behave, but you can decide the consequences for his behavior. Finally, the major consequences themselves do not have to be anything extraordinary in the child's life. Selectively using your attention and controlling privileges and freedoms are usually sufficient.

In the final section of the book we looked at a fairly complex though integrated approach to discipline. Again, we didn't focus immediately on how to solve a messy eating problem or a "not listening" problem, but instead on the process of normal family living. So often it is the things we don't consciously think of as discipline which greatly influence or shape a child's life. Understanding that children are trying to learn prediction and control, we saw how the use of daily structure, routines, and rituals can provide a form to the child's day. Discipline is not akin to calling out the National Guard in a state of crisis, but is something woven into every aspect of the child's daily life. The child learns discipline and self-regulation because the day has a normal rhythmic quality. In addition, using a simple routine of discipline to deal with basic family rules enhances the predictability of the parents in certain situations. Finally, we dealt with those special problems which occupy so much space in the minds of parents with misbehaving children, such as "What do you do with a child who has a temper tantrum in the supermarket?" or "What do you do with a child who is lying or stealing?" The temptation is to come up with a specific recommendation that will satisfy the parents' immediate concerns. Indeed, there are books on the market that will provide hundreds of specific behavior prescriptions to deal with many of these problems. The approach in this book has been different. Instead, I have encouraged parents to think about a logical process for dealing with special problems. When a child shows a chronic behavior problem, it is not a time to panic but, as with any behavior problem, a time to carefully consider how best to teach the child a more appropriate way of behaving. Therefore, the book's emphasis is on how to solve problems in a rational and realistic way. Of course there are some problems you may not be able to solve on your own. Then it is time to turn to others for help. It is important to understand when to turn to others for help and also to deal with your own feelings about obtaining this help.

What I have provided in this book is really a skeletal structure, a framework for a teaching process. Parents who are anxious to find the right way to cope with little Cindi's temper tantrums may be disappointed with this. I believe the best approach to solving specific behavior problems is not to read about them in a book but to communicate with others. Talk with other parents in the neighborhood, your child's class, your colleagues, or your clergyman. See what others have tried. Work with a therapist or counselor if you need to. First try to sort out where you are going with your discipline, what you are trying to teach your child over the long journey to young adulthood. Understand also that misbehavior is not bad or unusual. We have all experienced that embarrassment as our child flaps around on the floor of some crowded store like a tuna thrown on the deck of a trawler. We understand; we've been there. Realize that this tantrum or that mess can provide you with a chance to teach your child something important about the world. This book provides a jumping-off point for further discussions and explorations.

Some may scan this book and complain that it is all too complex. They may be discouraged by the burden of their freedom to make *good* choices. In truth, it may seem desirable to some to return to a more restrictive society in which roles are clear, authority is absolute, and moral decisions are automatic since they proceed from dogma. As long as you are a member of a privileged class, of course, this oppressive society may not seem too intolerable. But who is to be top dog? Who will be an underdog? In our two-hundred-year history Americans have fought very hard for various freedoms and we are not likely to give them up, but freedom is also dangerous and terrifying. We find we are on our own and responsible for our own decisions. There is no absolute authority to tell us what is right or wrong. We need to learn how to cope with freedom and to take responsibility for our choices and actions.

Learning to cope and to adapt to change is the central purpose of all growth and development. The twenty-year journey to adulthood is necessary to help children become strong enough to tolerate independence, to shoulder the burdens of freedom. For some children this is a difficult journey, and they need a lot of help from their parents. But even for those children who seem to pass effortlessly through, there are unseen challenges and adjustments. As children accumulate knowledge and experience, they must constantly readjust their conception of the world. Those simple constructions of reality which comfort a preschool child undergo some remarkable transformations as the child grows. We should be thankful the process of development is a slow one: there is so much to learn. Consider the process from a small child's point of view.

I can remember an incident from long ago, when I was much younger and the world was much simpler. I don't think I could have been older than two, since I remember standing in my crib and looking out my window to the gravel driveway below. It would have been the early evening, with the sun low on the horizon and the sky filled with the pinks and pale blues of dusk. I would be waiting to see the brown '52 Buick come down the gravel driveway as it did every night when my mother drove my father home from the train station. As they emerged together from the garage, I remember my father standing below in his blue seersucker suit, placing his hands in his pockets and staring up at the sky.

"It looks like it is going to be a light night," he said.

Now I am not sure what he meant by that statement. Perhaps that the air was light, not too humid for summer. Perhaps he meant there would be a moon out that night. I don't know. But as I understood him in my two-year-old fashion, it seemed to me there were certain nights that were "light"; that is, that the evening sky with its pale blues and soft pinks was as dark as it got. This was a comforting feeling for a child who was probably afraid of the dark. I went to sleep when it was light and I awoke when it was light. My first remembered conception of time and the world was confirmed.

But years passed and the heavens did not remain the same. When I was four and five years old the nights always seemed to be an inky black. Every now and then I would remember this one moment from that particular summer and I would wonder what had happened to the light nights.

At age five, like all other children, I went to kindergarten and began my formal schooling process, in which I learned new things about the world. By the time I was seven I had learned all about how day worked and had a big argument with my friend Nick over the rather abstract fact that the earth revolved around the sun rather than vice versa. It was during the summer after second grade that I realized that what I had taken for a "light night" was, in fact, the normal lengthening of daylight as we approached the summer solstice. I had lost my light nights forever, but I no longer needed them because I had learned more useful and helpful things about the world. Like all children, I gave up the simple for the more complex and learned to bear the weight of my freedom.

All children learn to do this and all parents as well. Please do not despair that the goodness has gone out of the world or that your children are not good. You are their great teachers and you will show them how to do good things in the world. But enough has been said. Your children are waiting for you.

They need you.

Acknowledgments

I am deeply grateful to a number of individuals who have stimulated ideas in me and provided guidance and critical feedback. I am also indebted to those who understand the Byzantine world of publishing and in whose trust I placed my book. For this trust I have been rewarded.

I have been strongly influenced by the works of many psychologists. Even the casual reader will recognize many of the names: Jean Piaget, the Swiss epistemologist; Hans Eysenck, the British psychologist; and Alexander Thomas and Stella Chess, the psychiatrists who engineered the New York Longitudinal Study and provided much-needed emphasis on the importance of temperament in development. In this respect, I must also mention Stanley Greenspan.

I have also been influenced by the psychologists with whom I have studied. Don Tucker, now at the University of Oregon, was my mentor at North Dakota. I also acknowledge the influence of Barbara Brandt, now in Southern California; Angelo S. Bolea in Columbia, Maryland; and John and Victoria Lavigne at Children's Memorial Hospital in Chicago.

Since I am a very poor typist, I have relied heavily on those who are more proficient at this skill. My thanks to Linda Schleicher, Colleen Cotter, and Jean Lottridge for typing the various drafts of this book.

I am also thankful for the help and the very existence of Fred Hills at Simon and Schuster, who has brought this book from rough draft to final copy. Ellen Levine, my agent, not only had the acumen to bring the book to Fred, but also provided encouragement and many helpful suggestions during the writing process. And I am always thankful for my lifelong friendship with David H. Bain, author—and new father.

I am deeply indebted to those who have taught me the most: the children and parents I have worked with over the past fifteen years. These include the children and staff at the Northwood Children's Home in Duluth, Minnesota; students and teachers in the Superior, Wisconsin, public schools; and the patients at the Child Evaluation and Treatment Program in Grand Forks, North Dakota. I owe thanks as well to the youth and staff at the Depot in Fargo. I am also grateful for my association with the Dean Clinic and especially Mary Dominski, M.D.; with St. Mary's Hospital; and with the children of Madison, Wisconsin, and the surrounding area. But it seems I owe the most thanks to my own children, who taught me true sympathy for other parents. They continue to teach me that I'm not as smart as I usually think I am.

Finally, I am grateful for the assistance of my wife, Charlene Zabawski. She provided invaluable help in organizing chapters and straightening the kinks out of my idiosyncratic sentences. Sometimes the feedback was not quite the undiluted praise I wished for, but it was usually right on target. I believe this book is substantially improved because of her keen critical eye and her many suggestions.

Index